FOREWORD

Bríd Dukes

The Civic Theatre's Tenderfoot programme was initially conceived as an audience development strategy, a way of getting young people to feel comfortable and "at home" in the theatre. Under Veronica Coburn's inspired and inspiring leadership it quickly became much more than that. Tenderfoot is now a process through which young people discover and explore many kinds of creativity, learn how to work and play together by making theatre with professional mentors. Veronica Coburn has been supported from the beginning by Liam Halligan and Gavin Kostick and a small army of sound engineers, lighting, costume and set designers and all the other artisans who make theatre possible. I am most grateful to them all and especially to our Civic Theatre staff who unfailingly pitch in and keep the show on the road. My thanks are also due to South Dublin Arts Office and the Arts Council Young Ensemble Scheme for their continued financial support with Tenderfoot. The publication of this volume of plays has been made possible by the joint cooperation of South Dublin Libraries, South Dublin Arts Office and the Civic Theatre for which we are very grateful.

Brid Dukes
Artistic Director

South Dublin Libraries and Arts; Civic Theatre Tallaght

ISBN 978-0-9575115-4-5

Design and Layout by
SilverBark Creative

Content by
Tenderfoot Project; Veronica Coburn

INTRODUCTION
Veronica Coburn

Tenderfoot is an apprentice theatre programme @ The Civic Theatre in Tallaght for transition year students. The programme runs for six months from September to February each year and forty students from eight different schools, representing the geographic and socio-economic make-up of the region, participate. Students are not required to have any experience, only interest. Selection is through low focus group workshops, held in the schools, to promote the widest possible access. There is no cost to students to take part in the programme. Tenderfoot provides young people who wouldn't ordinarily gravitate towards the arts an opportunity to initiate an interest in them.

A tenderfoot is an apprentice, a trainee, a learner, a novice, a fledgling, a new boy or girl. The model of the programme is one of apprenticeship, learning by doing - learning by working alongside experts in their field. In the course of the programme, the students, our tenderfeet, work alongside working theatre professionals, theatre artists – writers, directors, designers and production technicians to develop their art/skill, be that writing, production design, costume design, performance or stage management.

In the first phase of Tenderfoot a number of the students, approximately sixteen, participate in a targeted programme designed to introduce them to the basic conventions of drama, the work of existing playwrights and the discipline of writing for the stage. The aim is for each of the students to write an original play for the stage.

The final phase, a fulltime three week long work experience module in January/February of the academic year, sees all participating young people act as a youth ensemble as they design, stage manage and perform a number of the plays that have been written by their peers. The young people work under the guidance of professional mentors. The plays are performed in The Main Space in The Civic, a policy decision that values the distinct voice of young theatre makers.

Young people have the need and the capacity to make excellent art. The theatre that is produced in Tenderfoot is of interest to a general theatre audience. It is profoundly meaningful and resonant to a peer audience. One of the most exciting elements of Tenderfoot is peer reaction to the work.

Young people are very seldom considered as artists. They are more generally categorised as receivers rather than makers of art. They are taught about art. They are facilitated in their engagement with art. But what of a child's or a young person's need to create art? Surely the need to create is fundamental to the human condition and, if so, then why would it lie dormant until the age of consent? I posit the theory that children, up to a certain age, do not have a burning need to express formally ideas and/or feelings in an imaginative way because they exist in a world that is one part reality to one part imagined reality. They use their imagination to express ideas and feelings every day. Their art form is play. With puberty, with the arrival of the teenage years, with the growing presence of the trappings of the adult world, with increased pressure and responsibility, the balance of a young person's life shifts. This then is a crucial time and, in the interests of metaphysical health, it is of vital importance that opportunities are provided for young people to exercise/exorcise their ideas and feelings imaginatively. Why do people make art? Why have people always made art? Why did our prehistoric ancestors scratch rough images into solid rock? They did so to notate their reality, to record their reality and to interpret their reality. Surely, the need to do that is equally as strong for young people whose lives are in a constant state of change and uncertainty.

Tenderfoot is a truly unique programme that provides young people with an opportunity to behave as theatre artists, to be artists in a theatre context, to work alongside other young people in artistic endeavour and to have their work elevated through presentation in a professional forum. Tenderfoot gives young people an opportunity to come together for art rather than education, in a theatre, outside of school. Their produced work presents a unique and seldom heard voice in Irish theatre.

Tenderfoot works. It is an excellent youth arts programme that serves its participants well. It bridges the gap between education and the arts and it is a replicable model. Imagine a national arts landscape where there was a Tenderfoot programme in every funded theatre and arts centre in the country. The result would be generations of young people who feel they belong in their local theatre or arts centre and a generation of young people who have a meaningful relationship with the art of theatre.

Tenderfoot, and its principles, has a lot to offer teachers, schools and arts venues in the coming years. The principles that underpin Tenderfoot can be applied to facilitating students' engagement with drama in a school setting.

The twin pillars of good youth arts work are access and excellence representing the dual importance of process and product. Creativity and wellbeing, two of the six key skills of the new Junior Cycle Curriculum, fall in line with these central tenets.

Access. Art, theatre, is for everyone. In Tenderfoot we introduce students who have never previously participated in a drama activity to active drama workshops. The purpose of youth arts, the same as any art, is exploration, questioning, understanding, and imagining new possibilities. All young people are capable and interested in that, not just those who are good at English or those who are perceived as being good performers. Many students have no interest in acting or performing. That is perfectly understandable and acceptable. All Tenderfoot students, including those who gravitate towards design and stage management learn about theatre in a workshop environment. We facilitate their engagement in theatrical storytelling, in improvisation and in embodying other characters and lives because it is a way of understanding themselves and their world, and it is a way for them to imagine themselves in a new light. It is also a way for them to learn about their art form. It is active learning. Learning by doing. And it is contextual learning. Understand the whole art form before you specialise.

The same principle sees us bring our students to the theatre. If they are going to learn about theatre they should go and see some. We want them to see work that is full of the concerns of today. Such immediacy and relevance promotes an engaged experience. There is no historical, social or academic distance. Therefore, the possibility of a significant engagement is higher. We want them to experience theatre intellectually, aesthetically and emotionally. We want them to react to the words that they hear, words containing story and ideas. We want them to be affected by the things that they see and to understand that images also contain concepts and thoughts. And we want them to be moved in a shared moment of understanding between performer and audience. We want them to understand that the audience completes a piece of theatre.

Excellence in a youth arts context is about young people working and achieving to the best of their ability. The task of arts mentors, youth leaders, and now teachers, is to have useful knowledge of young people, of art form and current practice, to aspire on behalf of the young people they work with, and to provide resources and structures for those young people within which they can work to a level of personal excellence. In youth arts it is all about the making. The writing of the play, the crafting of the performance, and how that is, at some level, an articulation of the young artist. The quality of the work is also important because inherent in achieving a level of excellence is a sense of value. The implied rationale that this voice, this content, is worthy of form and rigour.

If the art of theatre, under the name of drama, is to be explored in every classroom in the country the Tenderfoot approach is very useful. It is inclusive, it facilitates engagement and it is clear in its rationale. A Tenderfoot Handbook is in development. It will outline the ethos, principles, structure, practical detail and benefits of the programme. The Tenderfoot Handbook will be accompanied by three short DVD documentaries outlining the programme from the mentors' point of view, the participants' point of view and the point of view of a peer audience. The handbook, with this volume of plays, will be an invaluable resource to teachers and others given the responsibility to implement the new Junior Cycle curriculum with its emphasis on artistic articulation and expression.

I am immensely proud to introduce this volume of plays. The plays within these covers are selected from over a hundred plays and monologues written by fifteen and sixteen year olds over a period of seven years. They appear for various reasons. Excellence, certainly. Relevance, to a peer audience in particular. Some of these plays when first presented had the effect of making its audience fall silent and listen with an attention that can only be described as profound. And range. Young artists, just like any other artists, display a variety of concerns. Some write about what they know. Some write about what they want to know. Others are delighted by words and form. What I like about this volume, in keeping with Tenderfoot's core value that art is for everyone, is that a young person might read or see one of these works and think "I could do that".

There are some people that I must thank. Our core funders for their shared vision and continued support through the years. Tenderfoot was originally funded by The Civic Theatre in Tallaght, the Arts Office at South Dublin County Council & Storytellers Theatre Company. Since 2009, the programme has been funded by The Civic Theatre in Tallaght, the Arts Office at South Dublin County Council and The Arts Council Young Ensemble Scheme.

I would like to thank my colleagues, the Tenderfoot mentors, who work alongside me every year. I am forever indebted to their capacity to understand and serve our dual remit with good humour, skill and grace. I must mention, in particular, Liam Halligan and Gavin Kostick, who have been by my side from the very start. Their continued commitment to the ethos and their belief in the value of Tenderfoot is greatly appreciated. I would like to thank the staff of The Civic Theatre for their unconditional support for the programme. Every year they welcome and facilitate the students in any way they can. We could not do what we do every year without their hard work, their care and their professionalism. And lastly, and most importantly, I would like to not just thank but pay tribute to the wonderful Bríd Dukes. It was Bríd Dukes who first imagined a programme for transition year students. It was Bríd Dukes who gave me the opportunity to embark on this rich vein of work. It has been Bríd Dukes who has ensured that Tenderfoot has continued to exist from year to year despite the recession and dwindling resources. Her commitment to the young people of South Dublin County, her belief in the importance of their place in our cultural institutions, and her capacity to put her principles into action is an inspiration.

And to all of our Tenderfeet across the years I am so pleased to have had the opportunity to work with and alongside each and every one of you. I am appreciative of all our writers who worked with me over the last few months in preparation for the publication of this volume. I am happy for those whose work made it between the covers and I encourage those who missed out this time to hope, along with me, that this volume will be the first of many.

Veronica Coburn

TABLE OF CONTENTS

PLAYS ABOUT FAMILY

ESCAPE
a play for 4 characters by Ciara Donohoe   11

STACY
a play for 7 characters by Janice Bangala   25

LIFE SENTENCE
a play for 6 characters by Orlagh Woods   53

I AM RUNNING
a monologue by Katie Black   82

PLAYS ABOUT FRIENDSHIP

STRIKE!
a play for 3 characters by Alison Bryan   85

WEIRD
a play for 5 characters plus extras by Tírna McGauley   98

TEAM CAPTAIN
a play for 6 characters by Ola Kusiak   124

PLAYS ABOUT THE TEENAGE EXPERIENCE

WHAT A WAY TO SPEND THE WEEKEND
a monologue by Katherine Cullen   137

TTYL
a play for 9 characters plus extras by Declan Moore   139

PARTY
a play for 7 characters plus extras by Sarah Hanlon   150

PLAYS ABOUT RELATIONSHIPS

PARK BENCH
a play for 3 characters by Ellen O'Sullivan   167

DEPARTURES
a play for 3 characters by Simon O'Mara   176

A PIECE OF ME
a play for 3 characters by Seoid Ní Laoire   186

PLAYS ABOUT THE WIDER WORLD

MKII
a monologue by Robert Barrett   202

TRAPPED BY FEAR
a play for 3 characters by Aisling O'Leary   206

P.R.
a play for 9 characters plus extras by Scott Byrne   222

ESCAPE
Ciara Donohoe

"I found the whole process of writing and producing a play fascinating. Seeing what you created come to life before your eyes was something I found really special. My involvement on the costume design team was an experience that really stuck with me through the years. It definitely built up my confidence and love of fashion and design. I now study fashion in college."

Characters

Eve, 14 years old
Calvin, 15 years old
Eve's mum
Eve's dad

Scene One

When the lights come up we see two young people sitting together, one on a wall and the other leaning against it. It is early in the evening and it is quite bright out. Eve is fourteen and comes from a lower, middle class home. Her father is an aggressive alcoholic and has recently turned violent towards her and her mother. Eve's only close friend is Calvin. Calvin is fifteen years old. He drinks and does low class drugs as does Eve. Eve has a noticeable cut on her lip. She is smoking a cigarette.

Eve: Calvin?

Calvin: Yeah?

Eve: Do you ever think of running away?

Calvin: Running away, like for good?

Eve: Yeah.

Calvin: Why do you ask?

Eve: Just wondering really.

She passes the cigarette to him.

Calvin: Well yeah sometimes I guess.

Eve: But your family seem so... I dunno'... normal.

Calvin: You don't know shit about my family.

Eve: Well you never talk about them.

Calvin: A depressed ma, workaholic da, annoying little sister and a brother in Belfast, there's not much to talk about.

Eve shrugs. Calvin takes out a small plastic bag with hash in it, rolls a joint and lights it.

Eve: Pass that here will you..?

Calvin: You're fucking fourteen Eve.

Eve: And you're only fifteen, it's hardly the first time Calvin, come on I really need it.

Calvin: That have anything to do with your lip?

Eve raises her hand to her cut lip.

Eve: I don't want to talk about it.

Calvin: He hit you again didn't he?

Eve says nothing.

Calvin: I swear to God that motherfu...

Eve: Calvin just shut up about it and pass me the fucking joint.

Calvin shakes his head and hands it to her.

Calvin: Your mam okay?

Eve: She's fine, now shut up.

The two sit in silence for a minute or two but continue passing the joint.

Calvin: So do you then?

Eve: Do I what?

Calvin: Ever think about running away?

Eve: Oh, well yeah all the time.

Calvin: Things will get better you know.

Eve: I really doubt it.

Calvin: Well hey, if they don't, who knows, maybe we'll end up running away. I could be a drug dealer and you could be a prostitute, perfect eh?

Eve laughs and then takes another pull of the joint and then sighs.

Eve: Calvin this one is shit.

Calvin: They're all like that now. It's what happens when you've been smoking it too long.

Eve: So the buzz just stops.

Calvin: Yeah.

Eve: So much for my 'means of escape'.

Calvin: Good oul' Jack can always help you with that though.

Eve: Jack?

Calvin: Jack Daniels.

Eve: Oh right yeah… That would be good though.

Calvin: What would?

Eve: Running away.

Calvin: I never knew you wanted to be a prostitute.

Eve: Shut up, you know what I mean.

Eve laughs. She then raises her hand to her lip because it hurts.

Calvin: Yeah, we'd have a laugh. Here, I better go, you want me to walk you home?

Eve: No I better give him another hour to cool down, I'll be fine.

Calvin: Okay, well text me later.

Eve: Sure.

Calvin walks off and the light fades to black.

Scene Two

Lights up to reveal Eve walking into her kitchen. Her mum is sitting at the table with a cup of tea.

Eve: Dad home?

Mum: No.

Eve nods and leans against the countertop. Her mum sniffs the air.

Mum: Were you smoking again?

Eve: No.

Mum: I can smell it.

Eve: Just leave me alone.

Mum: Look Eve don't be like that. I'm sorry about earlier but you know how your father's temper gets when you wind him up like that.

Eve: Don't fucking defend him Mum.

Mum: Don't you dare speak to me like that, it's things like this that set him off.

Eve: Oh okay, so it's my fault he hits us?

Mum: I'm not bloody saying that, I'm only trying to help.

Eve: That's rich coming from the woman who just sat there and watched her husband hit his fourteen year old daughter.

Mum: Eve don't say that... what do you expect me to do?

Eve: Stand up to him for once in your life.

Mum: Don't be so stupid Eve, I couldn't do that, he's my husband. You're making him out to be some kind of monster.

Eve: But he IS a monster, he can't control himself.

They hear the door closing and they both jump. Eve's mum gets up and runs over to the kettle to put it on. Eve's dad strolls through the kitchen door.

Mum: Tony, cup of tea?

Tony: Nah, I'm fine.

He sees Eve. She looks away, avoiding his stare..

Tony: Look, sorry about earlier but you know how much you wind me up when you're cheeky.

Eve: But I wasn't being cheeky.

Tony: Excuse me?

Eve: Nothing.

Tony: Didn't think so. And look, don't go mouthing off about that lip of yours to everyone, it's none of their bloody business what happens in this house, you shouldn't have wound me up, that's how these silly little accidents happen.

He walks over and takes her chin in his hand to survey her lip. Eve flinches.

Tony: Barely a bleedin' scrape.

Mum: So where did you go then Tony?

Tony: And what's that supposed to mean?

Mum: Oh... well I was just... making conversation is all.

Tony: Being fucking nosey is all, more like.

Eve's mum looks down into her now cold cup of tea.

Mum: Sorry.

Tony: I went out for a quick drink, that okay?

Eve's mum stays silent.

Eve: Haven't you drank a lot already today though Dad?

Tony: Excuse me?

Eve: I was only asking.

Tony: No, you were being a cheeky bitch. Get out of my sight before you regret opening your mouth.

Eve walks out of the room and the light fades.

Mum: She was only looking out for you Tony, maybe you shouldn't be so hard on her.

Tony: Are you calling me a bad father?

Mum: Well... Of course no'... not.

Tony: Do you even understand how much I've done for this family, sacrifices after sacrifices, and all I get is grief when I reward myself with a few whiskeys. This bloody ungrateful asshole of a family.

Mum: Tony don't get upset love, we appreciate you.

Tony: Don't fucking patronise me.

Mum: I wasn't..

Tony raises his voice.

Tony: And don't answer me back, now we know where that little bitch gets her smart mouth from.

Mum: Tony. . .

Tony: I SAID SHUT UP...

Light fades.

Scene Three

We see Calvin sitting on the same wall as before. He has a makeshift plastic bottle bong in his hand. It is around nine in the evening and it is quite dark. He takes out his phone, punches some numbers, and holds it up to his ear.

Calvin: Hey Eve what's up? . . . Well I'm at the usual place, come on over, I have a little present for you . . . Haha, 'k, see you in a sec, hurry, it's fuckin' freezing.

After a minute or two Eve arrives. She sits on the wall beside Calvin.

Eve: Hey, that your bong?

Calvin: Yeah I'm done with it. I thought you might want it.

Eve: Nah, would be too dodgy keeping it in mine. Why don't you want it anymore?

Calvin: Won't be using it anymore, onwards and upwards is what I say.

Eve: What do you mean?

Calvin: I'm off that cheap shit. It's a joke.

Eve takes out a cigarette and lights it.

Eve: You're off it for good?

Calvin: Yeah.

Eve: So what are you taking now then?

Calvin: Well, E's are a good buzz.

Eve: Ecstasy?

Calvin: Yeah.

Eve: What's it like?

Calvin: Fucking amazing, it's like tapping into a secret world, everything feels so good. You've never had anything like this, it's heaven.

Eve: Could you get me some?

Calvin: Eve, I'm not a dealer.

Eve: It's not dealing, just sharing.

Calvin: Well, I'm getting some on Friday, think you can wait till then.

Eve: Oh I dunno', that's two days away, like I'm pretty desperate… Of course I can wait, I'm not a feckin' junkie.

Calvin: Yeah, we'll see.

Eve shoves him lightly.

Calvin: Another three weeks left of summer, feckin' brill', ha?

Eve: For you maybe, you don't have to live in my house.

Calvin: Anything happen last night?

Eve: Lost his head but I left in time.

Calvin: Oh right… Sure the E will soon have your mind off that.

Eve: Yeah, can't wait now, it better be all you're making it out to be.

Calvin: Oh believe me, it is, you'll be off your fuckin' head.

They both smile and the light fades to black.

Scene Four

Lights up to reveal Eve and Calvin leaning against the wall. There is an empty naggin of vodka beside them on the wall. It is dark and around eleven at night. They are both giddy and laughing uncontrollably.

Eve: And… he kicks… the dog over… the bridge.

Eve nearly falls over with laughter.

Calvin: Anchorman… what a fuckin' film. (*They both continue laughing until Calvin slumps down and leans against the wall. Eve follows.*) JESUS CHRIST!!

Eve jumps.

Eve: What, what?

Calvin: What the fuck happened to your face?

Eve: You calling me ugly?

The both giggle.

Calvin: No, ya thick, that… (*He pokes the bruise on her cheek.*) Looks like a bleedin' giant hickey on your cheek.

They both fall into convulsions of laughter.

Eve: Naaah, was my dad.

Calvin: Fuckin' ponce! If I had some like giant fuckin' gun it would be straight in that face o' his.

Calvin imitates shooting someone with a shotgun. They both laugh.

Eve: Thanks Cal.

Calvin: So E eh? How's it feel?

Eve: Oh my God amazing! Thank you so much.

She gives Calvin a huge hug. Still laughing. Nearly falls over.

Calvin: Ah here, I better get you the fuck home.

Eve: Calvin?

Calvin: What?

Eve: You swear a LOT.

Calvin: No I fuckin' don't, shut the fuck up...fuck.

They both start laughing and walk off giddily. Light fades.

Scene Five

Light rises to reveal Eve and her father in the middle of an argument. Eve is still drunk and they are both shouting.

Tony: Where were you till this hour?

Eve: Out.

Tony: Less of the cheek, I asked you a question.

Eve: With my friend.

Tony: That little knacker Calvin fella' yeah, thought I told you to stay away from him.

Eve: He's my friend, you can't stop me from seeing him.

Tony: And look at the state of you, your eyes are like saucers, what have you taken? Probably sleeping around for drugs you little junkie slut.

Eve: Shut up, I'd never do anything like that. Would be better than being a woman beating alcoholic anyway, the smell of whiskey off your breath, it's disgusting!

Tony: The cheek... *(He raises his hand to hit her, she flinches. He stops but leaves his hand in the air.)* You're not even worth it.

He lowers his hand.

Eve: No, go on, hit me, I'm not scared of you anymore, you know that? Come on, you pig.

Tony turns back around and hits her with the back of his hand. Eve's mum comes in behind her husband.

Mum: Calm down the pair of you.

Tony spins around and hits her too, she falls to the ground. He turns back to Eve.

Tony: Now look what you've made me done, you little bitch.

Eve goes to help her mother up but she doesn't let her.

Mum: No, just get out Eve, GET OUT!

Eve runs out of the house. She takes out her mobile.

Eve: Calvin where are you?... I'm fine I just... I just... Look can you come out?... At the playground?... Okay. I'll see you soon...

She hangs up and walks off quickly. She is crying. Lights fade.

Scene Six

Light rises to reveal Calvin and Eve sitting on steps beside a playground. It is late at night and very dark.

Calvin: I don't fuckin' believe that, what an asshole Eve... Here, you need to talk to someone, like, proper about it, sort it out.

Eve: How though, you don't understand he won't change, not for anyone or anything. Do you have anything on you?

Calvin: Em, I think I've another E.

He goes to search through his pockets.

Eve: Don't bother, I don't want it.

Calvin: Oh right, why'd you ask then?

Eve: Dunno', thought you might have had something more.

Calvin: What's wrong with E?

Eve: Well I dunno', it's good but it just messes up my head, makes me giddy. I just want to clear my head, relax...not think.

Calvin: You're not taking anything more than E Eve, you're not a junkie.

Eve shrugs.

Eve: I suppose.

Calvin: Promise?

Eve: 'K. Jesus, calm down.

Calvin sighs heavily.

Calvin: Well, what do you want to do then, about your dad?

Eve: What can I do?

Calvin: I dunno really.

Eve: I just need to get out of there.

Calvin: My brother's up in Belfast, he'd take us in no bother. It mightn't be forever but we can see from there, and anyway, he's always got like an unlimited supply of hash.

Eve: What, run away like? You serious?

Calvin: Why not, I've got nothing to lose anyway and neither do you.

Eve: Would your brother not say anything though, like to your ma and da?

Calvin: Nah, you joking? When he left he was like nineteen, hasn't spoken to my rents since. He'll prob'ly be happy for us.

Eve: Oh okay. When can we go though?

Calvin: Tomorrow night or something.

Eve: Tomorrow, just go into town and get the coach out or what?

Calvin: Yeah something like that, I can check the times tonight.

Eve: Shite, can't believe we're actually going to do this.

Calvin: This shit with your dad's been going on too long.

Eve: Shit, it's like twelve, I better head home, but thanks Calvin, I love you, ya know that?

Calvin: Fuck off you and go home.

They both laugh. Eve walks off. Light fades.

Scene Seven

Light rises to reveal Eve in her house. Her mum is sitting at the kitchen table.

Eve: Hi, you okay?

Mum: I'm fine.

Eve: And your cheek?

Mum: It's fine.

Eve: I'm sorry Mum.

She begins to cry a little.

Mum: I know pet, you just shouldn't wind him up you know that.

Eve: I know I just... I dunno'.

Mum: Are you okay?

Eve: I'll live. Where is he anyway?

Mum: I have no idea, out somewhere.

Eve: Since when?

Mum: Since last night.

They stay silent for a minute.

Eve: Mum, we can't keep living like this.

Mum: There's nothing wrong, he just has a short fuse, it'll blow over.

Eve: It's more than that though, I'll get us help.

Mum: We're grand Eve.

Eve: You sure you can't just leave?

Mum: Don't be silly love, he's my husband. I love him.

Eve: Does he really love you though?

The front door slams and Eve's dad walks through the door. He's visibly angry.

Tony: Eve, leave. I want to talk to your mother.

Eve: We were talking.

Tony: I didn't ask what you were doing. I told you to leave.

Eve: Dad, I...

Tony: What have I told you about talking back, giving cheek. Either leave the room now or I'll make you.

Eve doesn't move for a minute.

Mum: For God's sake Eve would you just leave, he just wants a chat, is there any wonder he loses his temper?

Eve: Bye Mum.

Eve walks out of the room. Lights fade.

Scene Eight

Light rises to reveal Eve sitting on the wall with a large backpack. She also has a handbag that is stuffed full. It is early in the evening. The light is dim. Her phone rings, she answers. We hear Calvin's voice on the phone.

Calvin: Eve?

Eve: Oh hey, Calvin, you nearly ready, we only have ten minutes to get to the bus stop.

Calvin: Here look Eve, I'm not going.

Eve: What?

Calvin: We're not going Eve, we haven't even thought the fucking thing over, we can't just get up and leave. I can't leave Louise, she's only five and with my ma like she is, I'm all she has. And you have to stay there for your ma.

Eve: Fuck you Calvin.

She hangs up the phone and sits for a minute, visibly angry. She then dials another number.

Eve: Hi em, Jack?... It's a friend of Calvin's, Calvin Kearns. Well what could I get off you today like?... What?... Heroin... Nothing else? Yeah 'k... Half five? Yeah okay. Bye.

Eve gets up and walks off. The light fades.

Scene Nine

Light rises to reveal Eve's parents still in the kitchen.

Tony: Look Teresa, I'm sorry, can't ya even look at me?

Teresa: What do you expect Tony. Look at me!

Tony: I know, it just, it was an accident, you know I didn't mean it. It just happened.

Teresa: There's only so many times something can 'just happen' Tony, we're falling apart.

Tony: I know.

Teresa: What happened to you? What went wrong? We were so good before, you were never like this.

Tony: A lot of things have happened

Teresa: Talk to me, I want to help you, I want things to get better. I can't stay in this house anymore, I'm a prisoner here. Look at poor Eve Tony, she's fourteen, she shouldn't have to deal with all this, she shouldn't have to look after her own mother.

Tony: And you don't think I know that? I love her, I love you, just too much has changed.

Teresa: Like what? Is there someone else?

Tony: No, course not, I love you, I just told you that. It's work..

Teresa: Well, things have never been perfect, everyone's struggling these days, it's nothing new, nothing we couldn't handle before. So what is it, you're not getting as many jobs as before?

Tony: I'm not getting any jobs

Teresa: What do you mean?

Tony: I was fuckin' laid off Teresa.

Teresa: What, when?

Tony: Almost two months ago now, I've been trying to get a job ever since, found meself in the pub one day and, well, what do you expect?

Teresa: What about the job centre?

Tony: Teresa, there just isn't any jobs for tradesmen anymore. I couldn't tell you, couldn't let you down, show you what a fuckin' failure I am.

Teresa: You're still my Tony. It's just the drink, but we can sort that out, can't we?

Tony: Of course.

Teresa: And things will be rough for a while but we'll get through that. Another job will come along soon. I can look for work too, there's always someone looking for a receptionist and what not. Tony, I missed ya.

Tony: I know, and things will get better. I love you an' Eve more than anything. I'll do everything to make things right this time, I promise.

Scene Ten

Light rises to reveal Calvin walking along with his phone to his ear. The rest of the stage is completely dark.

Calvin: Ugh, come on Eve, answer your bloody phone, stop being such a fuckin' drama queen.

The light rises further to reveal Eve lying on the ground. There is a syringe and a small piece of tin foil lying beside her. Calvin runs over.

Calvin: Eve, what the fuck. *(He shakes her, but she is lifeless.)* What the fuck have you done Eve, come on, wake up.

He slaps her cheek to try and wake her up but she doesn't budge. He leans his face to her mouth but feels no breath. He looks down to the syringe and picks it up. He slumps down against the wall and begins to cry.

Calvin: I should have fucking been here Eve, what the fuck have you done to yourself. *(He takes out his phone and dials a number. He is still crying.)* Can I have an ambulance... She's just... it was heroin... I think she's dead...

The light fades.

STACY

Janice Bangala

"I didn't want Stacy to be unrealistic and have a happy ending but I didn't want it to have a sad ending either. I wanted to find a perfect balance. I didn't want my play to be about a typical spoilt teenager who is disobedient. I wanted to show how teenagers can react to certain changes. I got most of my ideas from events that happened in my life, my friends' lives and some ideas just popped into my head."

Characters

Stacy, 15/16 years of age
Ma, Stacy's ma, 35 years of age
Eric, Stacy's brother, older
Amy, Stacy's best friend
Ben, Stacy's da, 40 years of age
Melissa, Ben's girlfriend, 20 years of age
BeerBellyMan, hotdog seller

Prologue

Two characters, Stacy and Ma, stand in a spotlight centre stage.

Stacy: Why me?

Scene One

June 4th. Evening. The start of summer. The scene takes place in Stacy's kitchen. Stacy is sitting down on a chair, she is slouched down in a bad mood. Her ma is standing opposite her. She is holding the back of a chair firmly as if she is trying to keep things in order or control. There are only three chairs at the table. Stacy's ma is well dressed. She looks as if she is going out somewhere fancy. Stacy is dressed casually. She is very upset but she is trying not to show it. Stacy is about fifteen or sixteen years of age. Her ma is about thirty five.

Ma: He wants you to ... (*Trails off.*)

Stacy: But... Ma, I don't even know him.

Ma: He's a good man.

Stacy: Stop being nice to the good for nothing/

/ indicates an interruption.

Ma: Don't you even dare. (*Gives her a warning with her eyes.*)

Stacy: How long?

Ma: Just for a little while

Stacy: How long Ma?

Ma: Just the summer

Stacy: Just? What do you mean just?

Ma: Have you/

Stacy: You must want me gone

Ma: No Stacy, it's not like that, he just wants to spend some time with you. Look at Eric's relationship with your da, it's been mended.

Stacy: As if our relationship's going to be mended! He left me ma, Eric runs back to him because he has no emotions, he might as well be a robot.

Ma: Eric does have emotions Stace, he just let go of the past and started a new path.

Stacy: Why do you forgive him so easy?

Ma: Because it's the right thing to do. (*Stacy sighs.*) He's trying.

Stacy: (*Folding her arms.*) I'm not shocked that you're on his side.

Ma: There's no side to be on, there's just reality. He'll take me to court, he has rights you know.

Stacy: Ughhhh.

Stacy gets up and walks to the fridge, opens it, and gets a drink. Someone walks in. It is Eric, Stacy's big brother. Stacy doesn't look at him. Eric has just turned seventeen. He's good looking, very cocky and all the girls like him. Eric is very sporty and very fit. Eric likes his father, Ben, and is very close to him. Stacy and Eric have a love/hate relationship.

Eric: Ma is she still being a whinge bag?

Eric sits in the chair that Stacy was sitting in.

Stacy: (*Mocking him.*) Ma is she still being a whinge bag?

Eric: Shut up Stacy.

Stacy: Make me.

Eric: I would but I'm not gunna bother withcha.

Ma looks at her watch. She seems nervous.

Stacy: Ma, why are you so nervous?

Eric: Yeah ma, you're so fidgety.

Ma: I have a date.

Eric: (*Laughs.*) Ha, I thought you said you were going on a date.

Stacy: That's what she said you dope.

Eric: Oh ok.

Ma: I won't go if it's bothering the both of yous.

Stacy: (*Trying not to look too shocked.*) What time's he picking you up at?

Ma: He's meant to be here ten minutes ago.

Eric: He probably stood you up.

Stacy: Ignore him, you look great.

Ma: Thank you Stacy.

Stacy: When is Ben picking me up?

Ma: (*Frowns.*) Tomorrow morning, did I not tell you?

There is a knock on the door. Stacy and her mam look at each other. Ma walks over to Eric.

Ma: (*Whispers.*) We'll talk tomorrow. Stacy?

Stacy: Yeah.

Ma: I won't see you in the morning, your dad is picking you up at twelve and I'm in work for nine.

Stacy: (*Sarcastically.*) Oh not even a send-off.

Ma hugs Stacy.

Stacy: (*Pleads.*) Do I have to go?

Ma kisses her on the forehead then opens the door to leave.

Stacy: Ma?

Ma: Yesss.

Stacy: Nothing.

Ma: (*Smiles.*) I love you too!

Ma exits.

Eric: (*In a silly voice.*) Ah ye little baby, do you wanna hug?

Stacy: As if. You're not going anywhere in the morning, I'll see you.

Eric: I won't wake up just to say goodbye, I swear.

Stacy: I know you will.

Stacy leaves the room.

Scene Two

June 5th. Twelve noon. Stacy is in the kitchen. Eric is still asleep. Stacy is sitting on the table, tapping the table nervously, biting her lips.

Stacy: I'm not saying hi first. (*There is a knock on the door.*) Wait, he's early. Shit, why am I talking to myself? Omg, I'm going crazy. Open the door Stacy! I'm officially losing it.

Stacy opens the door.

Amy: Ahhh you, thanks for saying goodbye. (*Stacy jumps on Amy and hugs her.*) You're suffocating me, suffocate me some more, I'm going to miss you.

Stacy: You'll come see me yeah?

Amy: Why wouldn't I?

Stacy: This isn't fair.

Amy: (*Rolls her eyes.*) Any news before I go?

Stacy: Nope, I'll probably suicidally kill myself.

Amy: (*Laughing*) Is suicidally even a word?

Stacy: (*Laughing.*) I make my own words.

Eric appears in the kitchen.

Eric: (*Winking.*) Morning Amy.

Amy: (*Smiling.*) Hello Eric, you're looking good.

Stacy: (*Stacy gives Amy a look then says to Eric.*) Put on a top and stop creeping on me like that, ye freak.

Eric: Nah, pretty sure Amy wants to see my body.

Amy: Don't mind.

Stacy: Ewww, why are you even here? It's a bit early for the likes of you to be up.

Eric: (*Ignores her.*) Dad!

Stacy: (*Surprised.*) Dad?

She turns and sees that her dad, Ben, has arrived. Eric and Ben do an arm shake.

Ben: How are ye boy?

Eric: Grand, you coming to the final?

Ben: Wouldn't miss it for the world.

Stacy: (*Nudges Amy and whispers.*) Ah, but he missed half of our lives already.

Amy: You're so negative.

Stacy: You would be too if you were in my shoes.

Ben: (*Looks at Stacy, scratches his head, and smiles.*) You're all grown up aren't you?

Ben reaches out to touch her but Stacy moves away.

Eric: Her hormones are awful, I warn ye.

Ben: (*Ben ignores Eric's comment.*) So, you ready?

Stacy: No.

Eric: She's ready.

Amy: Give me one last hug before you leave me.

Amy leaves.

Ben: Is she your friend?

Stacy: No, my best friend.

Ben: Oh, I see.

Eric: So, I'll be seeing yous both soon, don't worry.

Ben nods at Eric.

Stacy: Told you, you would get up and say goodbye.

Eric: Never said goodbye.

Stacy: (*Grinning.*) You got up for me, I know you did.

Eric: Ha, ha, whatever.

Stacy: Seeya Eric.

Eric nods.

Ben: Now are you ready?

Stacy: Do I have a choice?

Scene Three

Same day. Stacy arrives at Ben's house. Melissa, Ben's girlfriend, is watering flowers in the garden. Stacy doesn't know about Melissa. Melissa is blonde and beautiful and young. Stacy approaches carrying her suitcase.

Ben: Do you need a hand?

Stacy: No, I'm fine.

Ben: You sure?

Stacy: I said I'm fine.

Melissa: Oh, hello Stacy.

Ben: This is/

Stacy: The housekeeper?

Ben: (*Laughs nervously, scratches his head.*) Melissa, my....

Stacy: (*Sarcastically.*) Ohhhh, this can't get any better.

Melissa: I hope you don't feel uncomfortable with me here.

Stacy: (*Smiles.*) I'll be fine, girlfriends come and go.

Ben: (*Scratches his head.*) Why don't I make lunch?

Stacy: I'm just going to call Ma and tell her I'm here.

Ben: Okay.

Ben goes into the house.

Melissa: I hope we can be friends yeno?

Stacy: That'll be awkward since you're going out with my da, don't cha think?

Stacy takes out her phone and calls Eric. Melissa can hear Stacy's conversation.

Stacy: Ma?

Melissa: (*Whispers.*) I'll be back in a sec.

Stacy nods.

Eric: (*Imitating his Ma.*) Yes Stacy?

Stacy: Eric, stop.

Eric: Why you calling me Ma then?

Stacy: Why didn't you tell me there's a woman in Ben's life?

Eric: You never asked, you never want to hear about Dad Stace. She's a really nice person yeno, just give her a/

Stacy: I don't care if she's nice.

Eric: So why are you calling me?

Stacy: Tell Ma I made it safely and that I'm okay.

Eric: Why call me and not her?

Stacy: Cause I needed to ask you about that yoke.

Eric: She's nice, give her a chance.

Melissa: (*Melissa comes back.*) Lunch is almost ready Stacy. You must be hungry after that journey.

Stacy: (*On phone.*) See you later Ma, I love you.

Eric: Stacy, you have issues.

Call ends.

Melissa: I made BLTs. Eric said you liked them. I made them especially for you.

Stacy: BLTs?

Melissa: Bacon, tomato and lettuce sandwiches.

Stacy: I'm a vegan.

Melissa: You can just take out the bacon.

Stacy: I'm not hungry. Could you show me my room?

Melissa: I will. Yeah, of course.

They start towards the house. Melissa stops.

Melissa: Be easy on your dad, he's as nervous as you.

Stacy: (*Sarcastically.*) I'll try.

Scene Four

June 8th. One o'clock in the day. Sunny. A park. It has taken Ben three days to get Stacy to agree to do something with him. Stacy and her dad are sitting on a bench.

Ben: So how was school?

Stacy: School is over.

Ben: Yeah, I know but, when you were in school.

Stacy just looks at Ben. He scratches his head.

Stacy: Do you have nits? You should buy Head & Shoulders for that.

Ben: (*Laughs.*) Why would you think that I have nits?

Stacy: You're always scratching your head.

Ben: Hmm, never noticed I did that. (*Awkward silence.*) So any boyfriends?

Stacy: Seriously, why would I talk about that with you?

Ben: Why not? (*Stacy looks at him as though he is really weird.*) You like music?

Stacy: Yeah I do.

Ben: What type?

Stacy: Most types.

Ben: Like?

Stacy: Just music, jeez, you wouldn't know the stuff I like.

Ben: That's because you're not telling me.

Stacy: I don't have to, do I?

Ben: You don't have to but, I don't know why it bothers you to tell me.

Stacy: Why do you want to know in the first place?

Ben: Because I want to get to know you, we're both here for that.

Stacy: If this was my choice you think I'd be here?

Ben: (*Scratches his head nervously and changes the subject to avoid getting into a fight with Stacy.*) So that girl... em Amy, how long do you know her?

Stacy: Quite long.

Ben: How long?

Stacy: Does it matter?

Ben: She's your best friend.

Stacy: I know. I'm the one that told you that.

Ben: So do you like animals?

Stacy: Clearly if I'm a vegan.

Ben: Favourite type?

Stacy: Favourite type of what?

Ben: Animal.

Stacy: Don't have one.

Ben: You sure?

Stacy: Yeah, I'm sure.

Ben: What's your favourite colour?

Stacy: You're asking me questions I'd ask a five year old in primary school.

Ben: So you don't have a favourite colour?

Stacy: Jesus, it's blue, red and purple.

Ben: That's colours.

Stacy: Well done.

Ben: I said colour.

Stacy: They're my favourite.

Ben: You don't have a favourite?

Stacy: Oh my God! Go away, will ye?

A large man with a beer belly in white trousers and a white t-shirt walks by. There are ketchup and mustard stains all over his t-shirt.

BeerBellyMan: Hot dogs, get your hot dogs, they're hot, get your hot dogs, two for the price of one.

Stacy: I'm gunna get a hotdog.

Ben: Aren't you a vegan?

Stacy: I'm not. (*Smiles.*) I just don't like her. I'll be back.

She runs towards BeerBellyMan.

Ben: (*Shouts after her but she doesn't hear.*) I'll pay.

Stacy: Can I have two hot dogs please?

Stacy looks at BeerBellyMan. She sees that he is huge.

BeerBellyMan: €3.50.

Stacy: That's cheap.

Stacy gives him the money.

BeerBellyMan: Well, I'll higher the price for ya. (*Laughs.*) Ketchup or mustard?

Stacy: What?

BeerBellyMan: What sauce do you want on your hot dogs?

Stacy: Oh, ketchup for me. I'll guess ketchup for him as well.

BeerBellyMan: Ketchup it is, why don't cha ask 'um next time?

Stacy: I don't want to ask him.

BeerBellyMan: Why?

Stacy: Because he's not worth asking.

BeerBellyMan: But you're buying him a hot dog, shows you care.

Stacy: It's two for the price of one isn't it, I wanted a bargain deal. (*BeerBellyMan smiles at her.*) Why do you care?

BeerBellyMan: (*Gives her the hot dogs.*) I don't, I was just asking.

Stacy: Sorry, I'm not normally this rude, I'm just stressed out.

BeerBellyMan: Who's the bloke? New bf?

Stacy: Nah, my da, no, Ben actually.

BeerBellyMan: And you don't know if he likes mustard or ketchup?

Stacy: It's a bit more complicated than that.

BeerBellyMan: Okay.

He hands her the hot dogs.

Stacy: See you later BeerBellyMan.

BeerBellyMan looks at his stomach and then at Stacy in shock. Stacy returns to Ben on the bench.

BeerBellyMan: (*To himself.*) Interesting kid. (*Laughs.*) Wouldn't mind a beer, especially on this nice day.

Stacy hands Ben a hotdog.

Ben: It's beautiful isn't it?

Stacy: What?

Stacy looks around to see what he's talking about.

Ben: The park, the birds, the fresh air.

Stacy: (*Ignores him.*) There was ketchup and mustard but I didn't know what you like.

Ben: I'm a fan of ketchup.

Stacy: Same.

Ben: What took you so long?

Stacy: The queue.

Ben: So next week, do you want to go the beach, it's beautiful and the sea is amazing, it would be fun.

Stacy: With Melissa?

Ben: Yeah, if you don't mind. She's a nice person, she's trying her hardest, go easy on her.

Stacy: Could I bring someone?

Ben: Yeah.

Stacy smiles.

Scene Five

June 10th. Morning. Stacy is in her bedroom. She is lying on her bed writing in her diary. As she writes, her phone rings three times. She doesn't answer because she doesn't recognise the number.

Diary Entry: I'm going to start writing how I feel for the good of my health. Keeping feelings trapped inside isn't always the best idea. First of all, notebook, get prepared for a lot of negative energy and don't expect me to write perfect all the time b'cos I'm not in school so I don't have to. Now, where do I start? I must admit that it's not all bad. I was expecting worse. Ben's trying but I don't want to give in too easily. We're even going to the beach. That reminds me I have to ring Amy to ask her to come, hold on a little while, I'll be back dot, dot, dot...

Stacy puts her diary down, picks up her phone and calls Amy to ask her to come to the beach.

Amy: Hello?

Stacy: Heya.

Amy: Oh, how are ye?

Stacy: Had better days, you? I have to ask you something.

Amy: I'm actually doing well but I miss you, oh, is it serious?

Eric: (*In the background.*) Get off that phone of yours, you're always on it.

Stacy: (*Recognises Eric's voice.*) Eh where are you?

Amy: At home.

Stacy: Ummm, you sure you're at home?

Amy: Em, yeah, anyways, what did you need to tell me?

Stacy: Will you come to the beach with me on Saturday? Ben said I could bring a friend.

Amy: Um, maybe...

Stacy: What? Maybe? What have you got better to do? (*Amy doesn't respond.*) Well, call me if you're going.

Stacy hangs up. She calls Eric.

Eric: Yeah?

Stacy: Where are you?

Eric: At home.

Stacy: With who?

Eric: Me, myself and I.

Amy: (*Mocking him.*) You tell me to get off the phone and now you're on yours.

Stacy: You player, you couldn't keep your hands off her, you're so irritating. She's my best friend.

Eric: Call me when you make sense.

Stacy: When I get my hands on you, you're dead, you good for nothing... (*Eric hangs up.*) Oh no, he didn't hang up on me.

Stacy's phone rings.

Stacy: (*To herself.*) Oh here we go. Yeah, you're lucky you called me back or there was going to be murderrrrr!

Ma: Stacy, it's your ma! Who are you planning on murdering and why haven't you called me?

Stacy: I told Eric to tell you I'm alright.

Ma: Why didn't you call me?

Stacy: Why didn't you call me? Everyone expects me to make the first move, all the time.

Ma: Did you not get my missed calls?

Stacy: Oh, they were from you, why were you calling me on a private number?

Ma: I didn't even know it was on private Stace, anyways, I've been ringing cause I care.

Stacy: I know you do.

Ma: Call me later, will you, my manager is hanging around close by.

Stacy: Wait Ma.

Ma: Hurry it up.

Stacy: How did your date go?

Ma: (*Giggles.*) We'll talk soon. I have to go. Bye.

Ma hangs up. Stacy's phone rings again almost immediately.

Stacy: Seriously, who's calling me now? Hello.

Amy: I'll come on Saturday.

Stacy: You don't have to. I'm sure you have better things to do with Eric.

Amy: Wow Stace, that was a low blow.

Stacy: Says the liar. My brother is teaching you his bad habits.

Amy: Stace, I'll come on Saturday and we'll talk about it then.

Stacy: Hmmm, ok.

Amy: Seeya soon.

Stacy hangs up.

Stacy: (*Writing in her diary.*) Told you I'd be back but not back in the greatest mood. Forgot to tell you at the start my life isn't the simplest. Miss Girly Girl, who looks about 18, is going out with Ben, my dad. She's licking me hole, filling me with kindness. She probably hates me, but idgaf!! Wdf is happening like? I thought I was going to be the only girl in Ben's life. Me ma's dating, it's too much to handle. And Amy is going out with me brother. What's with all the sudden changes in my life? Last thing, Ben's gone out, it's just me and Melissa at dinner and she's making me bloody vegan food like vegetable rice, as if I'm gunna eat that. He told her I wasn't a vegan. I think she's messing with me head. I want some chicken like.

Scene Six

June 15th. Evening. Melissa has gone to do the shopping. Stacy and her dad are having pizza while they watch TV. America's Next Top Model is on the TV.

Stacy: Ugh, why do we have to watch this?

Ben: Aren't girls into this stuff?

Stacy: All girls aren't the same Ben.

Ben: I know but the majority like the same stuff.

Stacy: By now you should know I'm not the majority. I betcha Melissa likes this show though.

Ben: She does.

Stacy: We're no way similar.

Ben: You don't know that.

Stacy: Ugh, just change.

Ben: To what?

Stacy: To something good, something watchable.

Ben changes channels. The theme tune to The Fresh Prince Of Bel Air is heard.

Stacy: Now this is a show, none of that model crap.

Ben: (*Laughs.*) You're something else Stacy.

Stacy: Ssssshhhh.

Stacy, feeling comfortable, puts her legs up on the couch. She and Ben catch each other's eye. She puts her legs down.

Ben: It's okay, you can keep them up.

Stacy: I'm fine like this.

Ben: Here's the remote. You can change.

She changes the channel. The sound of a football match is heard.

Stacy: Did you know Man U are playing against Liverpool?

Ben: I did know.

Stacy: Then why aren't we not watching it?

Ben: I wanted to put something on that you liked.

Stacy: Well I want to watch the match.

Ben: Man U are winning. Go on United!

Stacy: Da?

Ben: Yeah.

Stacy: Do you love Melissa?

Ben scratches his head and gives Stacy a serious look.

Ben: Love is a strong word.

Stacy: Do you even know what love is?

Ben: Course I do! I love you Stace, I really do, whether you believe it or not.

Stacy: That wasn't my question Ben.

Ben: I do love Melissa.

Stacy: More than the woman who gave birth to your children?

Ben looks down trying to find the right words to say.

Ben: Your ma and I were really young. We didn't know what love was.

Stacy: Melissa's young enough.

Ben: This isn't the right conversation.

Stacy: You're going to have to realise that I'm not going to be a child forever.

Ben: I know.

Stacy: And that I'm going to want to hear some answers.

Ben looks at Stacy. Nods.

Scene Seven

June 17ᵗʰ. Morning. It's the day of the trip to the beach. Melissa and Ben are in the kitchen. Melissa is making sandwiches for the beach. A bag, in the process of being packed, is on a chair. Ben is helping her. The atmosphere is tense. No one is talking. The sounds of chopping can be heard.

Melissa: (*Not looking at Ben.*) She doesn't like me.

Ben: (*Laughs.*) She doesn't like me either.

Melissa: (*Glares at him.*) You find this amusing?

Ben: No.

Melissa: Good.

Ben: She'll adjust.

Melissa: I feel like the ugly step ma.

Ben: You're not ugly.

Melissa: Don't you get what I'm saying?

Ben: I can't read your mind, how do you expect me to know?

Melissa: Ben, don't you get it?

Ben: What Melissa? What do you want me to do about it?

Melissa: Do something, will ya?

Ben: What can I do?

Melissa: (*Louder.*) Grow up will ya. Grow up and be a dad for goodness sake. What if our kids turn out like this? This is chaos. What will happen then?

Ben: I don't know. This isn't about us. This is about Stacy.

Melissa: Well, she's taking over, you don't control her, you don't do anything, you just let her control you. You're the dad.

Ben: Well, what do you expect me to do, she has a right to be angry, Melissa?

Melissa: But she doesn't have the right to be rude.

Ben: You're right. I need to go harder on her… I just don't want to hurt her, I've hurt her enough.

Melissa: Getting some respect for you & me won't hurt her, she needs to know we're in charge.

Ben: You're right, I need to step up.

Stacy enters.

Stacy: (*Rubbing her eyes.*) Morning.

Melissa: (*Shocked.*) How long were you standing there?

Stacy: (*Looks at Melissa strangely.*) I don't know.

Melissa relaxes.

Ben: You should start getting ready Stacy.

Stacy: Yeah, I will. Em, can we go to the cinema instead of the beach?

Ben: No, Melissa made all this food for us we can't waste it.

Stacy: Ughhh.

Stacy turns to leave.

Melissa: Why did you change your mind all of a sudden?

Stacy: Because I wanted to.

Ben: Well, it's not your choice.

Stacy: (*Challenging them.*) Well, why don't yous go to the beach and I'll stay here.

Ben: That's not happening.

Stacy: Well, I'm not going to the beach.

Melissa: Why?

Stacy ignores her.

Ben: Answer her.

Stacy: Because I don't want to go, problem?

Ben: You're not always gunna get what you want in life.

Stacy: I learnt that when I was ten.

Stacy folds her arms and looks directly at Ben.

Melissa: We want to go to the beach and you want to go to the cinema, why don't we compromise?

Stacy: Yeah, whatever.

Ben: It's yes, okay, enough of that cheekyness.

Stacy: Why are you bossing me around all of a sudden?

Ben: I'm not bossing you around, it's called being a parent.

Stacy: When did you start being a parent?

Melissa: RIGHT!! Enough of the nasty talk, we'll go to the park, we can have a picnic in the park okay?

Stacy: Jesus Christ! You'd swear I asked yous to get matching tattoos with me to show how well our friendship is going. All I asked was to go to the cinema. I'll be in my room getting ready if you want to pick another useless argument with me.

Scene Eight

Same day. Ben, Melissa and Stacy are in the park. Stacy is looking out for Amy.

Ben: She'll be here.

Stacy: I know.

Melissa: Come sit down with us.

Stacy: I'd rather not.

Amy enters. Hugs Stacy from behind. Stacy gets a fright. Laughs.

Stacy: Amy!!!

Eric: Ha-ha.

Stacy: What are you doing here?

Eric: I was dragged by her

Amy: Heyyy..

Stacy: You brought the dog?

Amy: (*Laughs.*) He wanted to come see you.

Stacy: Yeah right.

Eric: I did, no lie.

Stacy: Where's Ma?

Eric: (*Looks puzzled.*) You wanted her to come?

Stacy: No, I mean yes, I mean, no, that would be awkward, but yes, I would of liked to see her if you get me.

Eric: Yeah, I do.

Amy sits down beside Melissa and Ben.

Amy: Hi.

Melissa: Hi, Amy is it?

Amy: Yeah.

Stacy: (*Pinches Eric.*) Ma all alone?

Eric scratches his head. Stacy looks at him doing that. It reminds her of Ben. She looks back at him and then again at Eric.

Eric: She'll be okay.

Stacy: Is she with the new bloke?

Eric scratches his head again.

Stacy: Stop scratching your head will ya! Answer me?

Eric: Didn't go too well with him.

Stacy: Is she okay, omg.

Stacy's eyes water up.

Eric: (*Puts his arm on her shoulder.*) Calm down, she says she's not upset, wants to be single. All she needs is the two of us.

Stacy: But I want her to find someone so she can get over Ben. When we're all grown up and leave, she'll barely see us.

Eric: Let's just take it a step at a time okay?

Stacy: (*Gives him the evil eye.*) Like the way you found Amy?

Eric: It's funny the way you change mood so quick.

Stacy: Stop trying to change the subject and tell me.

Eric: I actually like her you know, she's cute.

Stacy: You better not have/

Eric: I did nothing to her.

Stacy: Eric!

Eric: Just a few kisses.

Stacy: Eric!!

Eric: Swear, that was it. She wouldn't let me do anything else.

Stacy: Yeno, I have so much on my mind that I don't care anymore, but if you hurt her you won't live. (*Eric laughs.*) I'm not joking.

Eric: Why so serious? Let's just go sit down with the others.

Eric goes and sits down with Melissa and Amy and Ben.

Eric: Mel, you look great as usual.

Stacy stands apart watching them all. They start to eat.

Melissa: Ah thanks.

Ben: (*Jokes.*) Find your own woman.

Eric: (*Wraps his arms around Amy.*) I've got mine. (*Indicating sandwiches.*) These are nice Mel, by the way.

Stacy: (*To herself.*) Mel?

Melissa: Thanks Eric.

Stacy hears a familiar voice in the distance.

BeerBellyMan: A dog is the only thing on earth that loves you more than yourself and I'm selling dogs, hot dogs, get your hot dogs!

Stacy: I'll be back.

Amy: I'll come with you. (*Silence as they walk.*) Sorry.

Stacy: For what?

Amy: For not calling and for going out with your brother.

Stacy: The calling me part you owe me big time. The brother part is just weird but you can't help who you like. I was a bit of a bitch so I'm sorry as well.

Amy: He's attractive.

Stacy: To you.

They meet up with BeerBellyMan.

BeerBellyMan: Howaryih?

Stacy: I'm good, this is Amy.

BeerBellyMan: (*Winking at Stacy.*) My name's BeerBellyMan 'cause my fat belly is full of beer.

Stacy: (*Apologetically.*) Sorry about that. I didn't mean to call you that, I'm just very/

BeerBellyMan: Never caught your name?

Stacy: Stacy.

BeerBellyMan: What can I get yous girls?

Stacy: Five hot dogs and five ice-creams.

BeerBellyMan: Well some people want champagne and caviar when all they need is beer and hotdogs.

Amy: We're having a picnic.

BeerBellyMan: Nice day for a picnic. What sauces do you want? (*Chuckles.*) Hopefully, you know this time.

Stacy: I take ketchup, Amy takes mustard, Eric takes mustard and my dad takes ketchup. So two ketchups and two mustards please!

Amy: What about Melissa, Stace?

Stacy: Oh yeah! I think she's a mustard and ketchup type of person.

BeerBellyMan: How about I give you one ketchup hotdog and one mustard hotdog, for free, and you find out for me.

Stacy: You're too kind.

BeerBellyMan: You share my kindness with Melissa.

Stacy: You should join us?

Amy looks at Stacy as though she's lost her mind.

BeerBellyMan: I'll be off soon, having a picnic with my kids and my wife.

Stacy: Oh. (*Winks back at him as she leaves.*) Never caught your name?

BeerBellyMan: Thomas, and Stacy, I like to give people a quote of the day and here's yours. Happiness is only found when you come to terms with your life, when you accept your life. Remember that.

Amy: That's a brilliant quote!

Stacy looks back at BeerBellyMan. She looks at Amy. She then calls back to Thomas.

Stacy: Bye, for now, Thomas.

Scene Nine

June 24th. Afternoon. Stacy is looking out of her bedroom window. The window is open. She is watching Ben and Eric play football. Amy and Eric have come to visit Stacy. Melissa and Amy are in the kitchen. They are cooking. The three scenes are all set on stage. The focus shifts between them.

Eric: You're real bad.

Dad: Haven't played in a while.

Eric: Excuses, excuses.

Eric scores.

Eric: 10 – 3. I'm gonna be a serious football player.

Dad: Oh I know!

Eric: Hand it over.

Dad: (*Takes out €20.*) Here you go son.

Eric: Whopper buzz.

Focus shifts to Melissa and Amy in the kitchen.

Melissa: This is my favourite recipe.

Amy: (*Laughs.*) Beans on toast?

Melissa: Yeah, it's my fave food.

Amy: Seriously Melissa, how do you look good every day?

Melissa: (*Laughs.*) To keep a man interested you must put in effort and also, I like looking good.

Amy: Eric says he likes me the way I am.

Melissa: Oh, of course he does pet.

Amy: It won't always be that way will it?

Melissa: Never ever stress yourself over a boy, Amy.

Amy: It's just that this is my first relationship and Eric was sort of a player before.

Melissa: This is my first ever serious relationship so I know how you feel, don't stress too much, that's what I tell myself, everything will be okay in the end.

Ben and Eric come into the kitchen. They are laughing about their football game.

Eric: You're getting old.

Ben: (*Winks.*) I let you win, trust me.

Stacy: (*Opens her diary to write.*) New day, I feel quite good, and guilty. I don't want to feel good when my ma isn't around. I've never missed me ma so much. Feel like crying but I'm happy, is that possible? I think it's cos Amy and Eric are here. I'm happy Ben's here too. Melissa is a nice person but she's not my ma, I don't have to love her. Yesterday, I took a walk late at night by myself and I actually thought of what BeerBellyMan told him. He reminds me of that guy Jesus who talks through parables or something, he told me that happiness is only found when you come to terms with your life, when you accept your life. It was like he was trying to tell me a hidden message, but what in my life am I not accepting? I feel like he understands my situation even though he hasn't a clue about it at the same time.

Focus shifts back to the kitchen.

Eric: It's bleedin' half one and she's not here. I have a match at half two.

Amy: Why is your match so early?

Eric: I don't know.

Ben: I can drop you if you want me to.

Eric: (*Looks at Ben.*) She'll be here.

There's a knock on the back door. It's Stacy & Eric's ma. She has come to collect Eric & Amy. Melissa shouts up the stairs. Ben goes to the door.

Melissa: Stacy! Eric and Amy are going soon.

Stacy comes down to the kitchen. She sees her ma at the door.

Stacy: Ma!

Stacy rushes to her ma and hugs her. Cries.

Ma: What's wrong Stacy?

Stacy: Just missed you, were you okay on your own?

Ma: I was fine pet, don't be worrying about me.

Stacy: Come in!

Ma: Eh, no, let's just get your brother and/

Stacy: Come in!

Stacy pulls open the door and indicates to her ma to follow her. She does so reluctantly. The atmosphere changes. It is awkward. Nobody says anything.

Eric: So Amy, let's go.

Ben: She doesn't have to leave.

Stacy: Yeah, she doesn't.

Eric: Me match hello?

Amy: That doesn't start yet.

Eric: Your point is?

Amy: (*Rolling her eyes.*) Just saying.

Eric: Sorry Amy.

Stacy: Wow, he said sorry.

Melissa: He doesn't want to be late. Let them go.

Stacy takes Melissa's comment the wrong way. She interprets it as Melissa wanting her ma to leave.

Stacy: Who asked you?

Ma: Stacy, stop that.

Stacy: Well, what did she mean by that?

Ma: Watch your tongue Stacy. You're talking to adults, not your friends.

Ben: Go to your room Stacy.

Stacy: I'm not five! You can't tell me what to do.

Eric: Stacy, calm down.

Stacy: Why is everyone acting as if I'm the person who causes all the trouble?

Eric: But you are.

Ma: Eric, don't start! Amy, Eric, let's go now. Stacy, I'll call you later, we'll talk about this, I'm not letting you off.

Ben: Neither am I.

Ben and Ma exchange a look. Ma leaves followed by Eric & Amy. When they're gone Ben turns to Stacy but she turns and leaves. Goes back to her room.

Ben: Stacy, come back here now!

Focus shifts back to Stacy's room. She enters. She is angry and upset. Picks up her diary.

Stacy: (*Writing in her diary.*) I've been here three weeks. This house is driving me insane!

Ben enters.

Ben: Stacy, go apologise to Melissa now.

Stacy: No, she deserved it.

Ben: She did nothing.

Stacy: She sent my ma home.

Ben: You did.

Stacy: (*Screams.*) Ben, get out, will ya!

Ben: Don't tell me what to do in my house.

Stacy: Ben, get out of my room!

Ben: What have you got against her? Go and apologise now.

Stacy: You can't force someone to apologise.

Ben: Go apologise now and stop being a spoilt brat!

Stacy: You're telling me to apologise? Do you actually hear yourself?

Ben: It's the right thing to do.

Stacy: (*Trying not to cry.*) Do you not realise that I am struggling here? How can you not see it? I'm standing here, heartbroken, you don't even know what you've done to me Ben. I'm a big mess. I'm afraid to love you because I'm terrified of losing 'run away da' again. (*Stacy cries.*) I hate you Dad, I do, with all my heart, you're just a little boy who doesn't even know what he's doing, so tell me Da, why should I go apologise to your woman when you haven't even apologised to me.

Ben looks at Stacy. He is baffled. Stacy gets up and leaves.

Scene Ten

Same day. Stacy is in the park. She sits on the bench where she and Ben sat in scene four. She is trying to write in her diary but it's raining.

Stacy: Yeah, proper Irish weather, raining in summer. (*Writing in diary.*) I don't hate him. I can't go back there anymore. (*Wipes her eyes.*) I don't even hate Melissa. Can you be born cold-blooded because I think I am. I know everyone's trying their best and I know everyone's waiting for me to forgive but... (*Page rips because of the rain.*) Ugh!

A man with an umbrella sits down beside her. He holds the umbrella over her.

Stacy: You don't need to Mister.

Thomas: Stacy. (*Stacy looks at him. She doesn't recognise him.*) It's me, Thomas.

Stacy: (*Getting up.*) I don't know any Thomas.

Thomas: (*Laughs.*) Or should I say BeerBellyMan.

Stacy: Oh, sorry, oh, BeerBellyMan, sorry.... I just want to go home.

Thomas: Do sit and tell.

Stacy: Me and my dad just had a fight, it's a long story but I said things that I did mean but didn't mean, you get me?

Thomas: No.

Stacy: Forget it. (*She notices that Thomas is not wearing his work clothes.*) You're looking well.

Thomas: Go on.

Stacy: (*Smiles.*) Here, look at this notebook.

Thomas reads Stacy's diary.

Stacy: I don't want to be the one in the wrong.

Thomas: You, Eric and your ma are the three musketeers. You're all for one and one for all. Except there were four musketeers. You need the fourth musketeer to succeed. United you stand and divided you fall. No matter what, even if you're in the wrong, they're going to love you so go back and do the right thing. (*Stacy looks at him and gives him a hug. Thomas hands her his umbrella.*) Take this.

Stacy: What about you?

Thomas: I'll be grand.

Stacy: Thank you Thomas, for everything.

Scene Eleven

Same day. The kitchen. Stacy's clothes are wet. She is talking to Melissa and Ben.

Stacy: Sorry Melissa, I didn't mean it, I just missed me ma and didn't want her to leave. You're a nice person and I know you've been trying your best.

Melissa: It's okay, Stacy.

Stacy: I'm sorry Da, that was out of order. I just missed her, I'm… sorry.

Ben: Stacy, I'm sorry. I don't know if I'll ever make it up to you but I'll try. I called your ma, she's coming to collect you in the morning,

Stacy: I'll start packing and, thank you.

Scene Twelve

June 25th. Morning. Stacy, Melissa and Ben are in the kitchen.

Melissa: Toast anyone?

Stacy: Me please.

Ben: I'll be back in a minute. (*He disappears for a moment and reappears with a present.*) This is for you Stace.

Stacy: Thanks Dad.

Sound of a car pulling up outside.

Ben: There's your Ma.

Stacy takes the toast and runs outside.

Stacy: Let's go home.

Stacy turns to say goodbye.

Ben: Love you Stacy, be good, bye for now.

Ma: Thanks for taking good care of her these past three weeks.

Stacy: It was only three weeks?

Ben: Yeah, you came on the 4th of June and it's the 25th today, anyways, I'll see you soon Stacy?

Stacy: Sure.

They both get in the car.

Ma: You okay?

Stacy: Yeah, I am, are you?

Ma: Yeah.

Stacy: I really missed you. Why didn't you visit me?

Ma: I couldn't bear seeing you in person, crying, asking me to take you home.

Stacy: Really?

Ma: Yeah Stace.

Stacy: Well, it was fun with Dad even though we had our ups and downs.

Ma: Dad, I see?

Stacy: (*Smiles.*) Yeah, Dad.

Ma: Well, we're going home.

Stacy: You don't know how happy that makes me.

Scene Thirteen

July 28th. Afternoon. Sunny.

Stacy: (*Writing in her diary.*) Yo Diary, it's Stacy. Haven't talked to you for a while. Melissa and Dad don't go out anymore, I still like her, maybe they weren't meant to be. You never know me dad and Mam might get back together;) Wink. Wink. They've been talking a lot. Eric and Amy are still together which is just disgusting but nothing I can do to change that. I just hate the way we're talking about boys and she brings his rotten name up. Me brother loves me but he doesn't like to show it. I'm going to visit Dad the week before school starts. He's a bit lonely, I feel bad, I kind of blame myself on the whole Melissa thing, but being honest Dad told me her age, she was twenty, my Dad's nearly twice that age, she's too young. Btw, BeerBellyMan, yeah Thomas, that's him, he has a son whose seventeen and since I'm sixteen, yeno that has to happen, his son is absolutely gorgeous and he's just like Omg, even Amy says he's a babe. That's another reason why I'm going. BeerBellyMan has his own business now, something to do with accounting and maths, like where the fuck did that come from, I remember him selling sausages. My life isn't perfect but whose life is? I'll never forget BeerBellyMan's wise words — you can't find happiness if you don't accept your life and that's exactly what I have done. I've accepted that my life's not going to be perfect but it doesn't have to be because no one's life is. Stacy.

LIFE SENTENCE

Orlagh Woods

"When I started in Tenderfoot I didn't know much about drama or theatre and it was really exciting to have the opportunity to learn about it first hand. I wrote 'Life Sentence' because I wanted to write about something outside my comfort zone that involved some research. I loved the whole writing process and was delighted when my play was chosen to be part of the production. It was an amazing experience to see it performed in front of an audience."

Characters

Robert, adult & teenager
Paula, Robert's wife
Rachel, Robert & Paula's teenage daughter
Clodagh, Robert & Paula's youngest daughter, Rachel's sister
Spencer, inmate in a juvenile detention centre
Guard Williams, a guard in a juvenile detention centre

Scene One

Light fades up. A modern suburban kitchen. A counter, table and four chairs can be seen as well as a doorway to the hall. Paula, a thirty something year old woman, stands over the kitchen table pouring cereal for her seven year old daughter, Clodagh. Paula wears a fluffy dressing gown. She isn't wearing any make up. Clodagh is in a school uniform, though her hair is still messy. There are glasses of orange juice and a plate of toast on the table.

Paula: How much milk, love?

Clodagh: No milk, Mam! They're nicer with no milk!

Paula: Not a chance Clodagh. Not on a school day, love. These chocolate things are bad enough, let alone without any milk. I may as well just hand you a packet of Maltesers as you head out the door.

Clodagh: Yeah!

Paula: No. *(She pours a considerable amount of milk into the bowl. Clodagh sighs.)* Now here, eat up. And then go upstairs and do your teeth and hair, okay?

Clodagh, with her mouth full of cereal, nods her head.

Paula: Rachel will you get down here already, you'll be late!!

The girls' father and Paula's husband, Robert, enters. He is wearing dark trousers, and a shirt. His top button is open and he does not wear a tie. He is carrying his jacket.

Robert: Morning love. *(Robert kisses Clodagh on the top of her head. She grunts in response.)* Paula have you seen my eh... *(Motions putting a tie on.)*

Paula: On the back of the chair.

Paula sits down beside Clodagh with a cup of coffee.

Robert: *(Putting tie on.)* Any chance of a rasher love?

Paula: There's three in the pan there, but leave one for Rachel. And will ye call that one down, she'll be late for school.

Robert: *(Puts rashers on a plate.)* Rachel! Rachel! Will ye get down now! Mam's made your breakfast c'mon!!

Rachel stomps on stage. She is sixteen years old. She is wearing her uniform and carries a pink school bag. Her hair is down.

Rachel: There was no need to shout. I've been ready ages!

Robert: Then what in God's name have you been doing up there for twenty minutes?

Rachel: Straightening my hair!

Paula: *(Laughing.)* Rachel, you're unbelievable. You'll be lucky to have a hair left when you're forty if you keep burning it with the straightener.

Rachel: I don't burn it Mam, I just de-frizz. If I don't straighten it regularly I'll end up looking scary!

Paula: How in the name of God does a bit of frizz suddenly make you look scary?

Rachel: *(Points at Clodagh.)* Exhibit A.

Paula: Alright, Rach. Just sit down and have something to eat will you?

Rachel slumps into a chair and takes a slice of toast. Robert puts his plate on the table beside Rachel and sits down. The whole family are now sitting at the table.

Paula: Are you going to after school study today Rachel?

Rachel: Yeah, until half five. I'll walk home then.

Robert: How's the studying going Rach?

Rachel: It's alright. I'm mostly just sick of the teachers blabbin' on about it all the time. It's all Junior Cert this and Junior Cert that. It's a wreck the head. Talk about unnecessary pressure. I mean, everyone knows the Junior is just a practice. It doesn't actually mean anything in the long run.

Robert: Well Rachel, they have to pressure you. Otherwise there'd be people who just wouldn't bother studying. And believe me, it is important. Every person needs a viable set of exam results to get a job.

Rachel: Whatever.

Robert: I tell ye, if you paid as much attention to your studies as you do to that bloody David fella, you'd sail through your Junior Cert. Easy-peasy.

Clodagh: Lemon-squeezy!

Paula laughs.

Rachel: I don't get why you hate him so much Dad. He's a proper nice fella once you know 'um.

Robert: I've told you before. He's bad news. No good for you.

Rachel: Dad, I'm gonna keep seeing him. I like 'um, so it doesn't really matter what you think.

Robert: Do I need to remind you that you're only 16 years of age?

Rachel: No.

Robert: Good. Now eat your breakfast.

Rachel: *(Quietly.)* Mam likes 'um.

Robert: What's that?

Rachel: I said Mam likes 'um.

Paula: No Rachel, I said he should be given a chance. That doesn't mean I like him.

Rachel: You like him more than Dad. He doesn't get it at all-

Paula: Rachel, just eat, okay. We'll talk about this later.

Robert: I don't want to argue over the breakfast table okay Rach? Just leave it now. *(Pause.)* Love, where's the paper?

Paula: It's on the counter there.

Robert stands up and walks to the counter. He opens up the paper. He reads.

Robert: *(Shocked.)* Oh God! *(Continues reading.)* Jesus Christ!

Rachel: Aw, here we go...

Paula: *(Worried.)* What's wrong Rob?

Rachel: It's always about you Dad, you and that bleedin' company.

Paula: Rachel!

Clodagh: *(Worried.)* Dad?

Robert looks up at the worried faces of his family. He is clearly upset but he tries to cover it for their sake.

Robert: Ehh.. nothin' love. Sorry. Just ehh... read it wrong that's all. Yeah... just emm...

Robert places a hand on the back of his neck. He is clearly lost for words.

Paula: *(Standing up. Paula looks at her husband. She sounds uneasy.)* Girls, I think you better head off now... You don't want to be late.

Clodagh: Aww... Ma-am! It's too early. Nobody will be at school yet!

Rachel: Clodagh come on, don't make a fuss. Let's just go.

Paula: *(Rummaging in her bag.)* Here Rachel, take this. *(Hands Rachel money.)* Stop at the shops will you. Get yourselves a treat for lunchtime. You can have a look around while you're there, okay?

Clodagh: *(Jumps up.)* Thanks Mam!

Girls pick up their bags and put on their coats. Robert is still at the counter reading the paper.

Paula: Rach, you hold Clodagh's hand at the road do you hear me?

I don't care if your friends are there. And walk her right to the gate and watch her go in okay?

Rachel: Yes Mam. *(Kisses Paula on the cheek.)* Bye.

Rachel exits stage. SFX door being opened and faint traffic noises. Clodagh is still on stage. Paula is helping her with her jacket.

Rachel: *(Offstage.)* Will ye come on Clodagh!

Clodagh: Bye Mam! *(Running offstage.)* Bye Dad!

SFX door closing. A short silence.

Paula: Rob, what's going on? *(Pause.)* Rob? C'mon now, sit down. I'll make you some tea.

Robert sits down, still upset. Paula clicks the kettle on and joins Robert at the table.

Robert: Oh Jesus Paul, I just can't believe it. I can't believe it...

Paula: What love, tell me?

Robert takes Paula's hand across the table.

Robert: Paul, do you remember when we met? Do you remember that summer when I was sent to the juvenile detention centre?

Paula: How could I forget? We nearly broke up then.

Robert: Yeah, well there's something you don't know. Something I never told you. It's nothing to worry about or anything, I just never thought I'd have to and now-

Robert looks as though he may cry.

Paula: Rob? What is it?

Robert: Is the tea on? *(Paula nods.)* Good. I'm gonna text into work, I'm taking today off.

Paula: Okay love, whatever you need.

Robert: I'll start from the beginning...

Light fades out.

Scene Two

Opens on a dim cell. It contains a bunk bed, a table and a chair but little else. A boy, about 17, can be seen lying on the top bunk whistling to himself. Rowdiness can be heard outside the cell. After a few moments, a guard escorts another boy into the cell. He is also about 17. The boy is struggling but the guard is stronger than him.

Guard Williams: They weren't yours? You were holding them for someone? Yeah, yeah, we've all heard that one before pal. Anyways, it's over my head. I'm just transporting the goods. And this is your third offence this year Mr. Moynihan?

Robert: So! Like I said already, they weren't proper fuckin' offences.

Guard Williams: Oi! You be respectful Moynihan, ja hear? Or I'll have to teach ye to be respectful, d' understand?

Pause.

Robert: Sorry.

Guard Williams: You're lucky you're only here temporarily pal. You're lucky this is a short custodial sentence. But if you keep flauntin' that attitude of yours I'll make sure you're put on probation for the rest of the year when you leave!

Guard leaves. SFX of his shoes tapping down a long hallway. Robert does not see the other boy in the bed. He thinks he is alone. He slams his hand down on the small wooden table in anger.

Robert: Fuck sake!

The other boy jumps down from the top bunk and stands facing Robert. He is wearing trousers and a white vest. Robert gets a fright, turns to face him.

Robert: Jesus!

Spencer: I think that the guard told you to be respectful.

Robert: They never said I'd a cellmate, and what is it to you?

Spencer: Well surprise, surprise man! The name's Spencer Howard. And what this means to me, my friend, is a great deal. See, as you'll soon learn around here, if there's one fuck-up in a cell, that cell gets branded between the guards / know what I mean? Now I've been here a long time, and the idea of a little whip like you causing me more grief with the guards is not a thought I quite like, do you understand?

/ indicates an overlap of dialogue, the place where the next line begins.

Robert: No...

Spencer takes a step forward.

Robert: Whatche mean a 'branded cell'?

Spencer: What I mean, 'Mr. Moynihan', is *(counts on fingers)* surprise midnight trainin's, last ones into the canteen at dinner, less time in the yard, first ones into the showers in the morning, and overall just a substantially more difficult time for the both of us.

Robert: Oh right, yeah... I'm Robert.

Spencer: That's pretty Bobby.

Spencer jumps back up onto his bunk.

Robert: It's Robert. How long have you been here?

Spencer: Okay Bobby, eight long months around here man. And before you ask, yes, I know the ropes but no, I won't look out for you, show you around or try to make your time here any easier. We clear?

Robert: Yeah... I don't need looking out for. Besides this place is only for juveniles. It's not like a proper prison or anything.

Spencer laughs.

Spencer: Ha, you're all the same on the first day janno tha? Every one of ye says the same thing. But as you'll soon learn Bobby, this is no paradise. I know it says in the pretty pamphlet that the young boys will 'learn respect' and be under the supervision of 'helpful and professional' guards. But the one thing I will tell ye, those bastards don't care about any of us. They hate us all. And we hate them.

Robert: *(Apprehensively.)* So... This isn't a *real* prison. 'S just a detention centre... it's not like they can just attack you for nothing anyway...

Robert laughs nervously.

Spencer: No Bob, you're right. It's never for nothin'. Sure, that's not allowed. But they always find a reason. Always. *(Pause.)* Whether it's walking too quickly, walking too slowly, looking too tired, talking too quietly, breathing too loudly. They'll find somethin' Bobby. They always do.

Robert looks nervous. There is a wooden chair facing the bunk beds. He sits down.

Robert: Right... I'll keep me head down so...

Spencer: Not too far down, Bob.

Pause.

Robert: So ehh... what you in for then?

Spencer: *(Laughs.)* Burglary, assault, drug possession, drug abuse, threatening a police officer, take your pick. At this stage I forget which one I'm in for. The bastards keep postponing my court date. Not that I've much more to go home to...

Robert: Oh. Your old man's a mess or what?

Spencer: *(Sits up.)* Sorry?

Robert: Oh, no I just meant, like... ehh, is that why you don't want to go home. I didn't mean anything by it.

Spencer: *(Jumps down from bunk and walks right up to Robert's face.)* Listen you, you don't know me. You know nothing about me. If I hear you mention one word about my da I knock every tooth outta yer head. *(Shouts.)* Is that clear?!

Robert: Jaysus, will ye relax, I meant nothing by it! Sure my da's an alco, I was only makin' conversation!

Spencer: Well let's just clear the air then, you and me, we're not friends. We're not even fuckin' acquaintances. You are just some no-mark who'll be outta my hair just as soon as you got into it. And I couldn't give a shit about your sad little home life right? I've got me own problems. And trust me when I say, they're a bit more fucking important than *(mocking)* me poor da's back on the beer. I have a life outside here!

The two boys are now in a heated argument. They are standing face to face, shouting at each other.

Robert: Who said I even wanted to be your friend? Sure you're just a mess, you'd know by ye. I wouldn't come within twenty feet of you outside here. I have a life as well! So don't be actin' like you're the only one in the place with problems. Over there looking for pity like a-

Spencer: *(Shoves Robert.)* Like a what, Bobby?

Robert: *(Looks straight in Spencer's face.)* Like a bitch!

Spencer shoves Robert aggressively. Robert lifts his fist to hit back but does not get a chance to as they are interrupted by Guard Williams opening the cell door.

Guard Williams: Oi! Break it up!! Break it up now! *(He separates the boys.)* What's this about? *(Neither boy answers.)* Spencer!! Tell me what happened! *(Guard prods Spencer in the shoulder.)*

Spencer: Nothing guard.

Guard Williams: What's that now?

Spencer: *(Louder.)* Nothing guard.

Guard Williams: That's more like it. Christ almighty, seventeen years of age the two of ye? Jesus, you're supposed to be actin' like young adults here! And if either of you intends on walking out of here in the near future I suggest you put an end to this childish behaviour! *(Pause.)* Moynihan!!

Robert: Yes guard.

Guard: What happened here? *(Pause.)* Answer me!

Robert: *(Sighs.)* Nothing.

Guard: Right, I understand. Nobody wants to talk… Well, maybe you boys could use some time to find the right words, hm? Both of you, grounded to this cell for the next 48 hours. That means no canteen, no yard and no library. Use the time to work out whatever childish problems you have with one another! Because allow me to break it to you, for the foreseeable future… you're stuck with one another!

Light fades out.

Scene Three

Scene opens on the small cell. A small square of light on the dark stage. The rowdiness of the outside has died down. Spencer lies flat on the floor with his hands under his head staring at the ceiling. He is wearing earphones. He is listening to an old tape cassette. He whistles along with the tune. Robert enters. He is returning from the shower block.

Spencer: I hurt myself today
        To see if I still feel
        I focus on the pain
        The only thing that's real…

Robert: What's that?

Silence. Spencer does not hear.

Robert: Spencer!

Spencer: *(Takes the earphones off. Looks at Robert.)* What?

Robert: What's that you were singin'?

Spencer: You jokin'? You don't know Johnny Cash?

Robert: *(Clears throat.)* Oh yeah… course I know of 'um… I jus' dunno that song.

Spencer: It's 'Hurt'. One of his best.

Spencer starts to put the earphones back on.

Robert: Yeah? You like 'um?

Spencer: *(He leaves the earphones on the floor.)* Ah.. you could say that. He's a genius yanno?

Robert: Oh yeah. Me da used to like um... I remember that one 'Folsom Prison Blues'. Me da liked that one. Kind of appropriate now, eh?

Spencer: *(Chuckles.)* Yeah.

Pause.

Robert: Ju like music?

Spencer: *(Sits up.)* Yeah, definitely... It's what gets me through this place. I was on my best behaviour in here for two fuckin' months an' all they gave me was a scabby tape cassette player. I wanted me Walkman.

Robert: Haha hate that! I didn't think they'd even give ye that in this place.

Spencer: Nah, you have to fill ou' a form... and work for a reward like... You'll learn...

Robert: Oh... *(Pause.)* Here, I didn't mean what I-

Spencer raises his hand to stop Robert.

Spencer: Don't man... Don't even go there.

Robert: I just want che to know-

Spencer: It's over okay... It doesn't work like that in here. If shit goes down... you learn pretty fast not to dwell on it. It's a life lesson, Bob. Don't hold grudges, don't dwell on the past. *(Pause.)* That shit'll kill ye.

Robert: Okay.

Silence.

Robert: So, ehh...

Spencer: *(Spencer pulls a deck of cards from under his pillow.)* Je wanna game?

Robert: What? What game?

Spencer: *(Sarcasm.)* Fish. What game je fuckin' think, man, Blackjack. You play?

Robert: Oh yeah, absolutely. *(Robert drags the small table from*

the corner of the room to the centre. Spencer sits on the bottom bunk and Robert sits opposite him on the chair. Once everything is set up, he rubs his hands together.) You sure you know what you're getting yourself in for?

Spencer: Don't be so smug. I've had all the time in the world to perfect my strategies at this game my friend.

Robert: Okay, okay… What we playing for then?

Spencer: *(Reaches into his back pocket. Produces a handful of cigarettes which he lays on the table.)* These!

Robert: Aw nice! How ye get them?

Spencer: Rob 'um off the guards mostly, but some of the younger lads as well. They don't have a choice. Haha. Trust me though Bob, these may as well be gold dust around here. Don't come around too often.

Robert: Jesus, I'd well believe it…

Spencer begins to deal the cards.

Robert: Whoa, whoa, whoa!

Spencer stops.

Robert: What do you take me for, eh? *(Takes the deck from Spencer.)* You think I'd let you deal from your own deck?

Robert shuffles and begins to deal.

Spencer: What, you think I'm a cheat?

Robert: No… but I know you're a criminal. *(Robert produces a cigarette from his pocket.)* Takes one to know one.

Spencer laughs. The cards are dealt and the lads begin to play. They continue to talk.

Robert: Where you from?

Spencer: *(Laughs.)* I live in the city man. I suppose you could say I lead a nomadic lifestyle. Let's just say the cement beds in here are some of the best I've seen in a while.

Robert: Yeah? Jaysus man, that's rough…

Spencer: Ah no, I wouldn't have it any other way to be honest with ye. It's pure excitement never knowin' where the day'll take ye. Although lately I find myself typically endin' up back in this kip. But otherwise it's great like. No commitments, no responsibilities, and carefree.

Robert: I've never heard homelessness being described in such glowin' terms! You're sellin' it te me here man!

Spencer: Hah, well I never said I was homeless Bob.. I just said I moved around. Sure when you're a petty criminal who's pretty much up for anything, you make a lot of friends, know what I mean?

Robert: If you'da asked me that, this time last year, I'd have said no, but now? Fuck yes, I know what you mean. Ever since I got into "doin' people favours", I suddenly have no shortage of friends willin' to "do me favours".

Spencer: One of the few perks of the lifestyle Bob. Of course, the major down is they'll leave ye as soon as they found ye.

Robert: True that, true that. Since I got inte this shit I lost touch with all my proper friends. Another down I s'pose... Hold that thought, read 'um and weep pal.

Robert lays his cards on the table. Spencer inspects them.

Spencer: Fuck!

Robert: Pay up please...

Spencer reluctantly hands Robert two cigarettes from the pile. He throws his own hand down on the table.

Spencer: Ah yeah, but don't beat yerself up over that 'friends one' though Bobby. Once you get inte this crime business, you become a different species to the people that don't do it. They don't understand you anymore, and soon you stop understandin' them. The 'favours people' sort of become a substitute for real friends. All that matters is you find someone decent to look out for you.

Robert: I know that... sure I wasn't holdin' out much hope for those other fuckers anyway. Friends are overrated.

Spencer: Don't I know it mate...

Spencer stands up and begins to walk and Robert notices a mark on his shoulder.

Robert: Christ. What's that?

Spencer: What?

Robert: Yer shoulder.

Spencer: Oh nothing... just a birth mark. *(Spencer pulls at his vest to cover the mark.)* Anyway, where you from in the world Bob?

Robert: Eh, Goldenbridge. The bad part.

Spencer: Ah well, I took that for granted. What's yer house like?

Robert: What?

Spencer: Like, yer house, where ya live like?

Robert: Ehh, it's alri' I s'pose... just a two bed like.

Spencer: Yeah? Je have your own room?

Robert: Yeah, you could say that. I have to share with me two sisters though... when they're home. They live in London now so they're not here often.

Spencer: How old are they?

Robert: One's nineteen and the other is twenty... three now I think?

Spencer: I see, I see... And eh... attractive are they Bob?

Robert: Fuck off!

Spencer sits up and faces Robert. He leans his back against the wall.

Spencer: *(Laughs.)* Nah, I'm jokin' man... Ju see them a lot?

Robert: No, they rarely visit these days. They'd never come home if they didn't have to. I'm the only reason they have to come home.

Spencer: What about yer ma and da?

Robert: *(Looks down.)* No... She eh... Me mam died there six months ago. *(Pause.)* Me da's not worth shit.

Silence.

Spencer: That's rough... what happened to her?

Robert: Ehh... she eh... It was a car accident.

Spencer: Fuck.

Robert: Yeah I know. Me da took his anger out on the rest of us. Then when Sarah and Alison moved away, I was his only target. Just a big dope he is.

Spencer: He hits you?

Robert: Nah, he wouldn't try it. Just puts me down. He blames me for me mam's death like. Says I didn't appreciate her when she was alive. I don't know. I don't even think he knows... When he's not stoned he's drunk... and if he's not drunk, then he's sleepin' it off...

Spencer: He blames you? Ah no, you can't take that shit man!! It wasn't your fault... or anyone's fault. For fuck's sake it was... an accident like!!

Robert: I know! *(Upset.)* I know... But he doesn't get that. He's a drunk... That's all he'll ever be.

Pause.

Spencer: But da's are like that nowadays Bobby... All they care about is themselves. I wouldn't trust me own as far as I could throw 'um... He's in the army. Likes to treat me like one of his men.

Robert: Jenno, it wouldn't bother me so much, but he was the one who treated her bad. He was the one who was abusive to her. When she was alive... Man, when she was alive he treated her like a slave. But she.. *(chokes up).* She always put us first. She never once let him get to her. Even after all the rants, all the arguments, all the threats, she still was able to put on a brave face in front of us and say, "Right, well tomorrow's a new day!" *(Pause.)* She always said that.

Spencer: She sounds like a lovely person Bob. I know it's hard but ye have to be thankful that you had her at all. She obviously left you with a few life lessons. You have to be thankful for that man. Think about it. Some people have ma's their entire lives that treat them bad and put them down. Isn't it better that you had a great one for a short time than to have a really terrible one forever?

Robert: No, I know what you mean. Jeez for a petty criminal you're fairly fuckin' philosophical man!

Spencer: *(Laughs.)* Well, it sounds to me like them sisters of yours care about you about as much as anyone's sister could. Otherwise they wouldn't come home at all.

Robert: They do. They definitely do. I know I don't thank them enough. Them and Paula. I owe them each a massive thank you for all the shit they've put up with over the past six months.

Spencer: Who's Paula?

Robert: My girlfriend. Well... maybe ex-girlfriend. I dunno at the moment. Did I not mention her?

Spencer: No man you didn't...

Robert: Oh. Well anyways, we've been seein' each other for about three years now. She's great like. I don't treat her well enough though.

Spencer: Ahh... Do ye hit her?

Robert: Christ no. No, I don't mean that way... I just take her for granted sometimes. Little things like, but she notices... She notices.

Spencer nods.

Robert: *(Laughs.)* But sure, that's women for ye, what? Always highlightin' your flaws and all the rest. What about you anyway? You seein' someone?

Spencer: Ehh... no.

Robert: Single Pringle eh? That's the right idea. Less complication. But c'mere then, your last girlfriend yeah? Did ye ever have one of those arguments with her, where you actually forget what you're fighting over in the first place?

Spencer: Ehhmm... no. No I don't think so...

Robert: Serious? I'm surprised at that now. Woulda thought of you as a bit of an expert with the ladies bud... But maybe it's just us then. *(Pause.)* What about one of those times where she loses the head because you literally glance at another girl? Even if she's nasty lookin'?

Spencer: *(Nervous laughter.)* Ehh no. Don't think so either.

Robert: Ah here man. You're all quiet all of a sudden. What's wrong? Was your last girlfriend a bitch or something? Mess you up?

Spencer: Nah... No, it's not that, I ehh... don't have a last girlfriend.

Robert: What? Like... why?

Silence. Spencer's face says it all. He stares at the ground. He is burning red.

Robert: What... You're not... gay?

Spencer doesn't respond. His silence speaks volumes.

Robert: Oh.

Spencer: What?

Robert: No nothing Spencer... Nothing at all. I just... I never-

Spencer: Considered me the type? Yeah I know. I'm a fuckin' freak of nature.

Robert: What are you talking about? Relax will ye?! I never said that. You just caught me off guard. I'd a never a guessed like. Do people know?

Spencer: No!! And they won't ye hear?! You ever tell a soul about this I will make it my business to make your life hell, je hear me??!!

Robert: Calm the jets for fucks sake Spencer! You're the only one in here makin' a big deal of this.

Spencer: I'm fine.

Robert: So have you always known... *(Spencer shrugs.)* Right.

Spencer: Like, me da... I could never... He would never understand...

Robert: He's in the army? *(Spencer nods.)* Right.

Silence.

Robert: Man, I think you should tell um-

Spencer jumps up.

Spencer: Ah fuck off man. Don't even suggest that to me. *(He paces the cell.)* You're not thick in the head man! Surely you have enough of a brain to contemplate what he'd do te me! He's a sergeant, Bob!! Do you understand what he's capable of?

Robert: So! He's still your da!! It's not your fault you're gay anyway, he'll understand!

Spencer: *(Spencer accidentally knocks over the small table. The cards flutter everywhere.)* He'll fuckin' wha?! *(Spencer turns around and pulls his vest up over his shoulders. A large red scar is seen on his right shoulder.)* Like he understood when I failed me Junior? Hm?!

Robert jumps up at the sight of the scar.

Robert: Christ Spencer!! What did he do to you?!

Spencer: Did that with his lighter man. Held me down... *(Robert is upset.)* The fucker thought this'd teach me never to fail another exam in me life. *(Spencer pulls his vest back down.)* You can imagine how he reacted when I left school altogether.

Robert: Jesus Christ.

Spencer: Yeah. Maybe now you'll understand why I prefer to not go home when I have the option. Even this kip is better than home.

Robert: I'm sorry man...

Spencer: It's not your fault. But I'll tell ye one thing, as soon as I get the chance, I'll get my revenge don't you worry. He won't be stronger than me forever.

Spencer sits back down. His back against the wall.

Robert: I take it it's just you and him then?

Spencer: Yeah. Me mam left when I was a baby. I wish I'd brothers and sisters though.

Robert: What about telling the guards about your da? Your man who brought me in doesn't seem too bad?

Spencer: Williams. He's new. The other guards'll soon teach him the appropriate levels of discipline in here though, don't worry. Anyway, who do you think they'll believe Bobby, hm? A fuck-up like me or the honourable Sergeant Howard? Nah, he came here to visit me a few times and they were all just kissin' his boots.

Robert: Man, I wish there was something I could do for you...

Spencer: Don't worry about it. I'm safe in here anyway. Me and the guards, there's an uneasy peace between us. It's lookin' like I'll be in here a good while this term. It doesn't matter anyway...

Robert: It doesn't matter? Spencer, you have to face this. It's who you are-

Spencer: No Bob!!! No, it's not who I am! It's never been who I am. This place is who I am! It's all I'll ever be.

Robert: It doesn't have to be like that... You know that.

Spencer: This is the only place... The only place I can put it to the back of me head. You can't be gay in here.

Robert: Why not?

Spencer: There was this one fella... When I was in here the first time, about two year ago. He... *(Spencer chokes up.)* He was only twelve. And he came in and he was... just so fuckin' gay. Like, you know the type. Just real loud about it, real camp... *(Pause.)* I ehh... We all... Everyone hated 'um really. They all teased 'um. They stole his stuff and hid it, they called him names, they never let him sit with them at lunch. The poor fella... he always took it. He never fought back... I was good to 'um, yanno, I found his stuff, I gave 'um advice, I sat with 'um. But then one night he told one of the other lads that I was his best friend. Now, of course, to them that meant we were a couple or something was goin' on, and it wasn't! *(Pause.)* They all started askin' me about it and I had to do something. They respect me in here man, I couldn't jeopardise that!

Robert: What did you do to 'um...

Spencer: I battered 'um. In front of everyone. I waited for 'um with two other lads in the bathroom, where the guards wouldn't see. I took his clothes and I left 'um there. I broke two of his ribs, Bobby. I made sure he never misunderstood our friendship again.

Silence.

Robert: Oh my God! How could you do that?! You were his friend, his best friend, his ONLY FRIEND!!

Spencer: I know that!! Do you think I don't know that!! Jesus I never stop thinking about it... That's why people can never know about me, ye hear? They can't, Bob... I can't be another him.

Robert: *(Shaking his head.)* What you did to that kid? It disgusts me. *(Pause.)* But I won't tell. *(Spencer looks up. Robert extends his hand.)* Don't dwell in the past remember?

Lights fade down.

Scene Four

Bright light fades up. Spencer is asleep on the top bunk. Robert is curled in a ball on the bottom bunk. Rowdiness can be heard outside the cell. After a few moments there is a loud bang on the cell door. The boys slowly wake up. Robert yawns. Spencer leans over the top bunk and looks in on Robert.

Spencer: Mornin'.

Robert: Jesus. What time is it?

The cell door opens. Guard Williams enters carrying a tray with the boys' breakfast.

Guard Williams: Sleep well boys?

Robert: *(Mid yawn.)* Like a log, guard.

Guard Williams: *(Laughs.)* Yes, well... it certainly seems calmer in here. No more fisticuffs eh lads?

Spencer: Ah jaysus, no. It's like you said, we're mature young men and we'd better start acting like it... That right Robert?

Robert: What did you say?

Spencer: Ehh... I said isn't that right?

Robert: *(Smiling.)* Yeah... That's right.

Guard Williams: Well good, I'm very glad to hear that lads. You're good lads, I know yis are. But yis let yourselves down yesterday. I don't want yous becoming as difficult as the feckers in cell 204... You know your man Spencer...

Spencer: Woodsy?

Guard Williams: Woodsy! Yeah that's it. Now between you and me lads, he's a lost cause that Woodsy. Just can't seem to keep out of trouble. But you two? I see it in yis boys, you can turn yourselves around. *(Pause.)* Now yis know I can't go back on the punishment I gave ye..., but I'll tell ye what, cos of your good behaviour yesterday I'll let each of yis have a reward this weekend, hm?

Spencer: Aw sound!

Robert: Yeah, thanks a lot!

Guard Williams: No bother lads, I'll send the forms in later. Sure I was young once too. Sometimes we all need a break.

Guard Williams goes to leave. At the door he turns back to face the boys.

Guard Williams: It's not like we put yis together by accident...

Guard Williams leaves and shuts the door behind him.

Spencer: Aw, sound job man... maybe they'll finally let me have me Walkman back. What are you gonna ask for?

Robert: I haven't a clue... maybe extra time on the phone, sumtin' like that?

Spencer: Oh Jesus Bob, calm down. Don't go too wild!

Robert: Ah, I wanna ring Sarah and Alison...

Spencer: Your sisters?

Robert: Yeah. Doubt the old man has even told them I'm in here yet. Surprised if he even knew I was here himself. I owe them a ring. They want an answer I think...

Spencer: An answer?

Robert: Oh yeah. I forgot to tell ye. It's stupid. Every time they come over they ask me to go back with them. They live in London now like. When they visit they always try to convince me to go back with them. Just to finish school. Go to college there or sumtin. Get away from me da really. The last time they were here they were pretty serious that I go with them. They must'a noticed the state of the place.

Spencer stands up.

Spencer: Sorry... Am I hearin' you right Bob?

Robert: What?

Spencer: Are ye as thick as you fuckin' look?

Robert: Hey!

Spencer: Why in the name a jaysus wouldje not go with them?! Does Paula know about this?

Robert: No. I haven't told her. I know what she'd say. She'd tell me to go. See, she knew me before me mam died. So she knew me when I was...

Spencer: Good?

Robert: Yeah, kinda. She'd want me to do anything if it meant I'd get back to who I used to be. But I don't wanna leave her. Sure I don't even know if she's left me yet. I can't go.

Spencer: Well, in my humble opinion it'd be the best thing for you both Bob. I actually think that if you agree to go to London for a few months, after your probation ends, and take some time out over the summer, it'd save your relationship.

Robert: Do ye think so?

Spencer: I wouldn't lie te ye. If you don't do it for yourself Bob, do it for her. You said yourself you haven't been treatin' her well. Do her this favour. Go away for a few months. Let her have a think about what she wants.

Robert: Yeah but what if it means her leavin' me Spencer? I can't take that.

Spencer: She hasn't left you yet man.

Silence.

Robert: No, I just can't go. I won't.

Spencer: Why are you so against this?

Robert: I dunno! *(He stands up.)* I know what you're saying is right! I know it! It's not even Paula I'm worried about really.

Spencer: What?

Robert: I don't wanna leave me da on his own...

Silence.

Spencer: Look Bob, I know it's hard to hear, but he'll never change. Not now. And you staying isn't gonna alter the chances of him makin' a turn around.

Robert: I can't leave 'um Spencer.

Spencer: You deserve better than him Robert! You deserve so much better. See if I could get away from my da? I'd be out like a light. You can't let this pass you by.

Robert: Who the fuck would I be in London eh? The new kid?

Spencer: Exactly! You'd be able to start again, you pleb! Be somebody new man! Christ you'll never have to see one of these places again!

Robert: I have no idea what I want to do with my life! Now she's gone. There's no plan for me.

Spencer: I doubt your sisters would agree with that. I bet they've had a plan for you since the day they left home.

Robert: I dunno...

Spencer: Look Bob, you said it yourself. Not one of your new so-called 'friends' will stick by you. They're not real friends. I mean you owe it to your mam to give this a go. Make something of yourself!!

Robert: What about you?

Spencer: What about me?

Robert: What will you do?

Spencer: If I could start again
A million miles away
I would keep myself
I would find a way. *(Pause.)*

That's Cash. That was the plan. As soon as I'm eighteen, to get outta here. Leave this poxy country and go to Australia, or New Zealand. Somewhere I knew nothing about... and learn about it like. Make a life for meself. But I dunno now... I don't see myself leavin' here for a good while yet. I s'pose I'll just decide when the time comes. Why?

Robert: I think that sounds deadly Spencer, and do-able. I think you should go for it.

Spencer: *(Laughs.)* Ah sure why would you care about a mess like me, eh?

Robert: I do care! *(Looks down.)* I just... You're the first real friend I've had in a long time.

Spencer sits down on the bunk opposite Robert.

Spencer: Friend? You'd call me that? Even after what I told you?

Robert: Yeah. I think I would. I know you're sorry. *(Pause.)* That okay with you?

Spencer: Yeah. I think so... (*Smiles.*) Jenno what? I'm really glad I met you Robert.

Robert: I'm glad I met you too, man.

Spencer: I have to say, you're the first one to come in here and not bullshit me man. I've seen plenty a' newbies comin' through this cell and everyone is the same. Most of them in on minor, first time offences. All scared of me. You were different. And I respected that straight away.

Robert: Nice way of showin' your respect Spence, shoving me into a wall.

They laugh.

Spencer: Ah well, I had to test you man. Had to see if you were the real deal.

Pause.

Robert: Spencer?

Spencer: Yeah?

Robert: Let's not do this again.

Spencer: What?

Robert: End up in here. This'll be the last time, for both of us. (*Spencer laughs.*) Seriously!

Spencer: It's not that easy, man. You don't know where I come from. The only way to keep the older lads off your back is to earn respect, and the only way to earn respect is to do bad things. And when you've been doin' bad things for as long as I have, you can't just stop.

Robert: Yes you can. You'll have to.

Spencer: What?

Robert: I'm telling you. If I'm makin' this effort to make something of myself, you will to.

Spencer: It's not as easy for me Bobby.

Robert: You can make it easy, Spencer. Stick it out at home till your probation ends when you get out. Keep your head down. I know it'll be hard. Then do it. Leave. Go somewhere a million miles away, go-

Spencer: (*Shouts.*) No, no, no! That's just a fantasy man! It's not true, and it will NEVER fuckin happen!!

Robert: Make it happen then Spencer. I know it'll be hard! It'll be hard for me too, but we both know that the best chance either of us have of turning things around is to get out of here and stay out of here.

Spencer: You sound like my school counsellor. What I remember of 'um that is.

Robert: I'm serious.

Spencer: Yeah? Well so am I. Who even says I want to turn my life around eh?

Robert: You said it. In fact you screamed it.

Spencer: What?

Robert: I know by ye that you don't wanna be here. And I know by actually talking to ye that you don't belong here. You can still make something of your life Spencer. It can still happen.

Spencer: Do you think I haven't tried? I've no safety net like you Bob. If I fuck things up this time I'll never recover!

Robert: All the more reason to try then. *(Robert stands up.)* One last time. *(He extends his hand.)* Make the effort.

Spencer stares at Roberts hand for a minute before reluctantly shaking it. Robert places his other hand on Spencer's shoulder.

Robert: Right, this is it now man, the beginning of everything.

Light fades out.

Scene Five

Modern Day. Light fades up on Paula. She talks in a low tone until the light fades up further to reveal Robert and then the rest of the room. This is when the conversation becomes audible. Robert is sitting with Paula at the table. She is still in her dressing gown. Robert is no longer wearing his tie. Paula is holding a tissue. There are four empty mugs on the table, implying they've been sitting there a while. The newspaper sits folded on the edge of the table.

Paula: And you stayed friends the entire time? That's pretty impressive Robert. I mean, even now you only meet up with Tony and Joe every few weeks. I remember coming to see you the day you were released. You looked so different. I knew you'd changed. But all this time I thought you went to London because you wanted to finish with me.

Robert: What? Ah Jesus no Paul. If anything I went to *save* our relationship. Spencer had spelled it out for me and I knew you needed time.

Paula: I did. I was so young then. And my mam and dad hated you remember? I think they needed that time more than me. When you got put away they swore they'd never let me see you again. I wondered at the time where it all came from though, the sudden urge to go to London, I mean, you'd been putting it off for months and months before you went in. I just assumed it was for the education opportunities.

Robert: (*Laughs.*) Ah you know me better than that Paul. I just needed a breath of air. Sure, I hadn't really dealt with me mam's death until then. Being with Sarah and Alison helped me through that. And then when I ended up starting the accountancy over there-

Paula: I didn't know that's where you got into accountancy Rob?

Robert: Yeah, Sarah signed me up for a night course in a college over there. I stuck at it and when I came back the first place I went was the accountancy office. I re-sat my leaving and did the exams. Look at me now.

Paula: You worked hard alright.

Robert: Yeah... Spencer had a lot to do with it.

Paula: You seemed very close.

Robert: We were.

Silence. Robert reaches over to take Paula's hand but she pulls hers away. She sits back in her chair.

Robert: What?

Paula: Nothing, it's fine.

Robert: Paula, what's wrong with you?

Paula: I just can't really believe you never told me this. Why would you keep it from me all these years?

Robert: I honestly never thought it'd be necessary. When I came back from London and you took me back, I was so bloody delighted and amazed that you forgave me, I didn't want to tell you anything that might jeopardise our relationship. I thought... I thought you'd hate the sound of Spencer. I didn't think it was relevant, Paul.

Paula: You didn't think it was relevant?! (*She gets up, walks to the counter. She is angry.*) In fairness Rob, what wife wouldn't be worried listening to that story?

Robert: What do you mean?

Paula: Well you keep saying how *close* you were to your best friend who did so much for you. I mean c'mon you spent over a *month* in a cell alone with a *gay* fella in one of the toughest detention centres in the country. No, you're right Rob that's not relevant at all.

Robert: Don't be ridiculous Paula!! Just because he's gay doesn't mean he was attracted to me for feck's sake!

Paula: I'm not being ridiculous Rob. I just can't believe I never knew this. All this time you told me you had a cell to yourself. Seriously there must have been some reason why you wouldn't tell me all these years, something you felt you had to *hide* maybe?!

Robert: I don't have to listen to this!

He gets up to leave. Paula blocks his way.

Paula: Ehh... Yes, you do. You're not just gonna run away from this Robert. I'm your wife!

Robert: Yeah, so what happened to being supportive and understanding, hm?

Paula: What is there to understand?! What, do you want me to pity you some more? Because if I remember correctly I spent the majority of my teenage years sympathising with you!!

Robert: Do you want some sort of twisted apology Paul? Is that what you're after? I'm sorry my life was a fucking mess? It wasn't good enough for you or something? If that's what you're after maybe you shouldn't have taken me back at all!!

Paula: All I want is an explanation!! And seen as how you lied to me all these years, I feel I deserve a pretty decent one!

Robert puts his head in his hands and sighs.

Robert: Christ almighty... Will ye sit down then at least? *(They both return to the table. Sit down again.)* Now, Paul all I can do here is tell you the truth about what happened. I don't know if it's what you want to hear, but it's all I can do. Spencer Howard was the best friend I ever had in my life. And while I was in that godforsaken place, I told him everything about my life. He was half the reason I turned things around in my life. But God as my witness, *nothing* happened between us. I am not gay. And Spencer was my friend. He wouldn't have tried anything. *(Pause.)* I need you to believe that.

Paula: I do believe you. I'm just in shock. I can't believe I never knew about any of this.

Robert: Jesus, and there were so many times over the years when I thought about telling you. But when it came down to it, I just couldn't pluck up the courage to do it.

Paula: What made this time different?

Robert: Giv' us over the paper. *(Paula reaches over and hands Robert the paper.)* Do you want to hear this? *(Paula nods. Robert simply unfolds the paper and opens it up. He takes a deep breath. Then reads.)* 'Dublin Thug Shot Dead in Gangland Feud.' *(Pause.)* 'The body of notorious drug-lord, Spencer Howard, was uncovered last night in the Dublin Mountains. Howard, who was well known to Gardaí in recent years, had been shot twice. It is thought he died instantly. Gardaí believe his death is gang-related. Howard has since been described by those who knew him as 'violent' and 'disturbed'. He leaves behind four year old twin boys. It's thought-

Paula: Stop Rob. Just stop, I don't want to hear anymore. *(Pause.)* Robert, I'm so sorry.

Paula reaches over and takes Robert's hand.

Robert: I just can't believe it. I keep reading it over and over, wishing I could take it in. I feel sick over it. I never even got in touch with him. All these year I never even picked up the phone. I promised him I would and I didn't... *(Pause.)* Christ, and now I'll never get the chance again.

Robert puts his head in his hands.

Paula: Yeah but don't forget that he promised you as well. He swore he'd make the effort when he got out.

Robert: Yeah, but how do I know that he didn't? I bet he did make the effort. In fact I know he did... He'd some bastard of a dad though, Christ, I thought mine was bad for ignoring me.

Paula: Don't say that Rob.

Robert: Yeah, but if I had made the effort... If I rang him. I might have been able to... do something. I don't know.

Paula: No, you can't do that to yourself love. This was not your fault. Not in any way. You couldn't have prevented this. *(Silence. Robert starts to cry.)* Did you say he had kids?

Robert: Twin boys it says.

Paula: But I thought he was-

Robert: Yeah he was. But obviously he never told anyone. It's so sad. Lived his whole life hiding from the person he really was.

Paula: But do you really think he'd go as far as to have a relationship with a woman? And sleep with her like?

Robert: Absolutely. It sounds mad going to all that trouble just so other people won't suspect anything. But that's how Spencer was. You heard about the little fella in the detention centre. He didn't think twice about beating him up. He probably went out with her so the lads wouldn't ask questions, and slept with her so she wouldn't ask questions. Most likely the boys were unplanned.

Paula: Jesus. Four years old with no dad to look after them. That's heartbreaking.

Robert: I know. I think I'll go to his funeral. I'd love to meet them. I bet they're the spitting image of him.

Paula: That's a great idea.

Pause.

Robert: Thank you... for everything Paula. You put up with a lot of shit throughout the years. I'm so grateful to have you.

Paula: Well I wouldn't have stayed if I ever doubted you. I'm very proud of you.

They hold hands. Lights fade.

Scene Six

The kitchen. It is late evening. Paula is dressed to go out. Rachel is sitting at the kitchen table, doing homework. Clodagh, the only one still in her uniform, sits on a stool in the middle of the kitchen, while Paula brushes her hair.

Clodagh: Ow, ow, OW!!! Mam! That hurts!

Paula: Well Clodagh, how else will I get the knots out?

Clodagh: Just leave them in then. They don't hurt if you don't touch them.

Paula: Oh, so you would be okay with me sending you into school every day with messy hair, is that it?

Clodagh: I don't see why girls even *have* to have long hair. I wish everyone was just bald like Grandad. Then I'd never have to get my hair brushed!

Rachel: How are you my sister?

Paula shoots Rachel a look that says "Enough". Clodagh sticks her tongue out at her sister. Rachel returns her attention to her homework.

Paula: Are you nearly finished, Rach? Dad made reservations for half six so you'd better get a move on if you still need to straighten your hair.

Rachel: Remind me again why we have to go out for dinner on a Tuesday?

Paula: Rachel your dad wants to take us out okay? No need to question it. We're doing a nice thing as a family.

Rachel: But why? We never go out for dinner.

Paula: Well we are today, okay?

Clodagh: Ow!! Mam!!

Paula: Okay Clodagh, just go and get dressed, that'll do. Wear the clothes I left on your bed okay.

Clodagh skips offstage.

Clodagh: Okay!

Robert enters as Clodagh leaves. He is dressed up.

Robert: Why is she so hyper?

Paula: I told her we were going out for dinner... and, of course, her hair's done.

Robert: Right.

Rachel: Dad, how do you do this algebra?

Robert: Give' us a look?

Robert looks at Rachel's book.

Robert: Yeah, you just bring the x's over to one side, an' then you're left with a simultaneous equation.

Rachel: Thanks.

Rachel continues with her work. Robert looks over at Paula who is mouthing something at him. She is saying "Talk to her!" Robert is reluctant but when Rachel suddenly turns around he is forced to.

Robert: *(Sits down.)* I'm sorry about this morning Rachel.

Rachel: It's okay Dad. I'm sorry too.

Robert: I don't want you to think I'm being too hard on you about these exams or anything. You know I just want the best for you. The last thing I want is for you to feel under pressure to get all honours. *(Pause.)* As long as you put the effort in, I'll be proud of you no matter what.

Rachel: *(Taken aback.)* Thanks Dad.

Paula catches Robert's eye from the counter and mouths "Ask her" to him.

Robert: Emm... look Rach, your mam and me were talking and, eh, well if you want to ask David out to dinner with us, that'd be okay.

Rachel: Are you serious?

Robert: It's about time I gave him a chance.

Rachel: Oh my God, I'll go text 'um. Thanks Dad, yous are gonna love him!!

Rachel hugs Robert, closes her book and runs off stage.

Paula: Fair play to you Rob.

Robert: This is going to be the most difficult evening of my life.

Paula: Just be nice, Rob. I've met him and he's not as bad as you think.

Clodagh can be heard calling from the hall.

Clodagh: Ma-am, can I wait in the car?

Paula: *(Shouts.)* Go on, yeah, I'm coming now! *(Pause.)* Are you alright love?

Robert: Yeah, I'm fine. I'll be fine.

Paula hugs Robert.

Paula: I'm heading out to the car. Follow me okay?

Robert nods. Paula walks offstage. Robert stands alone in his kitchen for a moment before opening a press and taking out the newspaper. He stares at it for some time.

Robert: The beginning of everything, eh Spence?

After a moment Rachel enters. She is happy.

Rachel: Dad!! Dad, he texted back! He's coming! He cancelled his band practice to come with us! I cannot wait for you to meet him Dad, he's just so talented and- *(She cuts off when she notices that there is something wrong with Robert. She calms down.)* You okay Dad?

Robert smiles at his daughter. They have a moment.

Robert: Course I am. *(He puts his arm around Rachel and they begin to leave the stage together.)* ...so tell me more about this David fella...

I AM RUNNING
A monologue by Katie Black

"Writing a monologue was a new experience for me, but the workshops and the atmosphere of creativity in The Civic gave me a new confidence in my ability to write something original. Seeing my ideas come to life on the stage in front of an audience was incredible. I am now studying English Literature at university and certainly owe an early interest in drama and creative writing to my experience in Tenderfoot."

Character

Girl

I am running. So fast, I don't have time to think. Just run. Away from it all. Away from the man's pale face, the flashing lights, the wail of sirens. Forget it all. Right, left, right, left. Breathe. That's all that matters, all there is. I turn a corner. Plough through some dried up leaves. There are leaves everywhere. They crunch under my feet. I like that sound. Crunch, crunch, right, left, right, left, breathe. Concentrate on the routine. The rhythm. Always the rhythm. The beat of life, irregular, regular, doesn't matter. You have to follow it. Keep the time. Time, what time is it? Early I think. No, don't think, can't think. Concentrate. The sky is grey today. Grey with wiry clouds floating miserably along. Why is it miserable, the sky? It should be happy, happy it is up there. Not here. Everything that happens down here, all the madness, all the chaos. The sky is separate. A different world in the sky, so it is. I always wanted to be a pilot. But keep running Bud.

Past the traffic now. All those horns. There's a different symphony every day, the symphony of the roads. Toot, toot, crunch, crunch, right, left, right, left, breathe. One after another. And the colours, so many colours. Red one way, yellow the other. Blurs and streaks, painted on the tarmac. And people stare. Their heads turn as I pass. And their faces, their faces are – no, don't look. Can't look. Concentrate.

I fly past the traffic, into open countryside. Green grass, the smell of hay, fruit and dust fills my nose. The air is getting fresher now. It's cold, crisp. It floods my mouth, my throat. It flows into my lungs, for a visit I think. Hello, goodbye. It's gone. In, out, toot, toot, crunch, crunch, right, left, right, left, breathe. Like a tune. A good rhythm. Keep to the rhythm. Keep running Bud. I can run from anything, I can hide. Hide from my thoughts. What would she say if she could see me now? Would she be proud? Would she...? No. Don't think about *her*. Not now. Keep going, keep in line, and don't stray Bud.

Past fields now. Fields with cows and sheep and trees. I used to go on walks with her. And we wouldn't look at the cows and sheep and trees. We'd be too busy talking. No, no, *no*. Too much thinking. Not enough speed. *Faster Bud*. Heartbeat is getting quicker. And I don't feel tired. I don't feel anything. I just run, that's all. I am weightless, these arms, these legs, this head, they are empty. Just air. And I'm sure I am floating, not running. Because running doesn't feel like this. Smooth, sleek, I feel in control. The feeling flows though me, invigorates me. I feel powerful, and for a moment, I'm no longer myself.

Powerful, strong. I'm master of my emotions. They can't affect me. I am new, fresh. I'm going to get away. Leave all of it behind. *(Pause.)* And then I remember, I am not. The feeling floods away, leaving me in the afterglow of its glory. And I feel myself falling, and all of the doors are opening. The locks have come away, and everything is out now. I am on my knees, and the tears are cold on my cheeks. The truth has caught me. I can't run away anymore. I'm in the spotlight. I've lost the game and I can't hide now. I'm *not* in control. I *can't* hold it in. It's staring me in the face. And I realize nothing will change it. Nothing *can* change it.

How could she leave me? Why did she leave me? On my own. Because nobody else cares. Nobody could care like her. Or ever will again. She's gone. It's a fact. And I can't hide from it anymore. But *why*? Didn't she have me? Her little Bud.

Me and her, against the world. Except now it's not. Now she's left me to face it alone. *Liar*. How could she *lie* like that? Lie to *me*. Me of all people! Well I'll show her. I'm not her little Bud anymore. I'm fine without her, just fine! Can you hear me Mam? I'm just fine! I don't need her. I never did. I'm wiping away my tears. I'm starting again. I'm leaving all this crap behind.

Pause.

But can I? Can I walk away? I'm trying to leave, but something's holding on. And I realize, I can't let go. I can't. Because I always did need her. And whatever she did, whatever amount of hurt she's caused me, that will never change. I need to go back. Back to reality, back to the truth. Back to the man's pale face, the flashing lights, the wail of sirens. Remember it all. However much it hurts. I have to be strong. I'm turning back now. I'm going home. I am running.

STRIKE!
Alison Bryan

"The concept behind the play emerged from thinking about how conversations change and develop depending on who is participating at particular moments. The bowling alley setting was perfect for exploring this, as it provided me with the opportunity to play with the idea of conversational development as one character leaves and another enters the central stage setting. The audience is able to not only gain knowledge of the events taking place from various points of view, but also gauge the relationship dynamics between the three characters. The form of conversation between Kevin and Derek is very different to that between Kevin and Niall, even though they are generally talking about the same subject. The audience are able to gain a genuine understanding of these characters through their actions and how they speak to each other."

Characters

Derek, teenager, the nice friend
Kevin, teenager, the annoying friend
Niall, teenager, the capable friend

It's around two o' clock in a bowling alley on a Saturday afternoon. Three boys enter from stage right. They are between 15 - 17 years of age. The three of them are wearing t-shirts, jeans, runners and they each have a pair of bowling shoes in their hands.

Derek: (*Pointing at the seats.*) I think that this one's ours... lane 6, right?

The three boys approach the bowling station and sit down on three of the four seats. They quickly slip off their runners and start putting on their bowling shoes.

Kevin: (*Sniffing one of his shoes.*) Jaysus! They cannot be serious! Guys, you gotta take a whiff of one of these... Smells like somebody died wearing them. Like hell I'm gonna be next...

Kevin starts waving one of the offending shoes around. He waves it in Derek's face.

Derek: Quit moaning. At least you got a pair that actually fit. Those were the last tens, I'm stuck with these nines... If you wanna swap...?

Kevin: Did I say I wanted to swap? Seriously though, these things *stink*. You'd think the people here'd do something about it wouldn't ya? So they can keep their customers and all that...

Derek: (*Looks around at the packed alley.*) Looks like they're doing pretty okay for themselves to me...

Niall, finished with his shoes, gets up and goes to the computer. He ignores what the other two are talking about and begins to casually put the names into the system for the game.

Kevin: (*Looks up at the computer and notices what Niall is doing.*) Here Niall! Why do you get to be the one to go first? You always go first. Every single time we're here who goes first? That's right, you.

Niall: It's cause every time we come here you sit there sniffing your shoes and moaning to Deborah there while I get my shoes on as quick as possible so's I can sort out the computer for us all. Now stop being an eejit and just get your shoes on.

Kevin: Yeah, fine, whatever...

Niall: So, you guys going to Catherine's party on Friday?

Kevin: (*Mumbling.*)... no...

Niall: Why? You and Karen wouldn't shut up about it all last week... I thought that it was the only thing on the planet you could think about... What's with the sudden change of mind?

Derek: (*Taking Niall slightly away from Kevin.*) Didn't you hear about what happened?

Niall: ...no...

Kevin: (*Obviously annoyed.*) She dumped me last night... okay? Just leave it.

Niall: Jaysus... You serious? Why?

Kevin: I guess I became too much for her... She couldn't handle all this...

Niall: (*Snorts.*) All what? A midget who's failing every class in school, who's an uncoordinated dork, whose claim to fame is that he doesn't ALWAYS get a gutter ball when we're bowling, after eight months of us going every weekend... No, you know why she really broke up with you... (*Niall gets up to bowl. He goes to get a ball and chooses a yellow one.*) ...It's cause you were such a feckin' prick and you treated her like rubbish. I'm surprised the two of you lasted as long as you did. If I was her I'd've ditched you much earlier than she did.

Niall goes offstage to bowl.

Kevin: (*Sulking and mumbling slightly inaudibly.*) What the hell does he know... Good for nothing... I'd like to see him...

Derek: (*Attempting to cheer Kevin up.*) Come on Kev... Ignore him. You know what a pain in the ass he can be sometimes... Forget about Karen and come to Catherine's party anyway. You could always just ask someone else. I heard that Laura was into you...

Kevin: That's a load of BS. I bet Rachel told you that. She's always talking rubbish like that.

Derek: Well... you should go anyway... It'll be a laugh.

Kevin: I don't want to...

Derek: Come on man! Everybody's going and I mean *everyone*. If you're not going to ask some girl to go then will you just come with me and Niall and Christy? You can get with one of Catherine's friends or something once we get there. Come on it'll be kick ass.

Kevin: (*Still sulking.*) Not if Niall goes with us... I don't want anything to do with him...

Noise of pins falling is heard offstage.

Derek: Oh come on Kev! Seriously! Don't let him get to you over something so small. He's an idiot and you're a feckin' prick. Just leave it. You can't miss this party... you just can't. It's going to be *the* party. Catherine's got her cousin's band to play, there's going to be no adults, as in no parents, and... well...

Kevin: (*Suddenly interested.*) What? What is it?

Derek: (*Avoiding Kevin's eyes.*) Ah, it's nothing...

Kevin: Come on, tell me.

Offstage the noise of pins falling is heard again. Then an annoying overly American voice is heard. It shouts "SPAAAAAAAARE!" Niall comes back from the lane.

Niall: Alright Derek, off you go.

Derek walks over to the bowling balls.

Kevin: Come on Derek! What were you gonna say?

Derek: It's nothing, just leave it. (*He chooses a red ball.*)

Niall: What's happening?

Derek walks off.

Kevin: Oh, Just Derek being Derek. You know how he is...

Niall: Yeah...

Kevin: Yeah... He'd started saying something about Cat's party, but he doesn't seem to want to tell me anything

Niall: Have you any idea what it is?

Kevin: None, whatsoever.

Noise of pins falling is heard.

Niall: Eh... you don't think... it couldn't be some girl, could it? Someone he hasn't told us about?

Kevin: How could there be someone? We're with him, like, 24/7, we know everything about him. Besides, he was saying for us - you, me, him and Christy - to go as a group just a few minutes ago...

Niall: Yeah... I guess...

Kevin: Yeah...

Over the loudspeaker the annoyingly over American voice shouts out "GUUUUUUUTTER BAAAAAAALL". Derek comes back.

Derek: (*Jokingly.*) Think you can do better than a gutter ball? Well, at least I got four pins down first time.

Niall: (*High-fiving Derek.*) Nice one man.

Kevin: (*Getting up and stretching.*) Aaah... Allow me to show you how it's really done... How a real man bowls... How he becomes one with the lane... One with the ball... One with the pins... And he..

Derek: Is knocked out by his best mates for being such a class A prat. Just go and bowl.

Niall and Derek laugh. Kevin picks up a green ball and walks off

obviously annoyed with the other two.

Niall: (*Laughing at Kevin's exit.*) Why the hell do we bring him every week?

Derek: He's our mate.

Niall: Can't just be that...

Derek: (*Grins.*) And he always buys the drinks afterwards.

Niall: (*Over the top.*) That's it!!

Both laugh. Pause. Niall looks over at Derek as if something's on his mind while Derek looks offstage to where Kevin is bowling.

Niall: Hey... Derek...

Derek: (*Cautiously.*) ...Yes...

Niall: Kevin said something about you being really into going to Cat's party... Any reason?

Derek: Nope, I just thought it'd be a good laugh for us all...

Niall: You sure? (*Looks at Derek intensely.*) 'Cause you can tell me anything, you know that, right? (*Moves his hand closer to Derek's.*) We're best mates... It's what I'm here for.

Moves even closer to Derek. Niall is nearly sitting on Derek's lap.

Derek: (*Backs away from Niall.*) Eh... thanks Niall... Eh... are you okay?

Niall: (*Bursts out laughing.*) I'm just messing with you Derek! God, sometimes you can be so easy...

Derek: (*Joins in laughing, slightly nervously.*) Eh... yeah, I know... But seriously, it's all good... I just thought it'd be good craic. And Kevin seems down, it might be good for him, take his mind off Karen and everything that's after happening with them.

Noise of pins falling is heard.

Niall: Yeah... I guess... Seriously though, I can't believe the two of them lasted as long as they did - I mean two whole weeks!

Derek: I know what you mean. Like, who'd 've thought it? Kevin managing to keep someone captive for so long?

Niall: Especially someone like Karen. Remember when we were younger and we'd see her at the Kilnamanagh?

Derek: In her skirts and heels...

Niall: With her bright red lipstick...

Derek: Yeah...

Pause.

Niall: How the hell did she have so much patience with him? Remember all the things that he used to say to her?

Derek: He'd call her Fatty and Zit-zilla, right?

Niall: Right. If either of us ever tried anything like that with a girl we'd've been killed. How'd he manage to get with her in the first place? Did she have an accident that caused her to lose her sight and half her brain?

Derek: *(Kind of quietly.)* I think it was a bet.

Niall: *(Eyes wide starting to laugh.)* Are you serious?!

The noise of pins falling is heard. Derek looks up at the computer and takes note of the score.

Derek: *(To Niall who is laughing hysterically.)* Here, shutup, would you? He's coming back now... I didn't say anything, okay?

Niall: *(Starting to calm down.)* Okay, okay. But are you serious about the bet thing?

Derek: Yeah, I am, now shut up!

Kevin comes back just in time to see Niall burst into mad laughter again.

Kevin: *(Gesturing to Niall.)* What the hell's gotten into him?

Derek: Nothing, nothing. He's just going to bowl now. *(Firmly.)* Aren't you, Niall?

Niall: *(Still laughing.)* Yeah... Sure... Whatever...

Niall gets up, picks up random ball and goes off laughing madly.

Kevin: What's so funny?

Derek: It's nothing. He's just laughing cause, cause I... I... told him my plan for Catherine's party...

Kevin: What? Dude, what the hell? You told Captain Dorkulus what's up with you and not me? I thought we were supposed to be mates...

Derek: Kev, we are!

Kevin: Yeah, well seems to me you'd rather spend your time with just him. Maybe you want me out of the picture..

Derek: For Chrissake Kevin! It's nothing like that.

Kevin: Yeah, sure..

Derek: Come on! Kev, it's nothing really...

Kevin: Well... what is it then?

Derek: (*Suddenly nervous.*) Er... eh... well... em... I was thinking... eh... you know Rache - no! I mean Rebecca... eh... since there won't be any parents at the - No! I don't mean it like that... Eh... well one of the girls who'll be at the party... eh... eh... I was thinking...

Kevin: Dude! Who is it?!

Derek: Just some girl... She's nobody really... Forget that I said anything at all, okay?

Kevin: Aw, come on man! Who is she?

Derek: (*Annoyed.*) Would you just leave it! It's no one...

Kevin: Okay, okay. Well now I *have* to go with you, we're gonna make this happen, no matter who she is. And if you're gonna hook up with somebody, I guess I'd better too. How about... Rachel? She's pretty hot...

Derek: (*Trying to be casual.*) Oh, Rachel? Rachel Downes? Yeah, I guess she's alright. But I heard that she... she's with someone at the moment. Heard he's a big bloke... Plays rugby...

Kevin: Yeah? Shit. Okay then. How about... Sharon? I heard that since Dean dumped her she'll go out with anybody... I'd say that if she gets with me it'd be a treat for her. I'll text her now...

Kevin takes out his phone and as he starts his text he jumps as offstage the sound of pins crashing is heard. Niall shouts and cheers offstage while the American computer voice shouts out "STRIIIIIIIIIIIKEEEEEEEE!!". Niall comes running back onstage cheering, 'power sliding' on his knees etc etc.

Niall: (*Excitedly.*) You won't believe what I just did!

Niall continues to dance around.

Derek: (*Sarcastically.*) Oh, I dunno... seems like you must've done something incredibly worthwhile, like curing cancer or come up with the solution to world hunger. (*Niall sits down, a big grin still spread across his face.*) It couldn't 've been something as pointless and stupid as getting a strike in bowling, could it? Although, that *is* how you react to doing so every week so I guess that, yes, you are that stupid and that is most likely the reason you're acting like such a feckin' prick.

Niall: (*Rolls eyes*.) Alright, alright, you made your point- you didn't have to be like that.

Kevin: Yeah Derek. You're up now, see if you can do any better than the Great and Powerful Niall O' Dwyer!!

Kevin indulges in a mock 'we're not worthy' bowing etc etc.

Derek: (*Getting up*.) You know I won't, but who cares anyway? It's only bowling. And I'll be as crap this week as I was last week.

Niall: (*Joking*.) That's the spirit. (*Derek goes over to the bowling balls and chooses a yellow one. He then goes offstage*.) Kevin, I know you and Karen only broke up, but how'd you get together in the first place?

Kevin: Oh, she asked me to meet her one day when we were standing outside the Borza with some people from school, so I said yeah, sure babes. That was 'bout it.

Niall: Okay, I was just wondering... And what happened? How'd she dump you? Why?

Kevin: (*Casually*.) Oh she just texted me... said that she couldn't handle someone as manly as me...

Niall: (*Under his breath*.) Yeah... right...

Kevin: (*Continuing as if he hadn't heard*.) I guess I just became too much for her.

Niall: Yeah. Sure. Whatever. So, what're you gonna do now? She's going to Catherine's party, isn't she? Might be a bit awkward for you two...

Kevin: (*Airily*.) Oh, is she? Doesn't matter anyway - Karen's old news anyway... I'm gonna ask Sharon Keating to go with me...

Niall: Desperate Shaz? (*Laughs*.) That's aiming a bit low after you were with someone like Karen.

Offstage the American computer voice once again shouts out "STRIIIIIIIIIIIIIIIKEEEEEEEEE!!". Derek walks back on stage calmly. Pause.

Kevin: How the hell did you do that?! You never get strikes!!

Derek: (*Shrugs*.) I dunno... Guess it just must've been that we've been playing for so long. Or it could just've been my lucky day. It doesn't matter anyway, it's only bowling. See if you can make it three strikes in a row Kev!

Kevin slowly gets up and approaches the bowling balls, chooses a yellow one, like Derek had, whispers a kind of chant inaudibly and

STRIKE! Alison Bryan

kisses it for luck before walking offstage.

Niall: (*Patting Derek on the back*.) Well done man.

Derek: Cheers.

Niall: So, what were you saying before you put my strike to shame? Before bowling history was made? Before that miracle happened? Something about Kevin and Karen... Are you serious? Was it really a bet?

Derek: Well... What I heard was that Karen's mates - you know, Laura McGrath, Sharon Keating, Rachel Downes and Lisa Byrne? Yeah, well, I heard, get this, they were sick of how Kevin - well, you know how he is around them - such a total dickhead.

Niall: Yeah... I know what you're talking about.

Derek: Yeah, well, apparently Laura was the one who was *completely* pissed off with him, so she bet Karen a tenner that if Karen went out with him for two weeks, tried to sort him out and all that, well if she managed to, Karen'd win the tenner. But, yeah, didn't work.

Niall: A tenner? That's it? That's all Kevin's worth?

Derek: Yep.

Niall: Sure does suck to be him... Where'd you get all this info from?

Derek: (*Avoiding Niall's eyes*.) Eh... Rachel...

The computer shouts "GUUUUUUUTTEEEEEEER BAAAAAAALL!!" offstage.

Niall: (*Commenting on Kevin's bowling*.) Heh, the idiot. (*Goes back to Derek. Sighs*.) Look man, how long's it been? Just ask her. Do you realise how hard it's been trying to keep this from Kevin? I mean even today he was asking... Please, do yourself a favour and ask her - what's the worst that can happen?

Derek: Look, I just... can't. I was going to at Cat's party - that's why I wanted to go so bad... but I dunno... I don't have enough confidence like you... Who're you gonna take?

Niall: Lisa. Lisa Byrne, you know. Asked her last night when we all went to the Square, after the cinema. I think you'd gone by then.

Derek: Yeah, I had. Mam wanted me and Pete home by 9.30 for some weird reason... Lisa? Really? I didn't know you were after her. Way to go man! (*High fives Niall*.)

Niall: Yeah, well I guess I've kinda liked her for a while, and she must've felt like that bout me cause when I asked her she was all-

Niall is interrupted by the sound of the computer's voice shouting out "GUUUUUUUUUUTTEEEEEEEEEERR BAAAAAAAAAAALLL!!" once again. Kevin stamps back onto stage and slams down into his seat.

Derek: Jaysus, what's wrong man?

Kevin: (*Mumbling, looking down at his feet.*) Nothing, just got a gutter ball. (*Looks at Niall.*) You're up now.

Niall looks to Derek who shrugs. Niall then rushes off to bowl.

Derek: Kevin, clearly something's up. What is it?

Kevin: I... I just got a text from Sharon. It's a no-go. She's already going to Cat's party with Christy.

Derek: It's only Shaz Keating Kev... It doesn't really matter, does it? You can do so much better than her.

Kevin: (*Head in hands.*) I'm not going to Cat's. I'm such a fecking loser! I've lost Karen and I was so mad about her! She was perfect and now... (*Groans.*) If I can't even get someone like Desperate Shaz I must be messed up and a complete dork...

Derek: (*Trying to be funny.*) Ah, you're not that much of a dork. I would have pegged you as more of a geek. Come on Kev. What happened to you? Where's Kev the player? Karen's after making you a wuss man... You should still go. You could meet somebody there. There's going to be girls that aren't from the area there - Catherine's cousins 're from Kildare and they're bringing their mates...

Kevin: Seriously Derek, I do NOT want to go...

Derek: Fine, but you're gonna miss out.

Kevin: Fair enough. I just want to crawl into a hole and die anyway...

Derek: Kevin... seriously, you're starting to scare me... this is not like you... what really happened between you and Karen?

Kevin: You really want to know? You're not gonna have a go at me and call me a loser and laugh at me...?

Derek: Kevin, I'm your mate. You may be a dick, but if something's up I want to give you a hand...

Kevin: Okay... Well... Me and Karen were out on Grafton Street, near Subway, you know? Well... we were just standing there talking and then this guy came over to her. He started going on

about last night and so after he left I asked her what was up and who he was... (*Pins crashing are heard.*) She called me a loser and stupid to think she'd ever be interested in me. That it was all a joke and nothing to her. That she hates me and every minute with me was hell for her. Derek... I really thought I was in love with her... I thought she was, like, the one or something... I dunno what was up with me. She was right. I have no idea what I was even thinking. It's obvious now that it was all a joke. I can't believe I was so blind and stupid...

Derek: Kevin, she's just a bitch who's full of herself. Leave it. She is not worth you thinking about her. You should just forget her and get with someone else... Someone better...

Kevin: I don't know Derek... I'm still feeling pretty shit... I don't really wanna be in the same situation so soon after this... (*Pins falling is heard.*) Derek, don't say anything to Niall. I'd be mortified if he knew I was feeling like this... He hates me anyway and is always looking for a reason to prove I'm rubbish...

Niall returns.

Niall: Okay Derek... You're only three behind me... Try and catch up on this one!

Derek exits.

Niall: So Kevin, what was up earlier?

Kevin: Oh, just Sharon. She's already going with Christy. I was kinda gutted, but I'm a bit better now...

Niall: Ah... sure...

Kevin: (*Obviously feeling awkward after what has just been said with Derek.*) How's the bowling looking at the moment? You know I'm crap at reading the score boards...

Niall: Oh, I'm ahead of you by one and Derek's behind you by two.

Kevin: Derek's really getting better. Remember the first week he lost by fifty points?

Niall: (*Laughs.*) I seem to remember that you weren't too far ahead of him.

Kevin: I guess... Derek's a good mate, isn't he?

Niall: One of the best. I always feel like crap cause I can never repay him after everything he did for me when my parents were going through the divorce. I spent two weeks at his and we spent the whole time playing Grand Theft Auto. He really took my mind off of everything...

Pins are heard.

Kevin: I know what you mean. He's helped me with so much. Girls, friends, family, money... everything!

Niall: He's always there to help us...

Kevin: Wish we could help him...

Niall: Yeah... about that...

Pins falling is heard followed by 'SPAAAAAAAAAAAAAAAAAAAAREEEEE'.

Kevin: What?

Niall: Nothing...

Derek re-enters.

Niall: How the tables have turned. Look who's on top now.

Derek: Yep, yep! So Kevin, you look a bit happier now... Gonna come with us to Cat's party?

Kevin: (*Sighs.*) I guess I'll go if we're still going to go in a group. For you guys. Although I guess Christy's out now... Now that he's going with Sharon...

There is an awkward silence as Niall and Derek avoid each other and Kevin's eyes. They shuffle their feet awkwardly as Kevin looks from one to the other.

Kevin: (*Sighs.*) You're both going with somebody already, aren't you? Who are they?

Derek: Well, Niall's going with Lisa Byrne and me... well...

Niall: (*To Kevin.*) Look, Derek's been after Rachel for a year-

Kevin: (*Interrupting.*) What? Rachel? Rachel Downes?! How come you never told me?

Derek: Cause you'd do something about it. I know you would. I just wanted to leave it for a while... you know?

Kevin: I guess...

Niall: Yeah, well Derek's been mad about her for a good long while. He hasn't asked her to the party yet, but I know she's gonna say yes when he does. This is his one chance and he needs us. We're going to make this happen. (*Niall turns to Derek.*) Derek, you've always been there for us. I know I must sound like a sap saying all this, but this is our chance to help you. And none of our usual crap is gonna ruin this for you.

Kevin: (*To Derek*.) Dude... You are so in there! Go for it!

Derek: You sure? I mean, do you really think that she'd go for me? Really?

Niall: I've seen her looking at you when we're all out together - us and the girls. When she's round you she can never take her eyes off of you. Ain't that right, Kev?

Kevin: (*Nods*.) For serious man. She's always trying to get your attention.

Niall: (*Getting up to bowl again*.) Go for it Derek! Now's your chance! Text her now! She'll be delighted with herself to get someone like you, man.

Derek: Really?

Niall & Kevin: YES!

Niall chooses a bowling ball and goes to go offstage, but stops and turns back to address Kevin.

Niall: (*Grinning.*) Hey Kevin. You ready?

Kevin: Ready for what?

Niall: To see how a real man bowls.

Niall exits quickly before Kevin can get out of his chair. Kevin runs after Niall. Derek stays sitting where he is, takes out his phone and, with a small, slightly nervous smile on his face, starts to text.

WEIRD
Tírna McGauley

"A year ago, I was an entirely different person. I was terrified of the future. I was terrified of being me. Through Tenderfoot I discovered a side of myself I never knew existed. I became a playwright at 16, Shakespeare, eat your heart out. I realised that I could express myself through theatre, and the arts, and music, and writing. It was like breaking the surface after holding your head underwater. I could breathe. Thank God I don't have asthma."

Characters

Rose Byrne, 15 years of age, school uniform in scene 1, casual & party clothes thereafter
John Loughrey, 16 years of age, wears a black beanie with badges with his school uniform
Jack Kiernan, 16 years of age
Charlie Lucas, 16 years of age
Máire Jones, 16 years of age
Extras, partygoers for scenes 3 & 4

Scene One

Rose and John walk onstage, pushing each other, talking and smiling. They wear school uniforms, and carry a small schoolbag each. Lighting indicates that the scene is set outdoors.

Rose: I can't believe it's finally over!

John: Thank God, I'm wrecked with studying. Three whole years of learning shite-all and we're finally done! (*John counts off each subject on his fingers.*) No more English or Maths, or Irish, for TWO

WHOLE MONTHS!

Rose: (*Scowls.*) God, I hate that language.

John: Cheer up! We're done with our exams! Finished, vamoose, goodnight and God bless! And don't we have camping in Wexford to look forward to?

Rose: Jesus, I nearly forgot about that. It's gonna be... great. (*Pauses. Takes a deep breath. Smiles.*) I just kinda wanna get out this summer, y'know? DO something. Camping is gonna be fun.

John: I just want to kick back. Relax. Then it's only fifth and sixth year to go, the Leaving Cert, couple of years of college, and BAM - we're out of here for good. (*Rose moves away from John.*) Y'alright? Rose?

Rose: (*Looks at him.*) Yeah?

John: Are you OK?

Rose: (*Nods.*) Just tired. Sick of fucking exams. And y'know, college is gonna be a nightmare.

John: You're worrying about college? Now? Forget about that, and whatever the fuck else is bothering you.

Rose: Well I can hardly do that now. Can you imagine what my mam's gonna be like when I get back? A hug, a kiss, and then (*mimics*) 'Just because you're finished your Junior Cert doesn't mean you can doss! You have to get ready for camping, you have to pack, you have to sort out your room and all your school books, you have to study for exams you won't have for another three years, blah, blah, blah, blah, blaahhh...'

John: Good impression.

Rose: Cheers, I've been working on it. (*Pauses. Sits down.*) Could always leave.

John: Leave?

Rose: You know. Leave school. I'm fifteen, sixteen during summer. Legally... I could drop out.

John: Ah here, Rose, you can't be serious!

Rose: Why not?

John: You can't LEAVE. What about jobs, and college and all that? You can't seriously be considering giving that up.

Rose: (*Shakes her head.*) Maybe I am? I dunno. Everything we've done these past three years... It was all leading up to these fucking exams. The stressing, the panic attacks, EVERYTHING. And now it's all over. Answer a couple of questions and, what? That's it, we're done? I can't... I feel weird, y'know? I feel like everyone made this out to be a big deal, and then it's worth nothing. Don't you? (*Looks over at John.*)

John: (*Shakes head.*) ...not really. (*Rose scowls. John backs away defensively.*) Well, I don't! And anyway, it's not like we can do anything. This is what's supposed to happen. There's no point fighting it. And besides, if you leave school early, say in the next year, what would you do? What would you do for money and all? Your mam won't let you skive off her. You've gotta have a reason.

Rose: Like she'd care anyway. (*Pause.*) Can you not feel it, though?

John: Feel what?

Rose: I... I don't know. Something's off, something's just not right. I mean, yay, we're finished our exams - but it's like you said. Like we're stuck here for the next three years.

John: (*Pause.*) I said two years.

Rose: What?

John: You said we've got three years of school left, then the Leaving Cert. But we don't. We have two. We're not doing TY.

Rose: No, I said two years.

John: (*Stands up.*) No, no, you definitely said three years.

Rose: Well then I made a mistake. But anyway, doesn't matter. We're still stuck here for three - shit, no, two years.

John: (*Takes a few steps away.*) There! You said we've got three years. Three years, and if you're worrying this much about it, then you wouldn't make that mistake.

Rose: ..maybe it wasn't a mistake.

John: What?

Rose: Ms. Ryan talked to me before the final exam. She said... she told me that Jake dropped out of TY, and chose to do fifth year instead... And she offered me the final spot.

John: And? (*Rose pauses.*) Just one thing - did you even THINK of me, before you said yes?

Rose: John / I-

/ indicates overlapping dialogue. A slash occurring in one line indicates the start of dialogue at the slash point in the next line.

John: / Because I'm pretty sure that when it came time to choose between fifth year or TY, we said we'd talk to each other before we made a decision.

Rose: It was right before an exam, she caught me off guard, what was I supposed to say!?

John: You could have waited! You could have told her, 'Oh, give me a few minutes, I want to talk about it with my mates before I fuck off to a different / year!'

Rose: / It's only a year's difference, we'll still be in the same school, it's not like we're on different sides of a fucking… I dunno, galaxy or something!

John: Feels like it.

Rose: Oh grow up! I chose TY because I needed the extra year. You think I wanna be stuck here? Of course I don't, and it's not like I actually want to go into a whole different year without you, but I need this. I need to take some time off / to…

John: / Time off? Time off?! That's what summer is for! A couple of years and you'll be grand, Rose, you've no need to stay here an extra year!

Jack enters. He sees that they're arguing and waits on the edge of the stage, stage right, for them to stop. He can hear what they say.

Rose: Yes I do! You don't know what it's like! You're getting all honours results, you're grand, I'm lucky if I can get at least a single good grade! These exams were torture for me, this past year has been torture, and I've been stuck in the middle of it watching while you and Jack and everyone else got along grand! (*Starts walking towards John.*) I've had to sit around and struggle while you lot gloated about being fucking super geniuses. I studied, and studied, and fucking STUDIED, and even then it probably wasn't enough, because it's never enough! (*Pause.*) So there. That's why I chose to do TY. Because it was the only fucking choice I had. Because, right now? I need all the help I can get. (*Sits back down. Takes deep breaths.*)

John: You never… You never said you were struggling…

Rose: Oh, yeah, 'cause I walked into school every morning absolutely fucking WRECKED by choice.

John: You still could have said something.

Rose: What could I have said? 'Oh John, help me, I can't do all this on my own cause I'm a fucking idiot?!'

John: Look, it's not my fault! We all had our own problems, so don't start moping about like you had it worse off! Yes, it was easier for me when it came to doing the actual work, but for fuck's sake, Rose, we all had to study! We all had to go through being stressed and being tired, not just you. What about me, huh? What about when I needed help, or when Jack needed help, where were you? Going off on your own, or going off with Charlie, because that's what you always do!

Rose: What the hell are you talking about?!

John: You keep shutting people out, and then turn back to them expecting them to just drop everything for you. Everyone but Charlie. Does she know? About TY? Have you told her already? How did she react? Did she get upset? Did she simply nod, smile, whatever the fuck she does? You can be damn well sure that I'm not doing that! Go to TY, go stay here an extra year, do whatever you want, I don't care!

John starts to leave.

Rose: John.

John: What?

Rose doesn't know what to say. John turns and exits. Rose lets out a frustrated groan. Enter Jack.

Jack: Well, that escalated quickly.

Rose: Shut up, Jack.

Jack: Only trying to lighten the mood. Seems like there's trouble in Wonderland. Where's Alice gone?

Rose: Stop calling him 'Alice'.

Jack: Oooh. A fight like that and you're STILL defending him?

Rose: Well I'm hardly gonna badmouth him!

Jack: Why not! Come on, Rose. You're pissed, he's walked off, you've every right to rant... Well. Maybe not RANT. I think you've done enough ranting for today. But you've a right to give out about him, at least.

Rose: (*Looks away.*) I'm serious, Jack. Just... fuck off.

Jack: (*Pause. Sits down.*) Oh, no. I'm not leaving you mad and sad. And I'm not missing out on an opportunity to badmouth Alice.

Rose: Stop calling him that!

Jack: (*Dramatically.*) Never! Alice saved us from the Red Queen, and the vicious Jabberwock! HAIL THE CHAMPION!

Rose: (*Pushes Jack, grinning.*) Shut up!

Jack: There's that smile I wanted to see! Now come on, you Mad Hatter. (*Taps Rose's hat.*) Don't you think that, even if Alice won't attempt to save Wonderland, you should at least try?

Rose: (*Shrugs.*) I dunno. Should I?

Jack: Put it this way. If you don't, you'll end up losing a great mate. And over something so small? Seems a bit ridiculous, now. (*Stands up.*)

Rose: Where're you going?

Jack: (*Winks.*) Late for an important date.

Jacks starts to exit.

Rose: What's up with you and all this Alice crap, anyway? You've been like this all week!

Jack remembers something.

Jack: Wait, Rose! I came over to tell you there's a party on at The Rabbit Hole.

Rose: The Rabbit Hole?

Jack: My uncle's new club. Really cool, we figured tonight would be a good opening night. to celebrate the end of exams. Around 7-ish. Free in. You coming? Everyone'll be there.

Rose: Yeah. Yeah, sure.

Jack: Grand job. I'll text you later, let you know where it is. (*Winks.*) Later, Hatter.

Exit Jack. Rose takes out a phone and dials a number.

Rose: (*On phone.*) Heya, Charlie?...

Exit Rose talking on the phone. Lights dim.

Scene Two

Rose and Charlie are at Charlie's house. They are in Charlie's room. There are clothes all over the bed. Rose is sitting on the floor. She is preoccupied with her phone. Charlie stands beside the bed. Charlie holds two shirts up.

Charlie: Right, this one, or this one?

Rose: (*Doesn't look up.*) That one.

Charlie: This one?

Rose: (*Still not looking up.*) Yeah.

Charlie: (*Puts shirts on bed, frowns.*) How about this one?

Rose: (*Still not looking up.*) That's nice.

Charlie: But I like this one.

Rose: (*Looks up.*) Then wear... oh.

Charlie: Yeah, 'oh'. What's up with you?

Rose: Nothing. (*Looks back down at phone.*) I'm grand.

Charlie: Rose Byrne, did you know that you are a terrible liar?

Rose: Charlotte Lucas, did you know that I don't care?

Charlie: Oi! It's CHARLIE.

Rose: Charlotte!

Charlie: Charlie!

Rose: Charlotte!

Charlie: Charlie!

Rose: Charlotte!

Charlie: Oh fuck you, Roseanne.

Rose: (*Dramatically.*) You wound me, Charlotte! (*Lies down.*) I should just go home, curl up in a corner, and cry because of how mean you're being! (*Charlie hits Rose with a pillow.*) Hey!

Charlie: Slipped outta my hand, man!

Rose: That's what she said.

Charlie: (*Points at the door.*) Get out.

Rose: Alright, alright. Go with the blue one, by the way.

Charlie: Right. So come on, then. What's up?

Rose: What d'you mean?

Charlie: Well, you were grand this morning, then Jack said he saw you talking to John, and, I dunno what happened, but ever since then you've been really weird and quiet. What's up?

Rose: (*Sits up.*) I told you, I'm fine.

Charlie: (*Points at Rose.*) LIAR!

Rose: Oh my God, will you just let it GO?!

Charlie: Not until you tell me what's up!

Rose: HE'S PISSED! Pissed because I'm doing TY, apparently! So what if we're doing a different year!? So what if I want to take the time to do this for myself!? He's got no fucking right to start yelling his head off at me about it! And then he starts complaining about you, and I don't know where that came from! It's like when I needed help I went to you, and... I dunno, but he sure as hell wasn't happy about it! And he ranted about how, 'I never told him,' and how 'I should have talked to him first,' and I swear to GOD, Charlie, he's driving me up the fucking wall!

Charlie: (*Pauses.*) Well. Of all things, definitely wasn't expecting that.

Rose: (*Scowls.*) Cheers, Charlie.

Charlie: Alright, alright, calm down. Don't you think, if you took John aside and talked to him, you might get him to understand? TY's not a big deal.

Rose: I TRIED that. I TRIED explaining I had to do TY to try get my grades up, he wouldn't listen! Arsehole.

Charlie: Alright, no need for that. I'm serious, though. At Jack's thing tonight, John should be there. Talk to him in PERSON, for fuck's sake, cause you know texting or whatever is just useless. Try get him to understand, at least. You never know, he might cop on.

Rose: (*Scoffs.*) I doubt that.

Charlie: Well I'm not having you sit on my bedroom floor moping about it!

Rose: (*Lies down again.*) Leave me alone to die.

Charlie: I swear to god I'll throw another pillow at you.

Rose: Fuck you.

Charlie: Why d'you have to be so harsh?!

Rose: Because my life is ending, that's why!

Charlie: Drama queen.

Rose: Bitch.

Charlie: Cúnas!

Rose: Oh fuck off with your Irish, Charlie!

Charlie: (*Pause.*) Jesus, you really are upset!

Rose: No shit, Sherlock.

Charlie: (*Folds clothes.*) Well, I still think you should talk to John.

Rose: Are you deaf? I'VE TRIED. AND FAILED.

Charlie: Don't bite my fucking head off! I'm only suggesting you try again! (Pauses.) You know, if he's getting this upset about it there might be something more.

Rose: What are you on about?

Charlie: I mean... No-one gets that upset over someone only doing TY. Did you ever stop to think what he's thinking about? What he felt when you told him? Come on, even YOU can't be that oblivious!

Rose: Oblivious to what?! You're mental!

Charlie: Am I? Or are you just fucking blind?

Rose: WHAT ARE YOU EVEN TALKING ABOUT?

Charlie: IT'S JOHN.

Rose: Yes! It IS John!

Charlie: No, I mean -

Rose: What?

Charlie: Jesus, you're fucking thick.

Rose: Shut up.

Charlie: Just talk to him. I have more pillows, and if you don't at least TRY, I swear to GOD I will end you.

Rose: Jesus, you're scary when you're mad.

Charlie: Exactly. Now get ready, I think I need to buy something new for this party thing.

Rose: There's gotta be something here...

Rose starts looking through the clothes with Charlie. Lights dim.

Scene Three.

Rose and Charlie are at Jack's party in the Rabbit Hole, a club. The design for the inside of the club should be Alice in Wonderland themed. Pink, purple and blue lights mostly. Black and white wooden panel walls & a black and white chess board floor. There are themed ornaments hanging haphazardly on the walls. There is a bar upstage left. Music plays in the background. It is early, a few people walk around, mingling. Everyone's dressed in casual party dress. Everyone wears animal masks. Rose is wearing a brightly coloured butterfly mask. Charlie wears a pink/purple cat mask.

They stand, talking, centre-stage. Jack, wearing a white rabbit mask, walks over, carrying a drink. He takes off his mask and puts his arms around Charlie & Rose's shoulders.

Jack: Well! If it isn't the Hatter and the Cheshire Cat. (*Gestures around him.*) Welcome to the Rabbit Hole!

Charlie: (*Rose and Charlie take their masks off while Jack is talking.*) Is this why you're so obsessed with Alice in Wonderland?

Jack: (*Shrugs.*) Might have something to do with it, yeah. I helped set it up, gotta keep with the theme. Isn't it clever, though? (*Takes a card out of his pocket.*) I love the admission tickets. (*Holds it up to the light.*) Playing cards. Ingenious, wouldn't you say? (*To Rose.*) Seen Alice yet?

Rose: He's coming?

Rose looks at Charlie. Charlie nods.

Jack: Supposed to be. He's meant to help out with the music. So far he's left me all on my lonesome. I swear, if he doesn't show up soon, I'm gonna fucking kill him. Hardly the Rabbit Hole without Alice now is it?

Jack holds the ticket up to the light again, looking at it.

Charlie: (*To Rose.*) Is it just me, or is this whole Alice obsession a bit weird?

Rose: (*To Charlie.*) Just a bit. (*Out loud.*) Hey, Jack?

Jack: Yes, dear?

Jack puts the ticket in his pocket. Looks at Rose.

Rose: Have you seen Máire around?

Charlie scowls at the mention of Máire.

Jack: (*Coughs on his drink.*) Máire? Is, uh… Is she here?

Charlie: (*Bitterly.*) Yes, she is. Didn't you see her? She's wearing a fox mask.

Jack: I'm gonna go find her. See you later! (*Jack starts to leave. Remembers something. Turns.*) Oh, and John's wearing a blue owl mask, if you see him, tell him I'm on the lookout and I need him working the DJ set soon, alright?

Exit Jack. Rose bursts out laughing when he's gone.

Rose: Aw man, the poor child is lovesick!

Charlie: Oh, don't get me started.

Charlie walks over to the bar and orders a drink. Rose, laughing, follows her slowly.

Rose: Did you see his face as soon as I mentioned her? It's like we don't even matter. Running out the door like his life depended on it? Jesus! (*Laughs again.*) Aw, man, haven't laughed like that since the start of the exams! And you know - (*Notices Charlie isn't laughing. She has finished her drink.*) I... Charlie? You alright? What's up? (*Charlie shakes her head. Orders another drink. Rose pauses.*) You're... Something wrong?

Charlie: It's... (*Drinks.*) It's nothing. Absolutely fucking nothing.

Charlie orders another drink. Rose orders her first.

Rose: Jesus Charlie, go easy.

Charlie: Come on, let's find John.

Charlie puts mask back on and takes Rose's hand. Exit Rose and Charlie. Enter Máire. She has a fox mask hanging around her neck. Jack trails behind her. His mask is pushed up.

Jack: Come on! Please?

Máire: No, Jack!

Tries to walk away. Jack grasps her arm. Pulls her back.

Jack: Just give me one more chance, Máire, please?

Máire: (*Pulls away.*) I said NO. We tried this, and you fucked it up, and I'm not going back to that!

Máire tries to walk away again.

Jack: But I'm not like that anymore, Máire, I'm not! Come on! I had a girlfriend and all for, what was it, seven months? Just because you're.. I was.. It's different now! I'M different! Why can't you believe that?

Rose and Charlie re-enter and settle downstage. They are talking to a guy wearing a bear mask. The focus is still on Máire and Jack who are upstage.

Máire: Because you already lied to me once, how am I supposed to trust you again?!

Jack: Because that's what couples do! They make mistakes, and they learn from them, and then they.. get over it!

Máire: Oh, of COURSE she's here. Did you invite her?

A spotlight shines on Charlie singling her out. Jack looks over at her.

Jack: Charlie? Of course I did. Maybe things didn't.. Maybe we're not on the best terms, but she's still a friend.

Máire: I BET she's a friend.

Jack: Jesus, Máire, I told you, It was nothing. I was drunk. It was a drunken fumble.

Máire: She knew you were going out with me.

Jack: What the fuck do you want me to do?!

Máire pauses. Suspense builds.

Máire: Okay. How about this..

She starts speaking to him quietly. The lights dim around her and Jack and the light comes up on Rose, Charlie and the guy in the bear mask. The guy with the bear mask high-fives Rose, hands Charlie a slip of paper, and exits. Rose turns to Charlie and slaps her in the arm. As the lights come up Rose and Charlie start to speak. Máire & Jack's conversation continues in the background.

Charlie: Ow! What the hell was that for?!

Rose: You being an idiot, that's what! Decent guy walks over and starts pulling a move on you, and what do you do? Completely blow him off by saying, 'Sorry, can't date, it's against my JEDI RELIGION'.

Charlie: 'A Jedi must have the deepest commitment, the most serious mind. (*Looks at Jack.*) This one a long time have I watched. All his life has he looked away... to the future, to the horizon. Never his mind on where he was. Hmm? What he was doing. Hmph. Adventure. Heh. Excitement. Heh. A Jedi craves not these things. You are reckless!'

Rose: You just quoted Yoda.

Charlie: You're damn right I did. (*Downs another drink.*) The point was the same, though. A Jedi craves not these things.

Rose: Stop quoting Yoda! (*Takes Charlie's glass.*) Come on then, let's get some food in you so whatever the hell you're drinking doesn't go to yer head.

Rose and Charlie pass Jack and Máire as they exit.

Máire: So?

Jack: (*Watching Rose & Charlie walk offstage.*) No. No, not a chance in hell.

Máire: Good thing we're not in hell, then.

Jack: But Charlie / is -

Máire: / Who I need you to do this with. Maybe I still like you, okay?

Jack: But I think Charlie likes me.

Máire: Yeah, well I liked Charlie until she put her tongue down your throat.

Jack: (*Pauses.*) I can't do that to her.

Máire: (*Scowls.*) Alright. Fine. Let me know if you change your mind though, yeah?

Máire exits leaving Jack onstage alone. John enters carrying a glass and his mask. He watches Máire leave and then walks over to Jack.

John: Alright man? Sorry I'm late, my sister's an idiot. She's got her new fella over, and the guy's as thick as / a fucking -

Jack: / Look, man, as interesting as I'm sure this story is, I really don't care. And I mean that in a loving way. Now, come on. You're late, I need you to help me set up the stage stuff. (*Goes to exit but remembering something turns to face John again.*) Oh! And, uh, Rose was looking for you.

John: She's here?

Jack: Yeah, Charlie dragged her off somewhere earlier. Here, what's going on with you two anyway? I only caught the arse-end of the fight you had earlier. I've no idea what's going on, and Charlie's no help.

John: (*Shaking his head and shrugging.*) I don't even know. I mean, this morning, before the exam, she was grand, and then afterwards she just turns to me and goes, 'Oh, by the way, I'm doing TY. Surprise!' And I'm like, 'The fuck are you talking about?!' And she starts going on, saying how she's not prepared for fifth year and how she's been a stressed wreck all year, and how we haven't been helping her at all - which is a down-right lie! Who stayed at her house to pull a studying all-nighter? Who spent his free time trailing her around school and helping her out whenever it was physically possible? Who gave her revision books when hers were stolen? It sure as hell wasn't Charlie! It's like, I know I've got an easier time learning the stuff, but come on! I helped her every step of the way, as much as I could, and then she turns around and drops this on me! It's like... (*Sighs.*) It's like she doesn't even care.

Jack: Wow. How long were you holding onto THAT for?

John: Fuck off.

Jack: (*Defensively.*) I'm just saying!

John: I'll miss her. She's my best mate, Jack, she's... It doesn't matter what she is. I'll miss her, simple as. And don't give me that whole, 'You're overreacting, it's just a year's difference' thing, alright, 'cause I already got it from her, so I know all that already.

Jack: (*Shrugs, looking away.*) You could always just ask her out.

John: (*Turns towards Jack quickly.*) And WHY, in God's name, would I do that?

Jack: (*Turns to face John.*) Do you REALLY need me to answer that?

John: Well it'd be a GREAT help.

Jack: Don't act like you don't know what I'm talking about.

John: See, here's the thing - I DON'T know what you're talking about.

Jack: You're as oblivious as she is!

John: If you're saying you think I have feelings for / her -

Jack: / No, I'm not saying I THINK. I'm saying I KNOW. And so does half the school, apparently! Everyone knows that you two / are just -

John: / But there's nothing going on between us!

Jack: Exactly! Which is why I said to ask her out. Get the ball rolling. (*Makes a pushing motion with his hands.*) Kick things off. Preferably before we get our results, I've got a bet on with Charlie.

John: I'M NOT GOING TO ASK HER - wait. Did you just say you and Charlie are BETTING? (*Jack nods.*) On me and Rose.

Jack: I personally think you guys are gonna cop on soon. Like, before the results. Charlie thinks you guys will be on such a high from your results that you won't be able to control yourselves. She expects some romantic, running-into-each-others-arms-in-a-field-of-daisies shite. Or something. Anyway. The sooner the better!

John: What? No! I'm... I'm not asking her out! And even if I did, it would be on my own terms, when I was ready, not when it suits you to win a few quid off Charlie! And you're one to talk! I mean honestly, could the back and forth game between you and Máire BE any more obvious?!

Jack: Focus, Alice, we're not talking about me and / Máire -

John: / Oh, so you can comment on MY relationships, but I can't comment on yours?!

Jack: Yeah, that sounds about right.

John: It's not 'about right'! Honest to God, Jack. The two of you are / like -

Jack: / Look, me and Máire have a complicated relationship, alright? I fucked up, now she's pissed.

John: What did you do?

Jack: Nothing, I... I did something really stupid and.. She's still pissed, even though I've apologised profoundly and explained myself to her. And now she wants me to - (*Pause*.) Never mind. Doesn't matter.

John: What?

Jack: Nothing.

John: You two have history like... Jesus, I dunno, Tanya and Max.

Jack: From Eastenders?

John: Cop on, Jack. I don't watch the show. Rose forced me to when she was bored, Okay?

Jack: How am I supposed to take you seriously?

John: Fuck off.

Lights dim.

Scene Four

Later that night, still in The Rabbit Hole. More people are at the party. Everyone's had something to drink. Some people are properly drunk. Everyone still wears animal masks. Music in the background. Jack and Charlie stagger onstage. Jack is holding Charlie up.

Charlie: (*Slurred*.) Y'know what I don' get?

Jack: What don't you get?

Charlie: Why Rose's bein' a bitch. I mean, d'you see her earlier! Fuckin' twat. She wuddin' leave me alone aftur I rejected that guy.

Jack: What guy?

Charlie: Y'know... that one guy... (*Points at her own face.*) Wi' the face. He gave me his number'n everythin', but I didn' wanna go ou' with'm, and then that twat giz me a smack'n me arm! And I'm like,

'Whaa are you on abou'?!' And she's all, 'He was cool, he gave you 'is number, you need to stop quoting Yoda!' 'N I'm all, 'Nope, nope, nope.' (*Yoda's voice.*) 'Yoda I am, reject boys I must, train Jedi I haf'to!' The moral of the story, kids, is Jedi's before white guys.

Jack: I think you're drunk.

Charlie: And I think you're pretty, but we can't all be drunk.

Jack: (*Takes her glass.*) Okay, now, I REALLY think you're drunk. You should probably head home soon.

Charlie: (*Snorts.*) Home? Pffffftt. Home s'where my ma'n'da are busy procreating. Nah, nah, nah, 'm stayin' right here. S'where the party's at! You did a bang-up job, Pretty Boy. (*Grabs her drink off Jack and downs the remains.*) Now Pretty Boy. Hear me out, m'kay? (*Staggers closer to Jack, slings an arm around his shoulders.*) Pretty Boy. Hi!

Máire enters. She stands at the bar and watches Jack and Charlie. Jack looks over at her.

Charlie: (*Noticing Jack's not looking at her.*) Oi, (*slaps his cheek lightly*) eyes over here, Pretty Boy.

Jack: Okay, no, I'm taking you home.

Charlie: You're about as drunk as I am!

Jack: Charlie, NOBODY's as drunk as you are. I'm sober, anyway. I had to keep an eye out, in case things got too crazy.

Charlie: Aw! Prop'r gentlemen, you are. Fine. Lead the way!

Jack takes her arm. Máire watches on. Rose enters. Bumps into Jack and Charlie.

Rose: Alright, Jack?

Jack: Perfectly fine, Hatter. Escorting Cheshire here home.

Charlie grins dopily at Rose. Rose smirks.

Rose: Yeeaaahhh... Remind me to keep her on a leash next time, would you?

Jack: Remind you? Pfft, at this rate I'll be buying the leash myself.

Charlie: Kinky.

Rose: (*To Charlie.*) Oi. He didn't mean it like that. (*To Jack.*) Did you?

Jack: God no! Definitely... uh, definitely not.

Rose: (Pauses.) Right. How are yous getting home?

Jack: I'll call her ma, or her dad. I'll wait with her, one of them can come pick her up.

Rose: (Winces.) Oooh. She'll be slaughtered. Sixteen and pissed?

Jack: (Shrugs again.) Not my problem.

Enter John. He bumps into Máire. She is annoyed.

John: Sorry, I didn't - sorry, Máire. (Pause.) Are you OK?

Máire: Never better.

John: I doubt that. You look like you're fit to kick someone's head off. What's up?

Máire: Look, it's fine, nothing, I'm just not having the best night, alright? It's got nothing to do with you, anyway.

John: Doesn't mean you can't talk about it, though.

Máire: Doesn't mean I WANT to, though.

John: Alright, Jesus, calm down. I'm only saying if you need any help you can ask me, alright. Even if it involves Jack.

Máire: Oh, what do YOU know?! It's not like he's even bloody told you anything.

John: Au contraire. I know for a fact that he has feelings for you.

Máire: I've heard that before. Not interested.

John: Fine. Whatever. Can't say I didn't try. Anyway, why are you standing over here alone? Go talk to someone. It's a party. Kinda the whole point.

Máire: I'm talking to YOU, amn't I?

John: Well, yeah, but before that. I mean you were just kinda standing over here, away from everyone. Not like you at all. Usually you're at the centre of the crowd.

Máire: Well, this time I'm not. So just let it go.

John: Oh come on. The great Máire Jones, surrounded by people, but all alone. Tell you, something doesn't add up there.

Máire: Swear to God, John, just drop it.

John: Alright, fine. But don't be surprised if you miss your chance again. At least talk to the poor chap.

Máire scowls and John moves on. Focus moves to Jack, Charlie and Rose. Rose is on her phone.

Rose: (Looks up.) Have you got any food here?

WEIRD Tírna McGauley

Jack: (*Shakes his head.*) There's a chipper across the way, though. Why?

Rose: I'm not bringing Charlie home while she's plastered. I'll get a bag of chips and a burger or something into her, sober her up a bit.

Jack: You sound like this is normal for you.

Rose: Well, you know my dad.

Jack: (*Pause.*) Right, yeah. Eh.. D'you wanna bring her over, then?

Rose: Yeah. You alright here?

Jack: It's kinda getting quiet. I think we'll manage.

Rose: Alright. (*Puts an arm around Charlie's back, shifting her weight from Jack to herself. Charlie's still a bit shaky, but able to stand with only a small amount of support.*) You okay, Charlie?

Charlie: Never fucking better. Did you mention chipper?

Rose: Come on.

Exit Rose and Charlie. Jack starts walking over to John but is intercepted by Máire.

Máire: What's up with Charlie?

Jack: ..She's not feeling the best. Rose's bringing her out for some fresh air.

Máire: So she's pissed, then?

Jack: Pretty much, yeah.

Máire: And you?

Jack: Am I pissed? I haven't had anything.

Máire: No! I meant with Charlie. You made a move yet?

Jack: No. And I told you I'm not going to.

Máire: Oh, come on, who's it gonna hurt?

Jack: Well, I'm PRETTY SURE it's gonna hurt CHARLIE, for one.

Máire: Well, yeah. That's kinda the whole point.

Jack: Look, I'm not doing it, okay? I get that you're mad at us, but it's not HER fault. Give me hell all you want, but for fuck's sake -

John interrupts.

John: You guys alright?

Máire: You're like freaking Beetlejuice!

Jack: Well, no, we'd have had to have said his name for him to be Beetlejuice. I don't think we have.

Máire: It doesn't matter!

Enter Rose and Charlie. Everyone pauses.

Rose: ..Everything alright?

Charlie: (Slurred.) Never better!

Rose hits Charlie in the back of the head. Charlie yelps.

Jack: (*To Máire.*) Look, I'm not doing it, so just drop it.

Rose: Not doing what?

Jack: (*To Rose.*) It's nothing. (*To Máire.*) And I mean it. Stop.

Awkward pause.

John: ..Right. Well. I better, uh.. I better get going.

John starts to exit.

Rose: Wait! (*John stops, turns. Rose sits Charlie down on a chair, then walks over to John.*) I think we need to talk.

John: Can it not wait until tomorrow, because I really should / get-

Rose: / John. What the fuck is going on?

John: (*Pause.*) No idea.

Jack exits. Charlie follows. Máire exits after a while.

Rose: Because if you're still pissed at me about / TY -

John: / I just don't understand how you can sit around feeling sorry for yourself when we all went through the exact same thing! Why are you so different?!

Rose: (*Pause.*) I'm sorry. Okay? I'm sorry if, for ONCE, I took my needs into consideration before yours. I NEED this year. I NEED it, because**...**

Rose is lost for words.

John: What's going on?

Rose: What?

John: With you Talk to me.

Rose: I.. No.

John: I bet you talk to Charlie.

Rose: That's different. Charlie knows me. She's knows about my mam and.. stuff.

John: She knew about TY before I did?

Rose: She was there when Ms. Ryan offered me the place.

John: What else does she know? That I don't?

Rose: (*Sighs.*) Does it matter?

John: It does if you don't trust me.

Rose: Of course I fucking trust you!

John: So tell me!

Rose: I can't.

John: You can.

Rose: I CAN'T, John. Why can't you just /

John interrupts Rose with a sudden kiss. Pulls away after a few moments. Rose is stunned.

John: You can trust me.

Pause. Rose flees. John is in shock. Jack enters with Charlie.

Charlie: (*Voice still slurred.*) Here, John, where'd Rose go?

John: I.. She just left. She ran out.

Jack: Is she alright? (*Pause. No response from John.*) Are YOU alright?

John: ..I have to go.

Jack: What? John! John! Jesus.

Charlie: Jeeezus, like, wha's up with him?!

Máire enters. She stops at the side of the stage. Jack notices her.

Jack: I dunno.

Charlie: She likes him, yeah, an' he likes her, but they're both fuckin' idiots! Too fuckin' (*waves a hand in front of Jack's face*) blind to cop the fuck on, like.

Charlie stumbles. Jack steadies her.

Jack: You okay?

Charlie: Never fuckin' better, Pretty Boy. Here, Rose said she'd get me chipper!

Jack: I don't think she's coming back.

Charlie: Ah, here, I'm hungry!

Jack: Could see if there's anywhere else you could get food?

Charlie: Chipper, though!

Máire watches Jack intensely willing him to make a move.

Jack: Fuck. (*Kisses Charlie.*) Come on, let's find you some food, then take you home.

Charlie: (*Shocked.*) ..okay. Okay, yeah.

Exit Jack and Charlie. Lights dim.

Scene Five

The following morning. Rose and Charlie are centre stage. They are in a park. Charlie is lying down on a bench, Rose is sitting on the ground beside her. They are wearing summer clothes. Charlie is wearing a hat and sunglasses. Jack is on upstage left. He is in his bedroom. Máire is downstage right. She is in a different park. The three scenes occur at the same time with the focus shifting backwards and forwards between them. When one character texts another appropriate text alerts are heard. John enters later in the scene.

Rose: You dead yet?

Charlie: (*Muffled.*) You WILL BE if you don't shut the fuck up.

Rose: It's your own fault.

Charlie: I think Jack slipped me something. The more I hung out with him, the more drunk I got. I'm sixteen. TELL YOUR UNBORN CHILDREN, ROSE. THE CONSUMPTION OF ALCOHOL KILLS YOU THE FOLLOWING MORNING. IT'S BAD, BAD, BAD.

Rose: You do realise that your shouting isn't actually going to help you, like, AT ALL, right?

Charlie: (*Puts a hand on the hat.*) STILL BAD.

Rose: Yeah, remind me to never let you come to Jack's place ever again, Okay?

Charlie: (*Pause.*) Rose.

Rose: What?

Charlie: What happened last night?

Rose: Honestly? No clue. Everything kind of just got out of control.

Charlie: No, I mean with you and John.

Rose: (*Sighs.*) Can we not talk about this?

Charlie: You spill the beans or I spill your guts.

Rose: Charming.

Charlie: That's just how I roll. So come on. What happened?

Rose: (*Pause.*) He brought up TY. Again.

Charlie: Maybe he's upset because you're leaving him.

Rose: Leaving him?

Charlie: (*Looks at her phone, scowls.*) Think about it. For the past three years you two have been inseparable. Now you guys won't be doing the Leaving Cert together, or going on the same trips, you might not even get to go to the same debs. What's he supposed to do? It's grand for you because you KNOW this is what you need to do, but for him.. He's losing you.

Rose: When the FUCK did you get so psychological?

Charlie: Jack and I were talking about it last night.

Rose: Not the only thing you and Jack were doing last night? I mean.. You were kinda all over him, Charlie.

Charlie: He kissed me.

Rose: He kissed you?

Charlie: Don't sound so surprised.

Rose: Why do I get the feeling you were a LOT drunker than I thought?

Charlie: He kissed me before.

Rose: When?

Charlie: Last year.

Rose: How come you didn't tell me?

Charlie: I didn't tell anyone. It's sort of why Máire and him broke up.

Rose: Oh.

Charlie: (*Sits up.*) I didn't think he still liked me. I've always liked him. Máire tried to fuck things up. We were sitting outside because I was feeling sick from the drink and she came out and started chatting Jack up, like properly putting the moves on him, like I'm not even there. I mean I know we shouldn't have, when they were together, but they haven't been together in ages and he kissed me so I - and I dunno WHERE this came from - I just stood up and told her to piss off. At first she was shocked, and then she started bitching to me about how ugly I am and.. Y'know. All this rubbish. Jack stood up and told her to stop. And then he put his arm around me. She stormed off, proper narky, and he apologised and starts talking about how Máire's just a jealous cow, but all I can think of is his arm. Around me. (*Lays down again.*) And then he walked me home.

Rose: Wow. Have you texted him?

Charlie: Obviously. I've sent him a few messages, haven't heard back.

Rose: So text him again.

Charlie sits up, takes up her phone and sends a text. Jack's text alert goes off. He picks up his phone, sees who the text is from, sighs, and drops the phone on his bed.

Charlie: What about you?

Rose: What about me?

Charlie: Any news from John?

Rose: He kept texting me after I left last night, and he tried calling me this morning. I haven't picked up.

Charlie: And why the fuck NOT?!

Rose: (*Pause.*) He kissed me.

Charlie: HE WHAT?! (*Sits up quickly, then yells out in pain, clutching her forehead.*) Okay. Okay, fuck, okay, tell me what happened.

Rose: With what?

Charlie: WITH JOHN, YOU IDIOT.

Rose: Nothing happened!

Charlie: YOU JUST SAID YOU KISSED.

Rose: That's a something?

Charlie: THAT'S A VERY BIG SOMETHING.

Rose: That sounds wrong. Think about your words, Charlotte.

Charlie: IT HURTS TO THINK.

Rose: And that's YOUR OWN FUCKING FAULT.

Charlie: Stop shouting and tell me what happened!

Rose: I was giving out about needing to do TY and... and he just swooped in and kissed me. And at first I'm like, 'Wow, this is nice,' and then a second later, I'm like, 'HOLY FUCKING HELL WHAT IS GOING ON HERE'. So I panic, jump back, then peg it out the door.

Charlie: So, John kisses you, you ENJOY IT, and then you peg it?

Rose: Pretty much, yeah.

Charlie: Oh my God, you're a fucking idiot.

Rose: How am I an idiot?

Charlie: I'VE BEEN TELLING YOU ALL ALONG THAT HE LIKES YOU, AND THEN YOU GO AND PEG IT WHEN HE KISSES YOU. WHAT THE ACTUAL FUCK, ROSE?

Rose: I DON'T KNOW! I mean, yeah, okay, I like / him -

Charlie: / Knew / it -

Rose: / Shut up. I never thought he'd like me back. And then we have this big row, and he kisses me out of the blue, what the fuck was I supposed to do?! I panicked! Like I always do, apparently! This is ridiculous. He was the ONE THING that I had in my life that was constant. And then all this SHIT kicks off, and now I'm pretty sure I've lost him. First my dad, then my mam, then school, and now him. I just want one thing that... something that makes me happy, y'know? One thing that I can't fucking screw up. (*Leans forward, brings her knees up and covers her face with her hands.*) It's not fair. (*Leans backwards, shouting.*) IT'S NOT FUCKING FAIR.

Charlie: (*Pause.*) Text him.

Rose: What?

Charlie: Text him. Clearly he likes you, clearly you like him. So make a move. Get talking. Sort this TY shit out, then start going out, simple.

Rose: Not so simple.

Charlie: Oh, come on! You're as bad as each other! If you text him or call him or something RIGHT NOW, then you can start sorting this out! The sooner you sort it out, the sooner you can start GOING out, and the sooner me and Jack won't be stuck in this fucking back-and-forth tennis match you two have going on.

Rose: Alright. Alright, fine. I'll do it. I'll text him.

Charlie: (*Throws her hands up, cheering.*) Finally! At long fucking last, you're being responsible!

Rose: Fuck off, Charlie. (*Starts typing on her phone.*) So come on.

Any news from Jack?

Charlie: Nah. Sure it's only, what, quarter to one? He's probably still asleep, that's all. I'll, uh, I'll talk to him later. It's fine.

Rose looks at Charlie for a second, then goes back to typing. She sends the message. John enters downstage right. His text alert goes off as he does. He reads the message from Rose. He nearly trips over Máire as he passes her.

John: Sorry - sorry, Máire, I wasn't looking. (*Holds up his phone.*) Just got a message from Rose. I'm gonna go meet her.

Máire: What happened with the two of you last night?

John: I dunno. We just... we just got in a fight, really. I've been trying to talk to her all night, but she hasn't replied until now, so I really gotta go.

Jack picks up his phone and dials a number.

Máire: What'd you fight about?

Máire's phone rings. She looks at caller id and cancels the call. She puts the phone in her pocket.

Jack: Come ON, Máire...

Jack dials Máire's number again. Her phone rings again.

John: Are you... you not gonna get that?

Máire: It's nothing, just my... sister. I can call her back later. (*She cancels the call.*) So anyway, what happened?

Rose sends John another text.

John: Well, we - (*His text alert sounds. He reads the text.*) Sorry, Máire, I've really gotta go. I'll tell you what happened later, yeah?

John leaves Máire. He stops and sends a reply text to Rose. Jack tries calling Máire a third time. She cancels again.

Rose: (*Takes a deep breath.*) Alright. I've texted him twice.

Charlie: Gowan, Rose.

Rose receives a text. She reads it.

Rose: He's on his way. Any word from Jack?

Charlie: Nothing. He's being an arsehole! I mean, he does all that last night, yeah, and now he's ignoring me! Like, what the fuck!?

Rose: Maybe it's like you said, maybe he's just sleeping.

Charlie: Doubt it. (*Sits up.*) Look, I'm gonna go. My head's a fucking wreck, I can't stand being out here anymore. I'll text you later, yeah? (*Charlie stands to go. Rose stands too.*) Rose. (*Rose looks at Charlie.*) It's gonna be fine, alright?

Rose smiles and as Charlie turns to go Rose turns to see John approaching. Fade to black.

TEAM CAPTAIN

Ola Kusiak

"I couldn't believe it when my teacher told me I got in and the fact that I was chosen as a writer made it even better."

Characters

Liam, teenager
Jake, teenager
Mike, teenager
Mairéad, Mike's mum, in a coma
John, Mike's dad
Ms. Cordon, teacher in Drimnagh Castle Secondary School

Scene One

Two boys sitting in a school changing room before football practice. A third boy walks in.

Liam: Hey guys. What youse up to?

Jake: You know changing boxers. Same old, same old.

Liam: Ah, you know what I meant!

Jake: Jesus, don't get your knickers in a twist. Ha, you see what I did there?

Liam: So smart... Anyways, two more days and mid-term boys.

Jake: Full week of freedom. Going to bed at five in the morning, waking up at five in the evening. Eating whenever we want to. Watching...

Liam: Watching what? *(Laughs.)*

Jake: Fucking Teletubbies. *(He starts laughing.)* What do you think?

Liam and Jake both laugh.

Liam: *(Looks at Mike.)* How come you're so quiet?

Mike: No reason.

Jake and Liam look at Mike simultaneously.

Jake: You alright? No offence but you seemed fine before Liam came in.

Liam: I'm the problem now, huh?

Jake: I said no offence, didn't I?

Liam: Well you might as well have said 'no offence but I'm going to offend you'.

Jake: Besides I didn't say you were the problem.

Liam: It seemed like you were implying it.

Mike: *(Whispering.)* Just shut up.

Jake: What?

Mike: Nothing. Jake pass me the ball.

Jake: Here. Who do you think is going to be the captain this year?

Liam: Bet yah it's you Mike.

Mike: It's not.

Liam: Don't be so modest. We all know you're the best player on the team. There's no-one new or anything.

Jake: You're bound to get the spot.

Mike: Can youse just leave it?!

Jake: *(To no-one in particular.)* Somebody's on their period.

Liam: Dude, seriously what's wrong?

Mike doesn't answer. There's silence between the three boys. Jake realises that there's something really wrong with Mike but he can see that he, Mike, doesn't want to talk about it.

Jake: Oh yeah, I meant to ask you, what did coach say when you asked him what time the match starts at?

Mike: He wasn't there.

Liam: Was his folder there? He could've written who the captain is in that.

Mike: It was there.

Jake: And?

Mike: And nothing. Just leave it!

Jake: Seriously calm down.

Liam: Yeah, you're gonna be the captain anyways.

Mike: No I'm not! Okay?! I saw what he wrote.

Jake: So? Don't be such a drama queen. Tell us already, or should we bow before your highness first.

Pause.

Mike: C'mon. We're going to be late to practice...

Mike walks out holding the football in his hands.

Scene Two

Mike is sitting beside a hospital bed. There is a woman lying in the bed. She's in a coma.

Mike: I just walked out of the changing room then. I felt like they were putting so much pressure on me, you know? Like I had to be the captain... I didn't tell Dad yet. I can already see that disappointed look he's going to give me. I'll tell him soon. Maybe even today when we get home from the hospital. I wish you could be there with me. Like the old times. I would tell you first, then I'd leave the house until you called me. Let you ease the info to Dad. D'ye remember the time you were at Aunt Maggie's house for a couple of days and the day you left I got an F for my chemistry test. All hell broke loose when I told Dad. When he finally calmed down, we both agreed that we're better off leaving those kind of things until you're around. *(Pause.)* What am I meant to do Mum? *(He lets his head rest on the bed for a while.)* You know I'm starting my mid-term next week. I'll be able to visit you every day.

Dad walks into the room.

John: Chatting away I see.

Mike: Yeah, just telling Mum about my week so far.

John: Aren't you lucky Mairéad? *(Smiles.)*

There's silence in the room.

Mike: Can I've a fiver? I'm starving.

John: Yeah, sure. Get me something as well.

Mike: Grand.

Mike walks out of the room. John sits in the chair that Mike was sitting in.

John: If only I knew the things he tells you. He's stopped talking to me. *(Pause.)* He's been odd this whole week. I think he's hiding something. Remember that time you went to Maggie's house after her miscarriage? That day he failed his biology exam. Or was it chemistry? I think it was chemistry. He was never good at it. What was I... oh yeah, I got so mad. I'm not even sure if it was because he failed or was it because everything was just piling up inside of me. Well, whatever it was I remember Mike and I agreed not to discuss these kind of things when you're not around. I can tell he's keeping something from me. Anyway...

Mike comes back into the room.

Mike: They didn't have anything good. Can we just get takeaway on our way home?

John: Pizza again?

Mike: I was thinking more like Chinese or Thai?

John: Thought you didn't like anything like that.

Mike: Tastes change.

John: Okay? I guess we should get going then. I'll see you tomorrow dear.

He kisses the woman on the forehead.

Mike: I've detention tomorrow Mum, so I won't be here, but I'll be here on Friday. Bye.

They leave the room.

Scene Three

Mike and John are sitting on a sofa centre stage. They are eating Chinese takeaway out of the cartons. SFX of a football match on T.V. John searches for something on the sofa.

John: Where's the remote?

Mike: I don't know, you had it. Maybe you're sitting on it. *(To himself.)* Again.

John stands up and picks up the remote.

John: There it is. I was sitting on it again.

John turns off the T.V.

Mike: Why did you turn it off?

John: It was horrible. A bit pathetic to be honest. They spend so much time training. Maybe they should get a new coach. Speaking of, how did practice go?

Mike: *(He hesitates for a bit.)* Fine.

John: Are you officially the captain now or did Tom not announce it yet?

Mike: He didn't talk about that, we just focused on our passing.

John: Fair enough. That guy, what's his name, Liam, he's pretty good at passing. You should train with him some time outside of practice.

Mike is quiet.

John: Are you regretting not getting pizza too, because I know I am.

Mike: Yeah. This is disgusting.

John and Mike both smile. John messes up Mike's hair.

John: It's getting late. *(He stands up.)* Did you do your homework?

Mike: Umm...

John: Did you even start it?

Mike: Yes?

John: Great. You know, this is one of the reasons for your detention tomorrow. Mike, when are you going to learn? This is all recorded, your grades, detentions, dockets. Do you realise that? If only.. *(Stops himself. Pulls back from anger. Walks off the stage.)* Don't stay up late.

Mike: Sure.

Mike is left alone sitting on the sofa. He looks in the direction that his dad left.

Mike: I miss her so much...

Pause. The lights dim.

Scene Four

The stage is divided in two. On one side is the detention room in Mike's school. Desks and chairs. On the other side is John's office.

There is a computer and a telephone on his desk. SFX. John's desk phone rings. He answers it. His colleague, Aíne, walks in.

John: Hello. John Costello from Walkinstown Bank of Ireland speaking. *(Nods to Aíne.)* I'm sorry but you would have to call customer service miss. Yes, I understand that you've been waiting for a long time. I'll have to check. Would you mind if I put you on hold? Thanks.

Aíne: Mrs White?

John: Who else? This is the fourth time she's called this week. Do you need anything?

Aíne: No, just came here to have a chat. Why? Am I interrupting?

John: Wait a minute. Hello. Yes, one of our customer service representatives is available. I'll just put you through. Thank you. Goodbye.

Aíne: Well, this is nice. I mean great conversation we're having here.

John: What? Oh yeah. What is it that you wanted to talk about?

Aíne: Nothing specific really. *(Pause.)* How are things at home?

John: Not bad, but at the same time not good. I don't know anymore. There isn't even a bad atmosphere in the house. There's nothing. Pure monotony.

Aíne: Ah, it can't be that bad. Is it?

John: Yeah you're right. There are good days. We sometimes start talking while watching a movie. Then I say something and it gets awkward. *(Sarcastic.)* I live for those days.

The phone rings.

John: I have to answer this. Hello, John Costello from Walkinstown Bank of Ireland speaking.

The focus switches to the detention room in Mike's school. Ms. Cordon walks in with Mike.

Ms. Cordon: Sit down Mike and be quiet. I'll be back in a minute.

She walks offstage. Jake and Liam enter. They sit down.

Mike: What are youse doing here?

Liam: My brother paid me to stay out of the house until six, so I thought I might as well come here. I think he's bringing some bird home.

Jake: Again?

Liam: What d'you mean 'again'?

Mike: Didn't he pay you on Monday as well?

Liam: Yeah, but that was a different one. He only paid me a tenner for the Monday one. For this one I got twenty.

Mike: With that speed you're gonna be rich by the end of the month.

Jake: Why can't my brother be a man whore?

Liam: Isn't he like four?

Jake: Mike how old is Matt?

Mike: He's five you dipshit.

Jake: Actually he's five, Liam.

Mike: Okay, so I get why he's here but why are you?

Jake: Like I'm stupid enough to let you have some alone time with Ms. C.

Mike: Dayum son, I've no words for you.

Focus switches back to John's office.

Aíne: Well, how's Mike?

John: To be honest, I haven't got a clue. He doesn't talk to me anymore. And when he does it's about food.

Aíne: You didn't go to the parent-teacher meeting. I was talking to Jack's tutor and he said that you never showed up. He was worried about Mike. His grades were fine, good actually, but Mike isn't paying attention in class and he's missing more days than usual.

John: I didn't even know there was a parent-teacher meeting.

Aíne: You can't wait until he talks to you. You're the adult so start acting like one. Talk to him. He needs you.

John: How am I supposed to tell him that it's going to be better with time, when I don't believe it myself?

Aíne: Then tell him that. Say what you're feeling.

John: Maybe you're right.

Aíne: Maybe? You're kidding right? Obviously, I'm right. When am I ever wrong?

They both smile. Pause.

John: Shouldn't you be doing something?

Aíne: Like what?

John: I don't know, working?

Aíne: Crap. Sandra's probably looking all over for me. Stupid reports. Did I ever tell you that I hate this job?

John: Every day.

Aíne: Good, at least you're aware.

Aine exits. John starts typing on his computer. On the other side of the stage Ms. Cordon walks into the detention room.

Ms. Cordon: Boys were youse… Boys? I don't remember all three of you here.

Liam: We were late.

Ms. Cordon: I don't have you on the list though.

Jake: That's because we only got it now.

Ms. Cordon: Now? What did youse do?

Jake: We… *(Looks to Liam for help.)*

Liam: Egged our tutor's car.

Mike and Jake look at Liam.

Ms. Cordon: Well then you obviously deserve detention. I need to photocopy some more worksheets. I'll leave the door open.

Walks offstage.

Mike: Bet youse she's not even photocopying anything.

Jake: Yeah, she's probably talking to coach. You know, the ol' hair flipping business.

Mike: Speaking of coach. Guys, I'm sorry for yesterday. I wasn't having the best day. I knew that coach didn't pick me. On top of that I had to figure out how I was going to tell my dad. Which reminds me, I still have to do that.

Jake: It's grand.

Liam: If it makes you feel any better I said 'no' to coach.

Mike: What?

Liam: I told him that everyone on the team, including him, knows that you should get the spot.

Mike: Why would you do that?

Liam: Cause it's true. Anyway, he only picked me cause he didn't want you to have to choose between football practice or visiting your mum.

John's desk phone rings. Aíne enters during the telephone conversation.

John: Hello. John Costello from Walkinstown Bank of Ireland speaking. Is everything alright? Should I be worried? Today? (*Smiles.*) I'll be there as soon as possible. Thank you so much. (*Hangs up.*) I need to go

Aíne: What's going on?

John: It's happening. I need to pick Mike up. (*Lifts the telephone receiver.*)

Aíne: I'll call the school, you just go.

John: Thank you.

He takes his coat from the back of his chair and exits. Aine dials a number. A telephone rings on the other side of the stage. Ms. Cordon answers it.

Ms. Cordon: Hello, Drimnagh Castle Secondary School. Lauren Cordon speaking.

Aíne: Hi, this is Aíne O'Reilly. I'm calling to inform you that Mike Costello's dad has to pick him up early from detention today.

Ms. Cordon: I'm sorry but students aren't allowed to leave detention early unless it's an emergency. There's a reason for detention.

Aíne: Yes, I know. It is a family emergency. Mike's father is already on his way to the school.

Ms. Cordon: Well, in that case, I'll let him off early.

Aíne: Could you give Mike a message?

Ms. Cordon: Yes, of course.

Aíne: Could you tell him his mum is waking up.

Ms. Cordon: His mum is what? I don't mean to be rude but that sounds a bit strange.

Aíne: I know but he'll understand.

Ms. Cordon: Okay.

Aíne: Thank you.

Ms. Cordon: Goodbye.

TEAM CAPTAIN Ola Kusiak

Aíne: Goodbye. (*She hangs up.*)

Ms. Cordon: Mike, pack up your stuff.

Mike: Why?

Ms. Cordon: Aíne O'Reilly called saying your dad is on his way to the school. Family emergency. Oh, and she asked me to tell you that… um… your mum is waking up?

Mike: What? Really?

Ms. Cordon: Yes. (*She looks confused.*)

Mike: Thanks Miss.

Jake: Your mum always had perfect timing. She'll help you tell your dad now.

Mike: (*Smiling.*) You always know what to say. (*Laughs.*)

Mike takes his bag and exits the stage. Jake and Liam stand up and pick up their bags.

Ms. Cordon: Boys, what do you think you're doing?

Jake: Leaving? (*He looks confused.*)

Ms. Cordon: Don't be smart with me. I said that Mike is leaving, not you two. Sit down and no talking.

Scene Five

John and Mike are sitting in the hospital beside Mairéad's hospital bed.

John: I called your grandparents.

Mike: Oh, yeah. When are they coming?

John: They're gonna try to get here today.

Mike: Cool.

John: According to your granddad, Granny is going crazy with the food. She's already made two cakes, she's in the middle of making meatballs baked in cheese and she wants to make dessert.

Mike: Isn't cake a dessert?

John: Not to your grandma.

Mike: Did you ask about the tulips?

John: I did. I made sure Granddad put them on the cupboard by the door so they don't forget about them. Your mum will be so happy to see fresh flowers, especially tulips.

Mike: Yeah, she will.

John: I got her chocolates on my way to get you.

Mike: Wasn't she on a diet?

John: I think she won't mind eating some chocolate now. I don't think any of us would mind eating some right now. We should be celebrating. Honestly Mike, I was terrified, horrified, petrified even. I mean whatever word floats your boat. You can use any or all and they still wouldn't be as strong as I felt. I thought that this day might never happen, that she might never wake up. Luckily I was wrong. This is the only time that I'm happy that I was wrong. And if me being wrong makes things like this happen then I'm happy to be wrong all the time.

Mike: Could you repeat that so I can record it and use it against you some day. *(He smiles. Then looks down.)* I was afraid she might never wake up as well. I felt all of the words you said. But now I feel like I've never felt before. Like I'm going to explode with happiness.

John: Try not to explode before she wakes up. Let her have a good look at you first. After that you're free to do whatever you want.

Mike: We have a deal.

John: She didn't even wake up yet and she's already made us agree on something.

They both laugh. Mike jumps in his chair. Smiles.

John: What are you doing?

Mike: Did you see that? Mum's foot – it moved.

John: What?

Mike: Mum's foot just moved.

John: Are you sure?

Mike: Positive.

A couple of Mairéad's fingers twitch.

John: Stay here, I'll get the doctors.

John exits. He is smiling. Mairéad's hand moves again. Mike smiles. The heart monitor increases in speed.

Mike: Someone's eager to wake up. *(Laughs.)* You're really looking forward to getting that chocolate.

Both of Mairéad's hands start to move..

Mike: Mum? Dad, where are you?

The heart monitor speeds up. Mike looks worried and runs out for help.

Scene Six

Mike is sitting on the floor in his bedroom. He's wearing a black suit. There's a knock on the door.

Mike: Who is it?

Jake: Jake. It's just me. Liam's downstairs talking to your dad. *(He walks in.)*

Mike looks at him. Jake sits beside him.

Jake: I know that this is going to be a stupid, clichéd question but I'm still gonna ask. Are you okay?

Mike: *(Sighs.)* Well, I wish there was a stupid, clichéd answer but I don't think there is. The worst part is that I don't know if I should be happy that she's not suffering or sad because I am. I've been thinking about it a lot since Friday. On one hand even though she was in a coma she was there physically. I could see her and just pretend that she was sleeping. That she'd just had a really hard day at work. Then on the other hand being at home without her, with just Dad, it already felt like she was gone. Always some sports thing on TV, no X Factor, no cheesy soap operas. And no homemade dinners. The only time I get a proper homemade dinner now is when I go to my grandparents' house or yours. I'm scared that this is going to be my reality now. That this isn't something that will pass with time.

Jake: I'm sorry. *(He hugs Mike.)* I'll always be here for you. Even on the days that you don't want to admit that there's something wrong. I'll know. Like you did in fifth class. When I was bullied. You helped me a lot then, even though I never said I needed help or wanted it.

Mike: Thanks. Wait, Liam is talking with my dad?

Jake: Yeah. Why?

Mike: What are they even talking about?

Jake: Before I came here they were talking about football.

Mike: Ah yes, football. The sport of real men.

The two boys laugh. John comes into the room.

John: Your grandparents are leaving, do you want to say goodbye?

Mike and Jake stand up.

Mike: I don't, but I know that I should, so I will.

Mike leaves the room. Jake is walking behind him. John stops Jake.

John: Could you talk to him. You know about the whole team captain situation.

Jake: *(To himself.)* Liam...

John: I think I put too much pressure on him about the whole captain situation. I don't want him to think that he can't talk to me about everything. Especially now that... *(takes a deep breath.)* that Mairéad is gone.

Jake: I'll talk to him.

John: Thanks. And could you not mention this conversation to him.

Jake: What conversation?

John smiles at Jake.

John: He's lucky to have a friend like you Jake.

Jake: I'm lucky to have a friend like him.

Jake leaves the stage. Fade to black.

WHAT A WAY TO SPEND THE WEEKEND

Katherine Cullen

"As a result of Tenderfoot I've met some incredible friends. I'm going into my second year of an English and sociology degree in NUI Maynooth and I am thinking of doing my MA in Theatre and Drama Studies with the hope of becoming a playwright."

Character

Girl

Girl: What a way to spend a weekend! I'm grounded, again! I hardly did anything at all! Like my ma and da were away for the weekend, so I had a free gaff, and my boyfriend Mark was coming down with his friend Kyle, coz Kyle just got a new motor and Mark wanted to come down and all the rest, and I was like, no, don't come down, cause my mam and dad were out and I'd just get in shite, and he was like, right, whatever, and I was like, grand. Next thing I know he's outside my gaff and I'm just like "Ah here! What are you at like?!" and he goes (*mockingly*) "just came down to surprise you baby" and all this, and I was, yeah, right, and kicked him out there and then. No questions asked like. Then I get this call from my mam and she's going ninety about some youngfellas driving around, into my house and all this, and asking me who they are and all, and I'm like, I don't know, and she's goin', yeah, you do, and I'm like, where are you getting this from and do you know who was telling her?! It was the bloody oul' one in the shop. They drove past like, twice, and she's like stalking them and ringing my mam and stuff. I didn't do anything, and now I'm grounded for two weeks, for nothing.

Okay, well, maybe I did let him in for a few, but only because they came all the way down and it would be bad not to like. But Kyle used the toilet and then they were gone like! Swear to God! Okay, well, they stayed for a bit but nothing happened or anything. Like we weren't even in the house! We went out into the field and we were just talking like. It's not like I was the one who brought the drink or anything. That was all Kyle and, like, I hate him anyway. He's a dope. I didn't know all these other young-ones were coming down too like. I hadn't got a clue. I was as surprised as your one in the shop like. They were proper weird! I was only drinking 'cause I was scared like. Here, one girl was doing shots of beer and I was just looking at her, like, what in God's name are you doing child, and she started shooting daggers at me and all this, and I was just like "Oh. Right".

I was so uncomfortable, so I said it to Mark that they were all weird, and said to him could we not just go back in, and he was like "No. Stop being dry" and all this, and I was like "I am not dealing with this" and got up to leave, and do you know what he did?! That cheeky little arsehole turns around to me and goes "Right so. Was only using ye for the ride" and all this. Well! I was snapping! Who says that to someone, in front of people like?! So I looked at Kyle, and not being up my arse or anything, like he's mad about me, but I'd had too much to drink, so I goes to him "Here! You're coming back with me", just to piss off Mark like, coz nobody talks to me like that, so I brought Kyle back to mine and all the rest.

The next morning I roll over and see Kyle and his stupid, dopey face and I'm like, sweet Jesus! kill me now! So like, I tell him he has to go and all the rest, so that's grand, but no! Mark being the immature little dope he is only went and stole two of the tyres off Kyle's car, so him leaving on the sly without next door noticing, turned into the bloody AA coming to save him and his shitty little two wheeler Micra.

That's when my mam rang me and now I'm grounded. For nothing like! She was going on about how I 'disrespected' her and all this so I can't go out. Ugh. Just don't get my mam sometimes.

TTYL
Declan Moore

"When I look back on my adolescence, there are a few experiences that I consider to have truly shaped me as an individual, there is no doubt that Tenderfoot is among these. From day one, I loved every second."

Characters

Killian, 16 years old, middle class, living in a bubble of technology, little or no relationship with parents
Rebecca, 16 years old, middle class, living in a bubble of technology, little or no relationship with parents
Rebecca's mam, works
James, Killian's classmate
Ben, Killian's friend
Lauren, Rebecca's friend
Teachers, history, music & IT
Other students

Scene One

We see two young people sitting at desks on either side of the stage. They are back to back. The boy has a guitar on his lap and is strumming out chords. The girl is doing homework. Both youths have laptops on their desks. They type their lines of dialogue. They do not speak them out loud. Their conversation, in text speak, is projected onto a screen on the wall behind. Complex text speak lines are accompanied by a translation. Translations in square brackets after text lines. Individual productions can decide which bracketed translations to use. The scene begins with a caption on the screen.

Screen: Thursday night. 11.40 p.m.

Killian: So... ur Michelle's frend? [So... you're Michelle's friend?]

Rebecca: S'pose I am, how do u knw her? [I suppose I am, how do you know her?]

Killian: I went 2 a summer camp wit her 2 years ago and we'v met up in town a few tyms. [I went to summer camp with her two years ago and we have met up in town a few times.]

Rebecca: Cul. [Cool.] Wuu2? [What are you up to?]

Killian: Nm, u? [Nothing much, you?]

Rebecca: Same, jst facebuk nd da. [Same, just Facebook and that.]

Killian: Kewl. [Cool.] Oh ye im playn gitar too, 4got 2 mention it. [Oh yeah I'm playing guitar too, forgot to mention it.]

Rebecca: U play gitar? Cul Ive always wantd ta but nevr was boderd enuf, wat sorta music dya play? [You play guitar? Cool, I've always wanted to but was never bothered enough, what sort of music do you play?]

Killian: loadza stuff, mostly rock tho lyk the Killers, Greenday etc. [Loads of stuff, mostly rock though, like the Killers, Greenday etc.]

Rebecca: Cul, r u in a band? [Cool, are you in a band?]

Killian: Nah I usedta b but we sukt so I decided to jst get betr nd play by myself. [No, I used to be but we sucked so I decided to just get better and play by myself.]

Rebecca's mother walks onstage. The following conversation is spoken.

Mother: Why aren't you in bed yet? It's a quarter to twelve, you have school in the morning!

Rebecca: Mam, chillax! I'll be done in a second!

Mother: Your aunty told me that she saw you active on Facebook at 4 a.m. on Tuesday!

Rebecca: Ah Mam, I'll be done in a minute, lemme just finish what I'm doing here.

Mother: BED! NOW! Or else you won't be going to town next weekend!

Rebecca: Fine!

Rebecca: (*Messages.*) Ye I g2g me mam is shouting at me to go to bed. [Yeah, I've got to go; my mam is shouting at me to go to bed.]

Rebecca's mother leaves. Rebecca thinks about sending another message to Killian.

Rebecca: Can I get ur fone numba? [Can I get your phone number?] (*Rebecca deletes her message. Pauses. Writes it again.*) Can I get ur fone numba? (*She sends the message.*)

Killian: Y dya want me numba? [Why do you want my number?] R u a stlker or sumtin? [Are you a stalker or something?] LOL [Laugh out loud.]

Rebecca: HAHA! Nah jst want to txt sumthn! [Ha-ha! No, I just want to text something.]

Killian: Okay, Im reckt and'll probly go2 bed soon 2. Me numba is 082-2438675. [It's okay; I'm wrecked and will probably go to bed soon too. My number is, 082-2438675.] I haven't much credit so I wont b able to txt 4 long. [I haven't much credit so I won't be able to text for long.]

Both characters close their laptop screens. Lights fade as they stand up and walk offstage. The projector stays lit showing that the technology doesn't sleep.

Scene Two

There are two mattresses on either side of the stage. Rebecca sits on one. She is staring at the screen on her phone. Killian sits on the other mattress reading a magazine. His phone is on the floor beside him. The projector shows the characters' text messages as they receive them. Each phone has a distinctive message alert.

Screen: Friday morning. 1.15 a.m.

Rebecca: So wat year r u in? did u do TY or just skip 2 5th? [So what year are you in? Did you do Transition Year or just skip straight to fifth year?]

Killian: Im in 5th, wasn't boderd spending an xtra year in d kip im in! U? [I'm in 5th year, I wasn't bothered spending an extra year in this kip I am in! You?]

Rebecca: Im doin TY, its nt lyk evry1 sez, in fact im probly doin mor work dis year on projects than I did 4 my whole jr cert. [I'm doing Transition Year, it isn't like everyone says, in fact I'm probably doing more work this year on projects than I did for my entire Junior Cert.]

Killian: wel mayb d Ty in ur skool is decent ours do absolutly nutin and Iv herd its absolute bllx! [Well, maybe the Transition Year course in your school is decent, ours do absolutely nothing and I've heard it's absolute bollocks!]

Rebecca: so wat sbjcts u doin? xXx [So what subjects are you doing? Kiss. KISS. Kiss.]

Killian: Erm...Geog, Home Ec, Frnch and Wudwork, K Im seriously outta credit, Il get some in the morn nd txt ye at skool. [Em... Geography, Home Economics, French and Woodwork. Ok, I am seriously out of credit, I'll get some in the morning and text you at school.]

Rebecca: K, g'nite xXxXx (Okay, goodnight. Kiss. KISS. Kiss. KISS. Kiss.)

Light fades as both characters put their phones down and lie down on their mattresses.

Scene Three

It is the next morning. Both Rebecca and Killian are in school. They sit at their desks in different classes in different schools. They are texting each other. They sneak their phones out every time they receive a message, Rebecca has hers in her pencil case, Killian has his in his pocket. He hides his phone under his chair when he texts. Their conversation is projected for the audience to see. We are in their world so the outside world continues as on mute. The teachers teach, we can see that they speak and move but we don't hear what they say. Lights fade up when a school bell sounds.

Screen: Friday morning. 10.10 a.m.

Rebecca: Wat clas r u in a d mo? xXx [What class are you in at the moment? Kiss. KISS. Kiss.]

Killian: Bludy History, I h8 it so much, the teacher jst gav me detention 4 no hmwork, wata wnkr! [Bloody History, I hate it so much, the teacher just gave me detention for not having my homework, what a wanker!]

Rebecca: Aw poor u, can u txt? xXx [Aw poor you, can you text? Kiss. KISS. Kiss.]

Killian: Ye, wat class r u in? X [Yeah, What class are you in? Kiss.]

Rebecca: Music, I luv it I can text down in the practice area nd nevr get cot xXx! [Music, I love it because I can text down in the practice area and never get caught. Kiss. KISS. Kiss.]

Killian: Luky u! hey im in town 2moro if u wanna meet up? X [Lucky you! Hey, I'm in town tomorrow if you want to meet up? Kiss.]

Rebecca: I can't, bt I will be next week! xXx Il b in any tym after 12. [I can't but I will be next week! Kiss. KISS. Kiss. I'll be in any time after 12.]

The teacher in Killian's class turns and sees him texting. Throws a stress ball at him. Killian's classroom comes to audible life as he does so.

Teacher: Burke! So, the Romans.....

Killian slumps down on his desk in a sulk. The sound of Killian's classroom fades as the focus moves over to Rebecca in her classroom. She doesn't know why he isn't texting anymore. She fidgets impatiently waiting for a reply. She checks her phone twice.

Rebecca: Helo?!?! Any1 der? [Hello?!?! Anyone there?]

Bell rings in Killian's school bringing the focus back. There is a surge in the sound of the outside world. Students begin to gather their things for a change in class. The sound immediately fades as Killian goes to his phone to continue the conversation with Rebecca.

Killian: K, soz bout that the wnkr cot me txtn! Ye I think I'll be in next week, We'll talk bout it l8r on Msn xXx [Ok, Sorry about that, the wanker caught me texting! I should be in next week! We can talk about it later on MSN. Kiss. KISS. Kiss.]

Screen fades to black as text conversation ends. Killian walks offstage.

Scene Four

It is the following Tuesday. Killian is in the IT room at school. Next to him is his classmate, James. Other students sit at other computer stations. His friend, Ben, sits at a desk in his pyjamas in another area of the stage. Spotlights fade up on Killian and James. The screen shows their conversation.

Screen: Tuesday morning. 11.30 a.m.

Killian: Howaya James! [How are you James?]

James: alri, ye I've got sooo much HW from Eng 2day! [Alright, yeah I have so much homework for English today!]

Killian: Hey man, dya know why Ben wasn't in 2day? [Hey man, do you know why Ben wasn't in today?]

James: No, bt he's online if u want me 2 add him to the convo? [No, but he's online if you want me to add him to the conversation.]

Killian: Sure go 4 it! [Sure go for it!]

A spotlight fades up on Ben when James adds him to the conversation.

Killian: Heya Ben! [Hi Ben!]

Ben: Hi xXx [Hi. Kiss. KISS. Kiss.]

James: Hey gayboy! Wats up wit d 'X's'? LOL. Y arnt u in skool? [Hey gayboy! What's up with the kisses? Laugh out loud. Why aren't you in school?]

Ben: Soz bout dat, I keep sending X's 2 every1. Sick, me ma tinks I have the flu! [Sorry about that, I keep sending kisses to everyone. Sick, my mam thinks I have the flu!]

Killian: Fuk! U better not giv it 2 me! [Fuck! You'd better not give it to me.]

James: I doubt u have it, evry1s just goin crazy tinkin they hav it! [I doubt you have it, everyone is just going crazy thinking they have it!]

Ben: W/e. So Killian, tell me bout dis gurl Rebecca! [Whatever! So Killian, tell me about this girl Rebecca!]

Killian: Wel Ive nevr actually met her face 2 face. [Well, we've never actually met face to face.]

James: WTF! How do u knw she aint just a 40 y/o pretending 2 b a girl? [What the fuck! How do you know she isn't just a forty year old pretending to be a girl?]

Killian: STFU! Shes defnitely a gurl! My m8 Michelle knws her! [Shut the fuck up! She's definitely a girl! My mate Michelle knows her!]

Ben: wel man, if u expect 2 get anywhere, you need to find out wat she's really lyk, I mean ppl r so much mor different in d real world! [Well man, if you expect to get anywhere, you need to find out what she is really like, I mean people are so much more different in the real world!]

James: Alri, I g2g, Iv got 2 do my HW b4 the end ov dis! [Alright, I've got to go; I've got to do my homework before the end of this!]

The spotlight on James fades as he leaves the conversation.

Killian: Ye man, dnt tel James, cuz you know how he is, but I tink im gonna ask this gurl out. [Yeah man, don't tell James this, because you know how he is, but I'm thinking of asking this girl out.]

Ben: Man, dats the stupidest ting! U dont even knw her! [Man, that's the stupidest thing I've ever heard! You don't even know her!]

Killian: Ye I do! Wev been txtin and stuf for nearly a week now! We're just so similar, I mean we both lyk similar music, we can always tlk on stuff like msn and she duznt live 2 far away. [Yes I do! We've been texting and stuff for nearly a week now! We're just so similar, I mean we both like similar music and we can always talk on msn and she doesn't even live too far away!]

Ben: Still man! It's kinda stupid. [Still man! It's kind of stupid.]

Killian: Wel Ive made an arrangement 2 meet up wit her in town this Saturday, Im gonna ask her den, dya wanna cum? [Well, I've made an arrangement to meet up with her in town this Saturday, I'm gonna ask her then, do you want to come?]

Ben: Well if Im feeling betr! [Well if I'm feeling better!]

Killian: Alri, well I g2g, the teacher is cuming over, if he catches me im ded! [Alright, well I've got to go, the teacher is walking over, if he catches me, I'm dead!]

Ben: alri, cya! [Alright, see you!]

Both spotlights fade. Then the screen fades followed by the lights.

Scene Five

Fade up on Rebecca's kitchen. The screen, during this scene, displays the notes that Rebecca and her mother leave for each other. The lights fade and restore between each message to show a passage of time.

Screen: Thursday. 10.20 p.m.

Rebecca: Mam, I'm going to town on Saturday so can you leave change for the bus.

Passage of time.

Screen: 11.15 p.m.

SFX hall door opening and closing. Mam enters, sees note, reads it and leaves a note in answer.

Mother: Your cousins are coming to visit?

Mam goes to bed. Passage of time.

Screen: Friday. 3.30 a.m.

Rebecca enters. She is wearing pyjamas. She gets a glass of water.

Sees note. Reads it. Leaves answer.

Rebecca: Ah mam… I need to go to town. I'm meeting some friends and we're going shopping.

Rebecca returns to bed. Passage of time.

Screen: 8.30 a.m.

Mam enters in dressing gown. Sees note, reads it, answers it.

Mother: But you have no money.

Mam takes a towel off the back of a chair and goes back upstairs. Passage of time.

Screen: 8.45 a.m.

Rebecca enters. She speaks audibly.

Rebecca: (*Out loud.*) Mam?

SFX shower. Rebecca tuts, see note, reads it and leaves an answer.

Rebecca: I know, I'm going because they may need help with their shopping.

Rebecca goes back to bed. Passage of time.

Screen: 9.15 a.m.

Mam enters ready for work. Sees Rebecca's note, reads note and answers it. She leaves money with the note.

Mother: Ok, you can go, but only if you're back by 4pm.

Mam leaves. Passage of time.

Screen: 11.30 a.m.

Rebecca enters dressed for town. Sees money, reads note and leaves answer.

Rebecca: Okay, thank you. See ya later. (*Smiley face.*)

Lights fade as Rebecca leaves.

Scene Six

It is after school on Friday. Rebecca is out shopping with her friend, Lauren. All dialogue is vocal. Lauren is looking at an item of clothing on a sale rack.

Screen: Friday. 5.30 p.m.

Lauren takes out her phone and laughs.

Lauren: Just got a brilliant snap from Damien!

Snapchat image of Lauren's boyfriend, Damien, is projected onto the screen. He is sitting on a friend who is passed out from drinking on a bathroom floor the night before. The snap's caption says "few too many, pal?"

Rebecca: Was your man alright after?

Lauren: Who cares?! It's hilarious!

Lauren takes a snap of herself, types a caption, and sends it to Rebecca. It comes up on the screen. The caption reads "Whos ur BF luv xoxox".

Rebecca: You are.

Lauren: Can't believe it's been this long since you've had a fella!

Rebecca: Ah, wouldya ever stop. It's none of your business, and what if I did have someone... sort of.

Lauren: Oh my God! Who is he? Tell us everything!

Rebecca: It doesn't matter!

Lauren: What do you mean it doesn't matter? What's his name? It's not that fella living around the corner from ye, is it?

Rebecca: Ah, I shouldn't have opened me mouth.

Lauren: Sweetheart, stop being so silly and tell us. I promise I'll keep it to myself.

Rebecca: Alright, fine. I'm texting this guy I met on Facebook. His name is Killian and he's absolutely lovely.

Lauren: Are you mad? Met him online? Dya even know how many stories there are on the news about this sorta thing? Girls meeting 'lovely' guys online and then they turn out to be murderers or rapists?

Rebecca: Stop, stop, it's not like that at all! I know him through Michelle. She went to some summer camp thing with him. I'm meeting up with him this weekend, cannot wait.

Lauren: Fair enough love, but ya need to be fucking careful with people on the internet. Don't have me worryin' aboutcha.

Rebecca: He seems really cool. He plays guitar and is great to talk to and...

Lauren's phone vibrates and she takes it out interrupting Rebecca.

Lauren: Uh huh... yeah... that's great love.

Lights fade as Lauren answers the phone.

Scene Seven

Later that evening. Rebecca and Killian are both at home. In their bedrooms. They are chatting for the last time before they are to meet. Their conversation is projected onto the screen.

Screen: Friday. 11.30 p.m.

Rebecca: Hiii! Still on 4 tmrw? X [Hi! Still on for tomorrow? KISS.]

Killian: Il b dere if u r. :) x [I'll be there if you are. *Smiley face.* Kiss.]

Rebecca: I wntd 2 ask u if u have snapchat? [I wanted to ask you if you have snapchat?]

Killian: Nah, it sounds stupid.

Rebecca: Ah, its gr8 crack xXx [Ah, it's great craic. Kiss. KISS. Kiss.)

Killian: I dnt tink its 4 me. X [I don't think it's for me. KISS.]

Rebecca: I tink u shud get it. Also I wnt to see wat u luk lyk b4 2mara. [I think you should get it. Also I want to see what you look like before tomorrow.]

Killian: Only if I get 2 c u 2. [Only if I get to see you too.]

Rebecca: Cors! [Of Course!]

Killian's screen can be seen going to download. He installs the snapchat app from the app store.

Killian: Alri, my name on it is Killiance246, wats urs? [Alright, my name on it is Killiance246, what's your's?]

Rebecca: Beccabubbly. [Bubbly Rebecca.]

Killian poses for a snap. He takes about two or three until he's happy with it. We see all of his attempts. He captions the one he's happy. The caption reads "Hey." He sends it to Rebecca. Rebecca smiles. She looks relieved. She sends a photo of herself too with the caption "#SELFIE X"

Killian: Happy now? Xx [Happy now? KISS. Kiss.]

Rebecca: Totes! :) xXx [Totally! *Smiley face.* Kiss. KISS. Kiss.]

Killian: G2g now, dead tired. X [Got to go now, dead tired. KISS.]

Rebecca: Kk! I'll c u 2mara! Xxx [OK, I'll see you tomorrow! KISS. Kiss. Kiss.]

Killain: Night xxxxx [Goodnight. Kiss. Kiss. Kiss. Kiss. Kiss.]

Rebecca: xXxXxXxXx [Kiss. KISS. Kiss. KISS. Kiss. KISS. Kiss. KISS. Kiss.]

Lights fade as both Rebecca and Killian settle down to sleep.

Scene Eight

It is Saturday. Killian and Rebecca are meeting for the first time. Killian is with his friend Ben and Rebecca is on her own. Killian and Rebecca both have their phones out. They are texting each other. Their texts show on the screen. Ben sees Rebecca approaching before Killian does.

Screen: Saturday. 12.30 p.m.

Killian: Jst off d bus now! X [Just off the bus now! KISS.]

Rebecca: Cul, Im at the end of Grafton! xXx [Cool, I am at the end of Grafton Street! Kiss. KISS. Kiss.]

Killian: Trinity side? X [Trinity side? KISS.]

Rebecca: Ye xXx [Yeah. Kiss. KISS. Kiss.]

Killian: Ok I c u! XxX [Ok, I see you! KISS. Kiss. KISS.]

They meet. Rebecca hugs Killian. They look at each other. Smile. The lights fade just as Rebecca is about to say something. The screen shows a long series of "............".

PARTY

Sarah Hanlon

"I really enjoyed my time in Tenderfoot and am incredibly grateful to everyone involved for the experiences it has given me. It made me come out of my comfort zone and most of all have confidence in my writing. It was one of the most fun and rewarding things I did throughout my secondary school experience and I'm very glad I got the opportunity to do it, and I greatly appreciate and am thankful to the people of Tenderfoot for seeing potential in me when I did not, both then and still to this day."

Characters

Danielle, 15 years old. Thinks that breaking the law, under any circumstances, is wrong. When she says no she definitely means it.

Courtney, 15 years old. Best friends with Danielle. Courtney is afraid of losing her friends or upsetting people. She will do anything to be liked. Courtney is naïve.

Daryl, 15 years old. Best friends with Danielle & Courtney. Daryl is a crazy hard partier. He doesn't care about anyone except himself. He will try anything once even if it means losing friends. All he cares about is having fun even if it means risking his health or breaking the law.

Lisa, teenager. Host of the party.

Shauna, teenager. Girl at the party.

Craig, teenager. Boy at the party.

Paddy, teenager. Boy at the party.

Other Partygoers

Scene One

Danielle, Courtney and Daryl are on their way to a party hosted by Lisa. Lisa is known for having the craziest parties. Danielle is having second thoughts. She doesn't know if it is a good idea for her to go. She has heard rumours in school that the party will be the wildest of the year, with no parental supervision and tons of alcohol and possibly drugs. Danielle knows she won't get into any trouble herself but her friends are pretty easygoing and when it comes to it they will do almost anything. Daryl is on a hyper buzz. It's not even ten o'clock yet and he has already taken ecstasy to get him into the party spirit. He has the night planned out in his head, go in, get drunk, take more drugs, dance with a selection of girls, pick his favourite and fuck her brains out. It's gonna be a whopper party in his mind. It's summer so it's only getting dark.

Danielle: Why did yous even ask me to come? I have better things to be doing than spending my valuable time with a load of wasters.

Daryl: Fuck off being a moan for once in your life D, it's just a party, I promise we'll have a great laugh, won't we Court?

Courtney: Yeah, it'll be deadly.

Danielle: Fine, I'll come, but I'm not staying long, an hour, two at the most, alright?

Daryl: Whatever then, but we aren't leaving for you, I intend on having a good time tonight, whether you're there or not.

Danielle: Fine then. (*Mumbles to herself.*) Prick.

They walk in awkward silence.

Courtney: Well this is awkward.

Danielle and Daryl both groan. They arrive at the party. Lisa opens the door. 'Just Dance' by Lady Gaga fades up. Lisa is already drunk. She is finding it hard to stand. She hugs each of them clumsily. They walk into the main room where the party is situated. The room is mostly bare so there is room to dance. There are a couple of tables filled with drink. There are also a few seats. A lot of people are already there. They are dancing, drinking and just talking to friends. Danielle, Daryl & Courtney split up. Daryl goes to the back towards the right of the room and immediately picks up a drink and starts dancing like a maniac. Courtney is unsure. She needs someone to tell her what to do. She isn't sure how to follow her own initiative so she just stands in the centre of the room watching everyone and feeling awkward. She bites her nails. Danielle walks to the left of the room and picks up a lemonade. She sits down and watches everyone dance. The light focuses on a girl. The girl's name is Shauna. She sees Daryl. She likes what she sees. She picks up a drink, gulps it back, then she walks over to Daryl and begins dancing seductively up against him for the rest of the song. When the song ends she gets nervous and just smiles at Daryl. She begins to walk away. Daryl pulls her back thinking that this might be fun.

Shauna: *(Shyly.)* Emm, hey.

Daryl: *(Confidently)* Hey, sup?

Shauna: Nothing much, I just thought I'd come over and talk to you... Or something.

Daryl: Alright, cool, cool, so do ya wanna drink or something? Don't worry, I brought my own. *(Smiles at Shauna and pulls out a full bottle of vodka.)* Lisa's drink tastes like SHIT!

Shauna smiles nervously and agrees. Daryl and Shauna walk over to the drink table. Danielle is sitting there.

Danielle: *(In an unamused tone.)* Hey.

Shauna: *(In an overly cheery voice.)* Hey.

Daryl: *(Just rolls his eyes. To Danielle.)* You alright?

Danielle: Nah, I'm pissed off, only been here two minutes and I'm bored stupid, and by the looks of it so is Courtney.

Shauna and Daryl look over at Courtney who is still standing awkwardly in the middle of the room, biting her thumbnail and looking around.

Daryl: Oh for fuck sake, look at her, she looks like a poxy spa, she can't do anything without someone forcing her to. *(Shauna giggles.)* Hold on a second. *(With a determined look on his face.)* I'll be right back.

Daryl: *(Daryl walks over to Courtney.)* Hey, whatcha doing?

Courtney: Oh hey Daryl, nothing much, just listening to the music, what about you?

'Fight For This Love' by Cheryl Cole is now playing.

Daryl: I'm wondering why you aren't dancing, you look like an eejit standing here doing nothing. Why don't you dance?

Courtney: I don't have anyone to dance with. Nobody has asked me and I'm too scarlet to ask any of the fellas.

Daryl: Okay, come here for a second, I'll find you someone, you wanna lose your virginity don't ya?

He pulls her by the wrist to the first fella he sees.

Courtney: Daryl what are you doing?

Daryl: (*Stops.*) Well, do you or don't ya?

Courtney: (*Embarrassed.*) Yeah, I think so, but I don't wanna seem slutty, you know what I mean?

Daryl: I'm getting you someone to dance with, a most likely fuck ha, and don't worry, all lads like a slut, so don't worry, just relax an' get it over with. You'll be happy when you do. (*He taps a fella on the shoulder.*) Alright mate, what's your name?

Craig: Ehh, Craig, why?

Daryl: Okay Craig, what do you think of my friend here? Do you like her?

Craig: Ehh, yeah, I suppose.

Daryl: Ha, perfect, alright then, I'll leave yous two future love birds to dance, okay?

Craig: Yeah, alright, I'll dance with your friend.

Daryl: Cool.

Daryl walks back over to Shauna and Danielle.

Craig: So what's your name?

Courtney: (*Self-consciously.*) Ehh, it's Courtney.

Craig: Are you okay?

Courtney: Yeah, I'm fine, I just get a bit nervous around strangers, sometimes.

Craig: Ha, don't worry, there is no need to feel nervous around me. I'm alright, I promise.

Courtney: (*She smiles.*) Yeah, for some reason, I actually believe you.

Courtney begins to feel more confident.

Craig: Well, that's good, because it's actually true. (*Craig looks into Courtney's eyes. She returns his gaze. There is chemistry between them.*) Sooo, do you wanna dance or what? (*Smiling.*)

Courtney: Yeah, come on. (*Pulls him by the wrist. They walk to the centre of the room. 'Break Your Heart' by Taio Cruz begins to play.*) I love this song!

Courtney and Craig begin to dance.

Daryl: See what I just did. (*Points to Courtney and Craig dancing.*) I'm like a relationship wizard or something. I have hooked those two and myself up tonight. (*Grabs Shauna's hand while saying this.*) I'm just amazing. All that's left to do is hook you up, which is easier said than done, because you're so bloody stubborn.

Danielle: Fuck off, I'm not stubborn, I'm just a bit picky, all the fellas like these (*motions towards everyone dancing*) are all spas.

Daryl: You know about six people here, including us, so I don't know what your waffling about, you're just being judgemental. I bet you're just afraid to get your heart broken.

Danielle: Ha, alllrrright then, whatever.

Daryl: See, look, you're not denying it so I must be right as usual.

Shauna: Look what you've done now, you've given him a big head.

Daryl: Shut up, my head's gorgeous.

Shauna and Danielle: (*In unison.*) Ha, allrrright.

Daryl: Fuck off.

Danielle: No, yous fuck off, yous are doing me head in, I just wanna be left on me own.

Daryl: Oh, fine then, you cranky bastard ya.

Daryl and Shauna walk away. They walk to the corner of the room where they were dancing earlier. 'Tik Tok' by Ke$ha comes on. It gets everyone in a happy dancing mood. Lisa stumbles towards Daryl and Shauna with a big cheesy grin on her face. She has, what looks like, a bag of cocaine in her hand. She waves it at Daryl who responds by producing an even bigger bag of cocaine. Also some hash.

Lisa: Oh, this is gonna be whopper! (*Cheerfully.*) When do you wanna start doing these?

Daryl: What's the point in waiting, we may as well do some now, get in the party spirit, right Lis? (*Lisa nods.*) You coming Shauna?

Shauna: (*Unsure.*) Aww, yeah, I may as well, it's not gonna kill me like.

Daryl: Good girl, good girl, so come on, yous coming to do this now or what?

Lisa, Daryl and Shauna go upstairs. Focus returns to Craig and Courtney who are still dancing. 'Tik Tok' by Ke$ha is still playing.

Craig: (*With a devilish grin on his face.*) You're a whopper dancer and all, but I'm bored of dancing, you wanna go upstairs.

Craig kisses Courtney.

Courtney: Ehh, I don't know.

Courtney begins to panic. She looks around for Daryl to ask for his advice.

Craig: Come on, I told you, you can trust me, I'm an alright fella, I swear, I won't make you do anything you don't wanna, okay?

Courtney: Alright, I suppose I trust you, but I don't think I'm ready to do anything like that with you, even though I really want to. I'm afraid you'll think I'm a slut, because I actually like you.

Craig: Yeah, no worries. I was actually thinking the same, I like you as well, so I don't wanna move too fast, like there's not really a point, I'd rather just get to know you first.

Courtney: Alright then. Ehh, why do you wanna go upstairs then?

Craig: Ehh, it's too loud down here, I can hardly hear you. I wanna go upstairs and talk in a quieter room, and start getting to know you like I was saying.

Courtney: Alright then.

Craig: So come on then.

Craig grabs two drinks off the table and leads Courtney upstairs. Focus falls on Danielle. She is still on her own. She is humming along to the song and drinking her lemonade. A boy, around her age, approaches her.

Paddy: Ehh, hey, sorry to disturb you but ehh, is anyone sitting here.

He points to the empty chair beside Danielle.

Danielle: Nah, no one is sitting here.

Paddy: Alright so, ehh, do you mind if I sit here then?

Danielle: No, I don't mind, you can sit here.

Paddy: Thanks.

Danielle: *(Stares at Paddy for a few seconds before asking.)* Do you have a brother?

Paddy: Ha, yeah, well actually two, why?

Danielle: Because I think I know him, is your brother Karl?

Paddy: Ha, yeah, he is, Karl and Andy, they're me brothers.

Danielle: Oh my god, your brothers are gorgeous, I would ride Karl! And Andy's not bad either.

Paddy: (*Smiles.*) Oh, and what about me?

Danielle: (*Smiles too.*) You're not bad looking either, and when you smile, you look just like your brother. He is massive!

Paddy: Yeah, so I've heard, so you really think I'm good looking?

Danielle: Ha, yeah I do, you're no Karl, but you're defo nowhere near ugly. So, ehh, what's your name?

Paddy: Patrick (*puts out hand for Danielle to shake*) but everyone calls me Paddy, so yeah, call me Paddy.

Danielle: (*Shakes Paddy's hand.*) So Paddy, I'm Danielle.

Paddy: Is your drink empty? (*Looks into Danielle's cup and sees it is.*) Alright mine too, so what you drinking?

Danielle: Emm, just Coke, ha, I know, I'm such a loser.

Paddy: No you're not, ha, I'm only drinking Coke as well, I don't wanna end up like all these wasters here.

Danielle: Yeah, that's exactly how I feel as well, weird coincidence.

They smile at each other.

Paddy: (*Gets embarrassed and coughs to break up the smiling.*) Alright then, I'm just gonna get the drinks and I'll be back okay?

Danielle: Okay, hurry back.

Danielle feels another rush of embarrassment as she realizes what she just said. Paddy walks to the drinks table, picks up two Cokes, and walks back to Danielle.

Paddy: Was I fast enough for you, did you miss me while I was gone ha?

Danielle: Ha, shurrup!

Paddy: (*In a joke threatening manner.*) You gonna make me Danielle!

Danielle: Ehh, yeah, I will actually, I'll get ya bet around! Ha.

Paddy: Ha, yeah alright, I'll get me brother to kill ya. (*Danielle grows quiet.*) Ha, well, that shut you up didn't it?

Danielle: (*Sarcastically.*) You can get your brother to do something to me alright, but it wasn't killing that I had in mind ha.

Paddy: (*Replies sarcastically.*) Oh fine, fuck off to me brother then,

I actually thought you were mine.

Danielle: (*Fake angry.*) Ehh, hello, I'm not yours, what do you think I am, your property, I'm not a fucking chair or something.

Paddy: (*Genuinely concerned.*) Aww, I'm sorry babes, don't get pissed at me, I was only buzzing with ya.

Danielle: (*Proudly.*) Ha you actually believed me! I knew I should have been an actress.

Paddy: Shurrup, I didn't actually believe you, I was only messing, I think I should really be the actress, ehh, I mean actor.

Paddy tries to hide his embarrassment.

Danielle: Oh my god, do you really think I can't see through your little act, you were well concerned, calling me baby and all, bless your little cotton socks.

Danielle pinches his cheeks. Paddy turns bright red.

Paddy: (*Laughing.*) Fuck off.

They sit in silence for a few seconds. They finish their drinks.

Paddy: Ehh, so do you wanna dance or something, or are you planning on sitting here all night?

Danielle: For your information I wasn't planning on even staying at this party for much longer. I didn't even wanna come in the first place but I'm glad now that I did. (*Smiles at Paddy.*) But yeah, I suppose one dance won't hurt.

Paddy: But there's no reason for you to go now, you're having a laugh aren't ya, watch, I bet by the end of the night you will still be here because you couldn't bear to part from me, ha.

Danielle: Ha, yeah alright, little Mr. Vain over here or what! And I bet ya I won't.

Paddy: Yeah, you know you love it, don't ya? And I bet money that you will be here at the end of the night still dancing with me.

Danielle: Oh yeah, what's not to love about your delusionalism, and nah, I'd feel terrible having to take your money.

Paddy: What the fuck, delusionalism, is that even a word?

Danielle: I don't fucking know, and does it actually matter, you get the point don't you?

Paddy: Ha, suppose, and yeah, having to take me money, me arse, you're just shitting yourself because you know I'll leave you with nothing at the end of the night, ha.

Danielle: Oh, whatever then, so we dancing or what?

Paddy: Yeah come on.

Paddy leads the way to the dance floor. 'Sexy Bitch' by David Guetta and Akon is playing. People are still dancing although they are getting sick of the upbeat songs.

Danielle: It's like this song knows me or something, it's right, I am a sexy bitch aren't I?

Paddy: And you were calling me vain, have you heard yourself?

They both laugh. Paddy realises he doesn't want to dance after all. He's more interested in talking to Danielle some more. He stops dancing.

Danielle: Why did you stop?

Paddy: I just don't actually feel like dancing, I actually wanna go upstairs.

Danielle: What the fuck, I hardly even know you, there is no way in hell I am going upstairs with you, do you think I'm some kind of slut or something?

Paddy: No you doorknob, I don't wanna have sex, I just wanna talk to you and get to know you better especially if you're going home soon.

Danielle: Are you sure you're not trying to trick me or anything and like date rape me or anything?

Paddy: Ha, you spoon, we're drinking Coke, I think you would know if there was something in it, and I'm only fifteen, isn't it like all old people who wanna rape teenage girls? And believe me, I wouldn't have to put something in your drink for you to drop your knickers, you'd do it right now if I wanted you tah.

Danielle: Oh my god, I didn't think there was anyone on this planet that was as full of themselves as me but you are just as bad, if not worse. And I'm not a slut so you can keep dreaming about me dropping me knickers because it's something you are never *EVER* gonna see.

Paddy: So do you trust yourself to be in a room alone with me or do you feel you will just turn into, like a sex beast or something? Because we look like spanners standing here. And believe me I won't date rape you like I was going to, especially since you figured out my plan, so you coming?

Danielle: (*Sarcastically.*) Yeah, I suppose I can resist the urges for about an hour, I'll try me best not to just jump on you mid-conversation, but I can't guarantee anything because you are just so sexy.

Paddy: I know that was supposed to be sarcastic, but I know you meant every word, ha.

They go upstairs. The lights go out.

Scene Two

The lights fade up. The stage is split into three sections, signifying three different rooms upstairs in Lisa's house. Shauna, Daryl and Lisa are in the room stage left. Craig and Courtney are in the room centre stage. And Paddy and Danielle are in the room stage right. The focus switches from room to room. The action starts in the room with Shauna, Daryl and Lisa. As the scene starts Daryl, Lisa and Shauna are finishing a line of cocaine.

Lisa: Oh my god, this is some good shit! Isn't it D?

Daryl: Yeah, it's alright. I've had better but it'll get me through the night in anyway so I suppose it's grand. You alright Shauna?

Shauna: Yeah, I'm fine except for the fact that I think my nose is actually melting!

Daryl: Oh shut up with your constant moaning! You have done this before right?

Shauna: Yeah, of course I have, but never this much at once, this is like my fourth line in like ten minutes, that can't be good for you.

Daryl: Well, I'm no doctor, but I'm pretty sure taking cocaine is not good for you at all, no matter what the dosage. So we may as well do a good bit because we only live once and we have already started with the coke so we are basically fucked either way, whether we continue or not.

Shauna: Well, I'm not really sure about your logic, but whatever, I'm still able to talk and stand so I couldn't be that bad. Pass me the bag.

Daryl: *(Throws the bag to Shauna.)* Alright, maybe my advice was a bit scabby, you should slow down a bit, it is cocaine. Take a break and move onto the hash for a while to cool down, okay.

Shauna: Nah, I'm grand, you were right. *(Does another line. To Lisa.)* You want some?

Lisa nods. Shauna throws the bag to her.

Daryl: Whatever, I'm not your ma, do what you want. Just don't use all me coke or you'll have to repay me in other ways. (*Points to his trousers and smiles.*)

Shauna: (*Licks her lips seductively.*) What kinda punishment is that? Jesus, I'd do that right now.

Daryl: Are you for serious?

Daryl is shocked at Shauna's forwardness.

Shauna: Yeah, it's only head! It's not a big deal or anything! And it's not like I haven't done it hundreds of times before.

She scoots towards Daryl who starts to undo his tracksuit bottoms.

Lisa: Okay, I'm starting to feel a little bit uncomfortable here now. I'm gonna leave, yous don't mind if I take the coke, don't yous? (*She gets no reply.*) Whatever then, I'm taking it, I'll talk to yous in a while, I think I need some vodka with my coke, ha.

Lisa leaves the room. As the door closes the focus switches to the room centre stage.

Courtney: We have been in here for ages and you have done no talking, what's wrong?

Craig: Nothing, I'm just thinking, you know?

Courtney: What are you thinking about? (*Smiles.*) Come on, you can tell me.

Craig: Don't get annoyed, promise.

Courtney: I promise, why would I get annoyed?

Craig: (*Shyly.*) I was just wondering if we could do anything, you know what I mean.

Courtney: Emm, I don't know, I thought we had it planned out that we wouldn't do anything like that tonight, in case it ruins things between us you know.

Craig: Yeah I know, but I kinda changed my mind, like I won't think you're a slut or anything, I just really wanna do something with you. But I suppose I can wait if you really want to.

Courtney: I really want to as well, believe me it was all I was thinking about before I got here, but now I really think it would be a lot better if we waited, just trust me about this, because I normally rush things like this and it never works out for me. I really don't wanna mess things up because I like you. I'd much rather wait if you don't mind.

Craig: Yeah, no problem babes, of course we can wait, you're probably right about it being better in anyways. So do you want another drink, you haven't had many tonight?

Courtney: Yeah, go on then, what is it, do you know?

Craig: Ehh, well, it's clear so I assume its vodka, hang on, I'll check. (*Sips drink and pulls face.*) Yep, it's defo vodka.

Courtney: Eww, I hate vodka but it'll have to do, pass it over.

Courtney puts her hand out to take drink from Craig.

Craig: Oh, wait, hang on a minute, your cup has a good bit more in it than mine, I'm just gonna even it out okay?

Courtney: Yeah alright.

Craig: (*Turns away from Courtney and begins evening out the drinks. When he knows Courtney isn't looking he slips a couple of pills into her drink and stirs it.*) Here you go, all done.

Craig passes Courtney's drink to her.

Courtney: Thanks.

Courtney begins sipping her drink.

Craig: Whatcha doing? Come on, be brave, gulp it back with us, I'll race ya, we need to make this party a bit more exciting.

Courtney: Ha, alright then. (*She gulps her drink back in the same time as Craig drinks his.*) Ha, I beat you! Scarlet for ya!

Craig: I must have ended up putting too much in my cup then because there is no way in hell you would have beaten me in a drinking contest, I'm a fella, like hello, you must have cheated, ha ha.

Courtney: Oh, you're such a sore loser, it's disgraceful! (*Grabs Craig's shoulder.*) Do you feel kinda dizzy or something?

Craig: No, I'm grand, you're probably just feeling sick from drinking too fast, ha, you're a lightweight.

Courtney: (*Panicking.*) No, that's not it, it's not like anything I've ever felt before, and I've been drunk before so it's definitely not that, I think I'm gonna collapse.

Craig: Oh fuck, hold on, I'll get help.

Craig runs out of the room. Courtney collapses onto the bed. Craig walks back in. Laughing.

Craig: Ha, about fucking time. (*Grabs Courtney roughly by the arm and moves her into the position he wants. He whispers to himself.*)

You better not fucking wake up.

Craig starts to unbutton his jeans. Focus switches to the room stage right.

Paddy: Ha, ha, so ehh, let me think of a question, emm, what's your favourite colour?

Danielle: Oh my god, what a shit question, does it actually matter what my favourite colour is?

Paddy: Shut up, it doesn't matter, but that doesn't mean I don't wanna know, so just answer the question.

Danielle: Emm, well I suppose, purple and black then, happy?

Paddy: Almost, so emm, tell me, why are purple and black your favourite?

Danielle: (*Rolls her eyes and sighs.*) I don't fucking know.

Paddy: (*Laughs.*) Chillax, I'm only messing with you, I honestly couldn't care less about your favourite colours. Okay, so your turn, ask me a question.

Danielle: Emm, alright then, do you have a girlfriend?

Paddy: Do you actually think if I had a girlfriend, I'd be at this party with my brother and up here with you now, I'd be killed! So to answer your question, no I don't have one, I broke up with my girlfriend of six months a couple of weeks ago.

Danielle: Aww, I'm really sorry for yous, what happened?

Paddy: She cheated on me with some ugly chap from me school, but I kicked his teeth in, ha, so it's all good. (*Smiles proudly.*) And by the way, what do you mean you're sorry for us, if we were still together you wouldn't be up here with me now.

Danielle: Yeah I suppose I wouldn't be, but still I hate when people break, it's so sad, even if I don't know the people, it makes me wanna cry.

Paddy: Oh my fucking god, you are such a girl! So ehh, what about you? When where you last with someone?

Danielle: I don't really like relationships, my friends think I'm stubborn and that I think I'm too good for other people but that's a lie. I'm just a bit picky because I don't wanna get hurt so I'd rather be alone, but I'd never tell me mates that, ha.

Paddy: Well, don't worry, your secret's safe with me, ha.

Paddy smiles at Danielle.

Danielle: *(Smiles back.)* So, ehh, sorry if I seem a bit nosey or anything, but ehh, are you a virgin?

Paddy: *(Overly dramatic.)* Ha NO, I was whacking some bird out of it last night, I had her in bits, she couldn't handle me, I was too big for her, ha, ha.

Danielle: *(Shocked. Disappointed.)* Oh, alright then.

Paddy: You do know I'm really messing, don't ya, I'm not like that, that's what all me mates are like, not me, so yeah, emm, I'm a virgin, and I'm proud of it and all. I'd rather be one than go around shagging sluts who spread their legs like butter.

Danielle: *(Happily.)* Oh yeah, that's cool, me too, I ehh, mean, I'm a virgin as well, ha.

Paddy: Deadly, I'm planning on waiting a good while like, not until marriage or anything, just until I find the right person, you know?

Danielle: Yeah, I feel the same way, so ehh, why didn't you think your girlfriend of six months was the right one?

Paddy: I don't know really. I just had a feeling I wouldn't like, be with her that long, I wasn't even expecting us to stay together six months, and if did lose me virginity to her, it would have basically been wasted because look at where we are now. I don't even speak to her anymore. *(Gets a bit emotional.)* I can't believe I'm actually telling you all this, I don't even know you!

Danielle: It doesn't matter that I don't really know you, that actually makes it kinda better in a way, for you to tell me things, because I won't judge ya, I'm kinda like your little therapist, ha. *(Puts on fake Russian voice.)* So tell me, what is the zha problem?

Paddy: Oh my god, you are such a loser!

Paddy is laughing now but his voice is still a little shaky.

Danielle: Aww, bless ya, showing your emotions. I suppose you are different from other fellas. *(Moves closer to Paddy. She smiles at him. He smiles back. She hugs him.)* You can tell me anything you know, I won't say it to anyone, because I kinda trust you, I don't know why, but I hope you trust me as well.

Paddy: I do, believe me, I really do.

Paddy kisses Danielle on the cheek.

Scene Three

It's the following Tuesday. It is four days after the party. Courtney,

Danielle and Shauna are all sitting on a park bench.

Shauna: So, ehh, how did yous think yous did on the maths test?

Danielle: Emm, I think it was alright, I just missed a couple of questions because I was more focused on Lisa's next party on Saturday.

Shauna: Oh my god, yeah I know, it's gonna be whopper! I can't wait.

Danielle: Yeah I know, so ehh, what's up with you and Daryl? Are yous going to the party together or what?

Shauna: Aww, he's a sap, he thinks he's the fucking cheese, young fella wrecks me mallet.

Danielle: Ha, so you're not going with him then?

Shauna: Yeah I am, you mad yoke, the chap has coke on a constant supply, I'd be mad to miss it. But I won't arrive with him because I don't want people to think that we are like, together or anything, I'll just get what I want off him and then ditch him.

Danielle: That's soo scabby! So who you going with then?

Shauna: I was going to go with you and Courtney if that's alright?

Danielle: Oh, well I was planning on going with Pad..., never mind.

Shauna: Oh my god, who is it? Tell me?

Danielle: Fine, I was planning on going with Paddy, a fella I met at the last party who I am really starting to like, we have been basically inseparable this whole week.

Shauna: Oh, so that's where you've been when you said you were 'babysitting', thanks a lot. Aww, I'm only buzzing, so little miss too good for love, finally has a fella, I am soo proud.

Danielle: Shauna, I know you like a week.

Shauna: So what, I see you around school all the time on your own, so I know, and also Daryl gets very blabby when he drinks so he told me a lot.

Danielle: Ha, well yeah, we are seeing each other, but we are taking it slow, I don't like relationships.

Shauna: Speaking of hooking up at the party, Courtney, how's Craig?

Courtney: *(Shrugs her shoulders.)* Don't know.

Shauna: Have you not seen him since?

Courtney: No.

Shauna: Why not? Yous were getting along great when I seen yous.

Courtney: I just don't want to see him, okay?

Courtney is getting annoyed. Her voice is raised.

Shauna: Okay, okay, so are you going to the next party?

Courtney: No.

Shauna and Danielle: (*Almost shouting.*) Why not?

Courtney: (*Shouts back.*) I just don't fucking want to okay? Can we please drop this?

Shauna: What the hell is wrong with you? You have been acting weird ever since the party?

Courtney: Who the fuck do you think you are, you don't know me, so stop acting like you do, I have been acting fine.

Danielle: Court, no you haven't been, you have been snappy anytime someone mentions the party, you know you can talk to me don't you? I am always here for you, if you need to talk about something.

Courtney: Thanks, but no thanks, I don't see why you think you can treat me like a fucking charity case, offering to talk when poxy Paddy isn't occupying your time for five fucking minutes. Speaking of Paddy shouldn't yous be off riding somewhere, that's the only way you could be soo happy about being involved with a fella, if you're getting something off him. It's not like he would have any type of decent conversation to contribute because men are all stupid bastards. I don't care how special and unique you think Paddy is, he will eventually fuck you over, and laugh at the outcome, and you would fucking deserve it because you are a shit fucking friend. (*Danielle and Shauna are in shock.*) So fuck off and leave me alone, it's not like you care about me in anyway. The fucking cheek of you trying to act like a friend to me now. Where have you been for the past week? Oh yeah, you fucked off with what's his face and this slapper. (*Points to Shauna.*) So don't act concerned now, you haven't been concerned all week, it's only when it suits you because it's all about Danielle! You're just a complete bitch, so fuck off to Paddy, and bring Slutty Shauna with you!

Shauna: Who the fuck do you think you're calling slutty Shauna?

Shauna stands off to Courtney. Tries to intimidate her.

Courtney: Do you think I am fucking afraid of you or something?

Don't make me laugh, now fuck off out of me face before I kick you around, I have bigger things to deal with than you right now, so piss off.

Shauna lunges forward to hit Courtney but Danielle stops her.

Danielle: Just leave it, come on, it's not worth it.

Shauna: Fine, whatever.

Danielle: Court, I know something happened to you at the party. I just hope that you will eventually realise you can trust me with what happened. I honestly just want to help you. I want my lovely bubbly friend Courtney back, not this broken, miserable version. I love you Court but you seriously need to face whatever happened to you, and when you do I hope you let me in, because I don't want to lose you. Your little rant about me was just coming from an angry place that is now gone, because Paddy, no matter how serious we get, will never take the place in my heart that is reserved for you, so please talk to me whenever you're ready.

Danielle leaves with Shauna.

Courtney: *(Alone.)* Fuckkk!!!!

Courtney puts her hands over her face.

PARK BENCH

Ellen O'Sullivan

"I can safely say that when I was fifteen I had no clue what went into writing a play. The thought that I might write one myself had probably never crossed my mind. Yet, through Tenderfoot, that is exactly what I ended up doing. I have such fond memories of my time in Tenderfoot and Park Bench is a play that I will always be proud of."

Characters

Adam, the hero
Louise, the heroine
Jen, the friend

Scene One

The scene takes place in a small local park at around 10.00 a.m. The park is empty except for a few children in the background and our hero Adam. Adam sits on a bench. He looks nervous. Every few seconds he looks up expectantly. Enter Louise.

Adam: Louise, hey.

Louise: Hey Adam what's up? I got your message, is everything okay?

Adam: Yeah, I just wanted to talk to you...

Louise: Talk away. Oh, but before I forget, I got those photos developed.

Adam: Cool, let's see!

Louise sits down and passes a stack of photos to Adam. They flick through them, laughing.

Louise: Ha, what's Ms Clancy like! Such a poser!

Adam: God, look at the state of me! Why did Romeo have to wear tights? Didn't they have trousers in the olden days?

Louise: *(Laughing.)* You look great! Oh and my mam says you can keep the tights!

Adam: Haha, thanks! Not sure I'll be wearing them any time soon though!

Louise: Aaaah, look at Jen! Where did she manage to find the wig? She had me in stiches being Nurse. It was gas! She's a really good actor.

Adam: Ahem! What about my magisterial acting talents?

Louise: Adam Nolan! Stop fishing for compliments! You were great though, you know that.

Adam: What about you? Romeo's nothing without his Juliet.

Louise: True! We worked well together! Jesus, it's hard to think it's all over now. Three months of my life I spent working on that play. I was saying the lines in my sleep! I had so much fun though.

Adam: *(Looking at Louise.)* Yeah, me too...

Louise: What's the look for?

Adam: *(Jumping out of a daze.)* Hmm what?

Louise: The look you're giving me? The 'meaningful gaze'?

Adam: Oh, eh I was just thinking.

Louise: About...?

Adam: Oh you know, this and that....

Louise: Right... So anyway, what did you want to talk to me about?

Adam: What?

Louise: For God's sake Adam, are you even awake today? What did you want to talk about?

Adam: Oh yeah, sorry. I suppose I better start then...

Louise: Good idea!

Adam: I'vc been thinking.....

Louise: That makes a change!

Adam: Shut up and listen, I'm trying to tell you something.

Louise: Sir, yes sir!

Adam: Well if you're going to be like that.........

Louise: Sorry Adam. Go on, I'm listening.

Adam: Really? This is important you know.

Louise: Really. I'm all ears.

Adam: Okay then. So, like I said, I've been thinking a lot lately. About life and.. and love.

Louise: Deep stuff then.

Adam: Exactly! So basically I thought, well we've been friends for a while now..

Louise: Yeah three years! God time flies when you're having fun.

Adam: That's what I mean. We've been great mates and we've had a load of craic over the years and now... well... I think... I- I- I mean.. I know... No wait, I'll start again. What I'm trying to say is, basically... eh...

Louise: Jesus Adam, would ya ever just spit it out? I haven't got all day!

Adam: (*Blurts out.*) I think we should go out.

Louise: (*Stunned.*) We should what?

Adam: Go out. Us. Together.

Louise: What? Why?

Adam: Why not?

Louise: Yeah but why now? Where's all this coming from?

Adam: I dunno, I guess I just felt a connection with you. Like, what's the word? Chemistry! I always felt the connection but working on Romeo and Juliet together just made me realise my feelings. You said yourself that we work well together.

Louise: In the play! It's called acting!

Adam: You can't fake that sort of connection Louise.

Louise: (*Under breath.*) Oh God.

Adam: (*Unsure now.*) Oh no... Tell me I haven't just made a complete fool of myself. Please say you feel the same way too.

Louise: (*Seeing his face and not wanting to upset him further.*) Sure I do. I feel a.. em.. what did you call it again?

Adam: (*Eagerly.*) A connection?

Louise: That's the one.

Adam: I knew it! This is so great! If you only knew how happy this makes me. I was so nervous this morning. I think my mam thought I was having a nervous breakdown or something!

Louise: You were acting pretty strange.

Adam: I just thought you'd say no. I mean, you're so pretty and you could have any guy you wanted, but you connected… with me!

Louise: (*Smiling slightly.*) Glad I could be of service.

Adam: So listen. I've to head now, I've art class at 11.00. I'll meet you here later, about seven yeah?

Louise: Guess so..

Adam: Great! See you then

Louise: Bye…

Scene Two

Louise sits on the bench nervously waiting. Enter Jen.

Louise: Hey, thanks for coming.

Jen: Yeah no problem. Not like I've anything better to do

Louise: Thanks Jen. You really know how to make a girl feel special.

Jen: It's a talent I have. Oh my God, did you see Ros na Rún last night? Isn't Ríona such an eejit? I mean, the whole village knows about O'Dowd, even Coilín, and he's not exactly in the inner circle!

Louise: I don't watch that crap.

Jen: Oh yeah sorry. I forgot you've no taste.

Louise: Says the girl who watches Murder She Wrote every day!

Jen: Jessica Fletcher is one classy woman I'll have you know!

Louise: Whatever Grandma!

Jen: I refuse to lower myself to your standards and reply to that comment.

Louise: Ha! Just 'cause you can't think of anything to say!

Jen: True! So what did you want me for?

Louise: I need help!

Jen: Is it that maths again? Cause all you have to do is cross multiply to find x.

Louise: It's not the maths.

Jen: Then what's wrong?

Louise: What's right?

Jen: Talented and astute as I am, I can't read minds. Do you want to elaborate?

Louise: Yeah, sorry. It's Adam.

Jen: Shit! Why didn't you say something earlier? What happened? Is he okay?

Louise: *He's* Fine

Jen: Thank God!

Louise: Mmm

Jen: Well if he's okay then what's the problem?

Louise: He asked me out..

Jen: (*Shocked.*) Wow, that's.. that's great!

Louise: No.. no, it's not! It's awful! What am I going to do Jen?

Jen: Don't tell me you were so thick as to turn him down!

Louise: Nope, I said yes....

Jen: Then what's the problem?

Louise: That's the problem!

Jen: Hold on.. Maybe I've gone stupid but I don't understand. You just got asked out by the nicest, cutest guy in school and it's a problem? What's up with that?

Louise: But I don't want to go out with him!

Jen: Nope, still confused. Adam's great! He's kind, funny, smart...

Louise: I know all that! I really like Adam, I just can't go out with him. It doesn't feel right.

Jen: So why did you say yes then ye mad thing!

Louise: Well, I dunno.... I was just shocked I guess. We were having a perfectly normal conversation and all of a sudden he started blabbering on about connections!

Jen: *Connections*...?

Louise: (*Ignoring Jen.*) He took me by surprise, I wanted to say no, I really did. But I was already confused and then I saw his poor little face and it just came out as yes! And know I can't break it off without hurting his feelings!

Jen: I see, this is a problem.

Louise: (*Wailing.*) That's what I was saying!

Jen: (*Putting her arm around Louise.*) Listen Lou, before we fabricate an escape plan, I think it's my duty as a friend to make sure you've really considered this arrangement.

Louise: Huh?

Jen: Girls go for fellas because they're hot or they're funny or they're kind. Adam's all three! He's also incredibly smart. He is, as they say in the movies, a catch. I know girls that are mad about him.

Louise: Like who?

Jen: (*Blushing.*) Well, em, I think Shauna and, em, Jodie and ehhhh..

Louise: You?

Jen: (*Turning redder.*) What?

Louise: I can't believe I never saw it before? Why didn't you tell me? *You* like Adam!

Jen: Course I do. I wouldn't be his friend if I didn't.

Louise: No! You like him the way *I'm* supposed to.

Jen: Wait a second, I never said..

Louise: (*Interrupting.*) Look who you're talking to Jen! You can tell me anything.

Jen: Well he's taken so it doesn't matter does it?

Louise: I knew it! This solves all my problems!

Jen: How?

Louise: Don't you see? My problem is that I don't want to be with Adam and yours is that you do! If we get the two of you together then he'll forget about me! Everybody's happy!

Jen: Genius! How's it going to work though?

Louise: I haven't got that far. I suppose we could... no, never mind...

Jen: What if we... nope, bad idea.

Louise: We need a fool proof plan. Something that can't fail. Except that my brain's gone blank!

Jen: Wait, I'm about to be brilliant.

Leans over and whispers to Louise. Girls laugh and exit stage.

Scene Three

Jen sits on the bench reading a magazine. Enter Adam. Jen keeps reading the magazine pretending not to notice him.

Jen: (*Notices Adam.*) Hey!

Adam: (*Looks up hoping that it's Louise.*) Oh, hi Jen. Have you seen Louise around?

Jen: I think she's on her way. I was talking to her just there. But Adam, I just wanted you to know that I think this is great, the two of you together.

Adam: Thanks Jen! Do you think she's really happy? I mean, she looked kind of weird when I left her this morning.

Jen: She's delighted! Seriously, she was just shocked this morning, she really wants this to go ahead.

Adam: You sure? I mean, I wouldn't want to force her into anything...

Jen: Adam, she's over the moon. When I was talking to her she wouldn't shut up about you! To be honest it was almost getting annoying!

Adam: Wow... glad she feels the same.

Jen: Oh she does! She was in the jewellers today and all.

Adam: Jewellers?

Jen: Looking at rings!

Adam: Rings?

Jen: As in, engagement rings!

Adam: WHAT?

Jen: Don't worry, she wants to finish school first. You'll have time to save for a ring. Plus, she only wants a simple one. And her parents will probably pay for a wedding.

Adam: Shit! Louise was never like this before!

Jen: (*Nonchalantly.*) Ah sure you know yourself. Love changes people. Speaking of her parents, are you free tomorrow?

Adam: What? Em, I'm not sure really, I think I might have football practice. Why?

Jen: Well you might want to cancel it, Louise said that her dad wants to meet you?

Adam: Why tomorrow? I mean, I've seen him before loads of times.

Jen: It's different now. You're the boyfriend, you have to do the boyfriend interview.

Adam: What do you mean?

Jen: You didn't hear it from me but he's kind of strict with Louise's fellas. He conducts a sort of interview before you can go out with her.

Adam: Why didn't I hear about this before?

Jen: (*Rolling eyes.*) Men! No intuition at all! If Lou broadcast this all over town, no boy would go near her! Don't worry though, you'd ace any test like that.

Adam: Thanks for telling me Jen, you're a good friend.

Jen: No problem! But, eh don't mention the engagement. And wear a suit. And maybe don't mention that you got a C in maths last week.

Adam: (*Growing visibly upset.*) Oh Jen! What am I going to do? Please help me, please!

Jen: (*Suppressing a giggle.*) Whatever do you mean?

Adam: I can't go through with this! It's too much! I thought I liked her as more than a friend. I dunno, maybe I got mixed up between life and art. I still really like her but maybe I fell in love with Juliet rather than Lou.

Jen: Stranger things have happened.

Adam: So what do I do know? This is such a mess! Why did I open my big mouth?

Jen: It's not your fault Adam, you're only human.

Adam: She's going to be so upset!

Jen: Too true. Let her down gently.

Adam: I'll try, it's going to be hard to think of the best way. You've always been good at this sort of stuff, what would you do?

Jen: Emm, I suppose just try and be tactful but truthful. Don't lie to her but don't be too abrupt either.

Adam: What does that mean? What should I say?

Jen: Something like... 'I don't think that we work as a couple and I don't want to ruin our friendship.'

Adam: (*Admiringly.*) How do you come up with these things?

Jen: (*Blushing.*) It's easy really. Any fool can do it.

Adam: Would you talk to Lou for me? I don't think I can do it like you can! It just sounds cheesy coming from me!

Jen: I don't know, I think she'd prefer it coming from you...

Adam: Please Jen? She'll take it better from you. You're her best friend, she trusts you, everyone trusts you!

Jen: I suppose you're right. It might speed up the healing process...

Adam: Exactly! So you'll do it?

Jen: Guess so.

Adam: Oh Jen you're a lifesaver! If there's any way I can repay you...?

Jen: (*Smiling.*) Oh don't you worry. I'm sure I'll think of something!

DEPARTURES
Simon O'Mara

"My experience at Tenderfoot is without doubt the reason I chose to pursue Creative Writing for my university degree and also the reason I have continued to write and involve myself with drama. I had an amazing time, learning valuable lessons about something I love and left with new confidence in my abilities and ambitions for the future."

Characters

Karen, 24
Sam, 22
Cassie, 25, glamorous

Scene One

Enter Sam and Karen into the waiting area of an airport, dragging bags behind them. Karen checks the list of departure times, then checks her watch.

Karen: It's delayed!

Sam: What?

Karen: They can't just delay the flight at the last minute.

Sam: It's probably the bad weather /

/ Indicates a line interrupted by the next character's line.

Karen: The storm's not that bad really. They're not going to get away with this, oh no!

Sam: Relax, Karen. It's going to be fine.

Karen: How can I relax?! It's not fine. The flight is not going to leave until twenty five past two at this rate.

Sam: It's only an hour delay. We've got plenty of time.

Karen: Only an hour! Only! Are you trying to annoy me?

Sam: You just need to relax.

Karen: But I have everything planned perfectly and now all that work is destroyed. We'll be an hour late arriving at the hotel so we'll miss the live music and we'll have to eat off the dinner menu which is always risky.

Sam: Just breathe in… /

Karen: It's going to be a disaster, I can tell.

Sam: Just take a deep breathe, in and out.

Karen: I know how to breathe, okay? It's a complete and utter disaster! Everything is ruined, absolutely ruined. We might as well just go home and forget the holiday.

Sam: Karen, it's not that bad /

Karen: I'm going to complain! I'll get the airline back for this though, you can count on that. By the time I've finished with them /

Sam: Relax, Karen. Come and sit down for a minute /

Karen: I can't sit down! I'm going to write a letter to someone, the Minister of Transport. No, better yet, The President.

Sam: Letters won't help us now /

Karen: Well then, I'm off to find somebody to yell at! They'll regret the day that they crossed me, I'll promise you that right now.

She storms off, leaving him alone with the bags.

Sam: (*Muttering to himself.*) I bet they will.

Scene Two

Sam crosses to a small cafe area. There is only one free seat. A high stool at a table for two. A woman sits on the other one. Sam takes the seat beside her. She looks at him, then looks away. She fidgets on the seat. She eventually turns to face him.

Woman: Did your flight get delayed?

Sam: Yeah.

Woman: Mine too. There seems to be a lot of that going around, doesn't there?

Sam: Yep.

Woman: Where you heading?

Sam: Athens.

Woman: That's funny. I was guessing Paris.

Sam: Why'd you think that?

Woman: I don't know. Just a hunch, I guess. I do that a lot. In fact, this is the first time that I've ever gotten something wrong.

Sam: *(Sceptically.)* The first time?

Woman: I'm very perceptive. How long are you staying in Athens?

Sam: One week.

Woman: Dammit! I was guessing two. You're starting to annoy me now.

Sam: Did you ever think that people might be humouring you?

Woman: No. I would have sensed it.

Sam: I never got your name.

Woman: I never gave it.

Sam: I'm Sam.

Woman: Cassie.

Pause.

Sam: Do you make a habit of talking to people in airports?

Cassie: No. You're special. Why Athens?

Sam: I don't know. Karen wanted to go so...

Cassie: The woman I saw you with earlier?

Sam: *(Embarrassed.)* You saw her?

Cassie: I see everything. Plus... *(leaning towards him)* she's kinda loud, isn't she?

Karen's voice is heard from offstage.

Karen: What do you mean "you don't know the answers". If you don't who does? I want answers, not the runaround.

Sam: It's just been a stressful day with the delays and everything.

Cassie: Airports are hell! The good thing is that you only ever come here to leave.

Sam: Where are you going?

Cassie: Siberia.

Sam: On business?

Cassie: No, just a holiday.

Sam: Not your typical holiday destination, is it?

Cassie: *(Whispering.)* I'm not exactly your typical kind of girl. In case you haven't noticed.

Pause.

Sam: How long are you staying there?

Cassie: *(Shrugs.)* Depends on how long it takes to see everything. I'm not really sure yet.

Sam: What about your plans to get home?

Cassie: Don't have any. I'll probably just get bored after a few months and decide to leave.

Sam: A few months?

Cassie: That's how long it took in Bucharest.

Sam: I see. Don't you have to get back to work?

Cassie: I quit last week, get rid of anything that gets in the way, you know?

Sam: Isn't a bit risky not to have any plans?

Cassie: Ah, but therein lies the beauty. Plans would ruin all the fun on my spontaneous trip.

Sam: I don't understand.

Cassie: Well, take this conversation. If we were people who knew each other and had planned to meet here, we would be talking about our dull lives and the weather and all that stuff. But, here we are, two people who don't know a thing about each other, who only met because that was the last stool left in the place, and 'cause of that we can talk about things like this. We can be honest 'cause chances are, we'll never see each other again.

Sam: Okay. But if you don't plan things, then you'll never get anywhere.

Cassie: I've been to over seventy five countries, seen some of the most beautiful sights in the world and I didn't plan any of that. I just let the events happen. If you don't mind me saying so, if your wife left a little more up to fate, she might get some more fun out of life.

Sam: She's not my wife.

Cassie: Oh really?

Sam: No, she's my girlfriend. We've just moved in together, a month ago, we've been going out for.. a while. This holiday is to celebrate… our relationship moving on.

Cassie: Yeah. But that's not my point. How did you guys meet anyway?

Sam: Well, we were friends for years and then… She's been kind of frantic lately, with the holiday and things… she's not like that normally.

Cassie: So, she's not always so… crazy.

Sam: I don't really know anymore. When we were friends, she was calm and funny and now … well you've seen now. Can people completely change or is it just a phase?

Cassie: Maybe you should look at things from her point of view. I mean, you've been friends for years and suddenly everything shifts and changes. She was comfortable with the old dynamic and now everything's up in the air. She's trying to control all of these trivial little things because she can't control the big things.

Sam: So you think she'll change back then? She'll be the old Karen?

Cassie: Who knows? *(Shrugs.)* I think she needs time to adjust to everything that's going on between you two.

Sam: Why can't she be like you? Less planning and more… action.

Cassie: You wouldn't like her to be like me either. I drove my last boyfriend insane. He was constantly complaining about how I never take things seriously and then one day he just left. He was right really. I should probably start to think about what I'm gonna do when I'm older.

Sam: Why don't you settle down then? Buy a house, get a job, start a family. Do normal things?

Cassie: I just don't want to wake up in ten years' time and wish that I'd enjoyed my youth more. You know, one of those bitter people who wishes they'd done it all differently. What if to 'settle down' is just a sugar coated term for settling?

Short pause.

Sam: What about your current boyfriend?

Cassie: What makes you think I have a boyfriend?

Sam: You're not the kind of girl that stays single for long.

Cassie: *(Laughs.)* Am I blushing? I feel like I'm blushing. I don't have a boyfriend right now.

Sam: I see.

Cassie: I had this office thing going on but I had to break that off. Clean break and all that.

Sam: Don't you hate having to do that every time you leave?

Cassie: It gets easier.

Karen enters. She can be heard ranting to herself. Sam and Cassie watch her, amused.

Karen: I have to do everything myself. Do I have to carry this entire holiday on my shoulders? Of course, he doesn't even see how much work I do. No 'thank you', no 'I appreciate it'. He doesn't even care how hard I'm trying.

Sam: It's weird that we can talk like this.

Cassie: It's 'cause we never have to see each other ever again. We don't have to be ashamed of anything. It's freeing, isn't it?

Sam: It is. Would it be weird if I said... if I said that I wish I had met you first?

Cassie: Calm down there, Romeo. It's only been ten minutes.

Sam: It's so much easier to sit her and talk with you than it is with Karen.

Cassie: That's because it's only been ten minutes. *(Sam laughs.)* After one day, you'd be so bored with me that you'd never want to see me again. You've only seen the fun side of all the crazy. I'm a lot more neurotic than I appear, albeit in a different, slightly quieter way to her.

Sam: So what should I do about Karen?

Cassie: Give her some time to get used to everything now that it's all changed. She's probably as afraid as you are. Only she doesn't have a quirky, but understanding, woman like myself to talk to. It's kind of tragic really.

Sam: And what if she stays like this forever?

Cassie: That one's on you. You have to ask yourself that question.

Short pause.

Sam: Do you think we'd maybe be able to see each other again? When you get back from... Siberia?

Cassie: Don't you think it would be better if we didn't? We could leave it like this. Two strangers in an airport meet, strike up a conversation, become friends or whatever we are, and then disappear into different corners of the world. It would be better than meeting up with these feelings clouding our better judgement.

Sam: Does that mean you feel the same?

Cassie: I don't think that either answer to that question would make you feel any better.

Sam: So I should just get on the plane and hope for the best?

Cassie: That seems like the only reasonable thing to do.

Sam: So, you think that Karen'll change back when the pressure stops?

Cassie: Are you looking for one of my psychic flashes?

Sam: *(Laughing.)* You are always right.

Cassie: Not when it comes to you. *(Pause.)* You'll be happy in the end though.

Sam: I better get going. My flight is probably boarding by now.

Cassie: Have fun in Athens.

Sam: Yeah...

Cassie: Try at least!

Sam: Enjoy Siberia. Don't stay too long.

Cassie: Who knows? Maybe I'll be back in a few weeks. Maybe I'll be back in a few months. Or maybe I'll be swept off my feet by a mysterious Siberian and never come back. I'll be coming to the dreaded age of thirty soon. The queue of men waiting to marry me will probably start to thin out pretty soon. How horrible!

Sam: Yeah. God forbid you might have to 'settle down'.

Cassie: I'll never be that old.

Sam: I better not keep Karen waiting. Might end up with a slightly angry letter waiting for me when I reach the hotel.

Cassie: Well she needs something to do on the plane! You're right, annoying her further would be a scary prospect. Although it might be funny for me to watch!

Sam: I guess this is it then.

Cassie: It's been fifteen minutes. Stop with the melodrama.

Sam: Okay. Bye then.

Cassie: Goodbye. Try not to take things too seriously.

Sam: I'll try my best...

Cassie: I guess this is it then! (*Pause.*) Have a nice flight. Try not to forget about the crazy lady at the airport.

Sam: It would be pretty hard to. You make a vivid impression.

Cassie: I'm setting an example. Never be afraid to take a chance, meet a new person, try something new, harrass someone you don't know in an airport.

Sam: Okay. I'll talk to as many strangers in airports as possible.

Cassie: That's my boy! Now get going before you're stuck here for another couple of hours, waiting for another flight.

She pushes him. He leaves. She watches him leave.

Scene Three

Sam and Karen stand in the departure lounge. The lighting is surreal. Sam is in a spotlight. He looks toward Karen. A spotlight fades up on Karen. She looks at Sam.

Karen: Sam I just wanted to say... I'm sorry. I know I've been a little stressed this morning, with the delay and everything and I snapped at you earlier and I'm sorry.

Sam: It's okay. I know you didn't mean it.

Karen smiles for a moment, momentarily calm. Then the lighting snaps back to normal and the scene snaps back to reality.

Karen: (*Agitated.*) If this plane doesn't leave soon then I am going to scream. I am just going to yell at the top of my lungs for everyone to hear. I mean the storm has settled down.

Sam: Yeah.

Karen: Who really cares about a little bit of wind and rain? We can handle a bit of turbulence, can't we?

Sam: Yeah, it's stupid.

Karen: I've made some calls and sorted out some new plans for when we arrive. Of course they won't be as good as the original plans but they'll have to do I guess. (*As Karen is speaking Sam looks over at Cassie. A spotlight forms around her. She is still sitting on the stool in the cafe. She is drawing on a piece of paper.*) There's a local restaurant I found that's supposed to do great seafood so we can go there instead of the hotel bar. They have live music on until nine, it probably won't be very good, but it's all I could do. I'm not a miracle worker. (*She notices that Sam is not listening to her.*) What are you doing just standing there? (*Sam's reverie is broken. The lights return to normal.*) Are you even listening to me?

Announcement: Boarding for flight no. EI8762 to Athens will begin at gate 42. Will all passengers for flight no. EI8762 for Athens please make your way to gate no. 42 as boarding will commence immediately.

Karen: The plane is boarding. It's not going to wait for you to finish your daydreams. Do you have your boarding pass?

Sam: I think so.

Karen: You'd better more than think that you have it! You never take these things seriously! If it wasn't for me none of this would come together. You need to start thinking about where you're going to be in ten years. You don't want to wake up in ten years and resent all this time that you've been wasting.

Sam: I was just thinking the same thing.

Karen: Good. So maybe when we get back you can focus more on the important things in life and not all these parties that you've been going to. That's fine when you're in your teens but at our age it's just a waste of time.

Sam: We're only in our twenties.

Karen: That's my point. We're too old for that kind of stuff.

Sam: Shouldn't we be trying to have fun anyway, no matter what age we are? That's what life's about, right?

Karen: Yes, Sam. Fun is fine but we should have sensible, organised fun.

Sam: Doesn't that take the purpose out of fun?

Karen: I can't talk to you when you're being like this.

Sam looks back at Cassie and then Karen nudges him.

Karen: We need to get moving. Boarding's started already.

Sam: I think I forgot my phone back at the cafe. You go on and I'll meet you on the plane.

Karen: Leave it to you! Alright, but be quick.

Karen exits and Sam goes back to the cafe to talk to Cassie. Cassie looks up as he arrives.

Cassie: I figured you'd be back.

Sam: So you heard her then?

Cassie: Continental Europe heard her. She's quite the little firecracker, isn't she?

Sam: How am I supposed to get on a plane with her?

Cassie: If you hadn't had a conversation with me here today, would you have got on the plane?

Sam: Yeah, I guess.

Cassie: Well then, there's your answer. Forget all about our little chat and get on the plane.

Sam: What if it's not a good idea?

Cassie: Nothing ventured, nothing gained. Just be patient with her.

Sam: What if we end up hating each other?

Cassie: You were best friends. You're not going to hate each other so quickly. So, get moving. Oh Lord. I've gotta catch my flight. Try not to kill her and enjoy your trip.

Sam: I'll try.

Cassie: I'd better get going and so should you.

Cassie picks up her bag and leaves. Sam moves towards the boarding gate and then pauses. He looks back over his shoulder in the direction Cassie went. Lights down.

A PIECE OF ME

Seoid Ní Laoire

"When I wrote *A Piece Of Me* I was full of questions and few answers. I was thinking about things; I guess the usual philosophical questions on reality, subjectivity and also happiness. I don't think the play arrives at any answers or even special insights. Writing *A Piece Of Me* developed me as a writer, but it was watching the director shape my words into something new, something physical and outside of myself that I learnt the most. My writing's weak points were suddenly glaringly obvious, as were its strengths. I remember peeking out from backstage and seeing the audience respond to words I had written and experiencing a connection that is impossible to achieve from a page. It is difficult for me to adequately describe the impact of my few weeks with Tenderfoot. It was one of those experiences that, when I look back on my life so far, carves out a milestone."

Characters

Erica
Psychologist
Chris

Prologue

Lights up. Single character center stage. Cello music plays quietly.

Erica: Reality is just another illusion. Like logic or reason it is a barrier that people create to feel safe and in control. What is reality? What makes something real? If you can touch me, hear me, am I real? Do I exist only in your mind or can I exist outisde of your reality? Don't be afraid to look past the safety nets, to see what is hidden behind them. Because it is *you* who decides reality.

Scene One

Takes place in a psychologist's office. The office is expensively decorated. It is conventional. Erica looks tired and unhealthy. The psychologist is sitting in his chair looking up at Erica. Erica is standing. She is looking away from him.

Erica: I'm not connected anymore. It's like I'm a balloon that was attached to something and someone just cut the string. And now I'm floating away and I don't know how to stop. I'm no longer connected to anything. I'm just... floating.

Psychologist: It's not unusual to feel out of control Erica. Do you know why you're feeling like this?

Erica: It's since Chris died. It's like he took a piece of me with him, and the part left behind has no idea how to function anymore.

Psychologist: You feel lost without him?

Erica: I don't know what I feel like anymore.

Psychologist: Do you think about him a lot?

Erica looks flustered.

Erica: Yes. He's never far from my thoughts.

Psychologist: Why don't you tell me about a time when you and Chris were happy.

Erica: Sunday was our day... We'd sit on the windowseat, still wrapped in our duvet and watch the morning unfold... Mrs Taylor watering her roses in her pink dressing gown, Amy and Tom's boys kicking a football against their garage door... the sunlight adding colour and warmth to the grass. At noon, everyone would head to mass... 'What about today?' I'd ask and he'd always chuckle and say, 'Maybe next week.' But next week was always the same. He wasn't a God man. We'd bake instead. We each had our bits, our jobs to do: I'd sieve the floor, he'd mix the eggs and the milk. The sound of the spoon hitting the bowl filled the air and set us a rhythm to work to. And you know, it was a bit like our Sunday mass... our own kind of worship.

Psychologist: So things were good, before.

Erica: Yeah they were. We had each other. That's all you need. Then none of the other stuff matters.

Psychologist: And you felt... complete with Chris?

Erica: Yeah. (*Pause.*) But even then some part of me knew it couldn't last. Happiness couldn't be that easy. I'd get this feeling, an inexplicable panic. He told me I was just working myself up. That we had forever ahead of us. But you never know how much time you have.

Bell rings to indicate that the next client is waiting.

Psychologist: Life is full of change, Erica. I know you feel vulnerable right now, the death of a loved one can shake our reality profoundly. But dealing efffectively with your grief is central to your recovery. You can get through this. And I'm going to help you. (*Erica nods.*) I'd like you to come back next week.

Erica: Okay.

Psychologist: Goodbye Erica.

Erica exits the stage and the psychologist takes out a recorder to record the meeting.

Psychologist: Tuesday, 11:30 a.m. Erica Roberts, attending sessions for two weeks previous to today. Suffering from grief-induced depression. No medication neccesary.

Swithces off recorder. Goes to sink and washes hands. Begins talking to himself absentmindedly.

Psychologist: Typical case. Should be done in a month or so.

Finishes washing his hands and returns to table. Presses button.

Psychologist: I'm ready for the next patient. Send him in. (*Gathers files.*) Two months, and he should be finished too. Ah, Mr. Keane, good to see you. How have you been feeling?

Scene switches to Erica who has just left the office. She sits on a bench under a tree outside the psychologist's office. A young man sits beside her. She doesn't look at him. Quiet cello music can be heard.

Erica: Why are you here? (*The man smiles at her.*) Leave me alone Chris.

Chris: You'd miss me if I was gone.

Erica: You are gone. That's the point. You're dead.

Chris: Then why am I still here?

Erica: *You're* asking *me*?

Chris: You're the one who's seeing me.

Erica: You're the one who's following me!

Chris: I've got to be better company than that moron in there.

Erica: At least that moron in there exists! I don't know why I haven't told him about this… He'd probably lock me up.

Chris: Chill out Erica. You were always such a worrier.

Erica: I'm having a conversation with a dead person right now and you think I've nothing to worry about? Ha!

Chris: S'pose you have a point there. (*Looks around the park.*) It's beautiful here.

Erica: I hadn't noticed. (*Looks at a tree.*) The trees have lost their leaves.

Chris: Winter's coming. But it'll be followed by spring.

Erica: I don't know… some winters are too dark and too cold for spring's light to penetrate. Some winters are everlasting.

Chris: And some people are determined to be pessimistic!

Erica: What reason do I have to be anything else?

Scene Two

Erica is in the office with the psychologist again. She looks pale and sickly. Some time has passed.

Erica: There's something I haven't been honest about.

Psychologist: Yes?

Erica: It's about Chris. I… I see him.

Psychologist: In what way? Do you mean you see him in dreams?

Erica: No, I mean I see him.

Psychologist: Oh.

Erica: I know you must think I'm mad. I think I'm mad.

Psychologist: There's no need to worry. It's a coping mechanicsm. It's natural to think you see Chris now and then.

Erica: Except it's not now and then. It's all the time.

Psychologist: Tell me what these experiences are like.

Erica: He is as real as you are.

Psychologist: Erica, sometimes when people are grieving deeply they can have unusual experiences like you're describing.

Erica: Yeah… okay.

Psychologist: I want you to try something for me. Whenever he appears to you, ignore him. Concentrate on where you are, what you're doing. If it helps, say to yourself, "I'm sitting at the kitchen table", or "I'm washing the dishes... This is real. A month ago I lost my husband. This is an hallucination."

Erica: Okay, I'll try.

Leaves the office. Psychologist takes out a recorder and begins recording.

Psychologist: Thursday, 3.30 p.m. Erica Roberts. Experiencing visual and aural hallucinations. No medication necessary - yet. I will review this decision next week.

Psycologist walks over to sink and the spotlight switches to Erica on the bench outside the office. Chris joins her. Quiet cello music plays.

Chris: (*Sarcastically.*) And what did the psycho-babbler have to say today? (*Erica ignores him.*) What's this? The silent treatment? (*Erica frowns. Continues to ignore him.*) Erica. Erica! Alright then. If that's the way you want to play it. (*Chris turns around and ignores her.*) Seriously, this is getting pretty boring.

Erica: Ha, I knew you wouldn't last!

Realises she's spoken to him and turns away again.

Chris: He put you up to this didn't he? (*Erica nods ruefully.*) Huh. Shows how much he knows. As if ignoring me will work.

Erica: What *will* work??

Chris: Getting sick of me are you?

Erica: It's lonely without you. The house seems so empty.

Chris: I told you we didn't need such a big house.

Erica: Ha, yeah, you did. (*Sighs.*) I'm scared Chris. I'm scared of the way I feel. I've never felt so... apart from people before. It's me and it's them and the gap between us is stretching wider and wider. I'm surrounded on all sides by emptiness. And if I step too far back, I'm afraid I'll fall.

Chris: You don't need to be afraid when I'm here.

Erica: You were my anchor. But now you're gone.

Chris: I can still be your anchor. I'll just be holding you to something else.

Erica: What do you mean?

Chris: Never mind.

Erica: I don't know why I'm telling you this anyway. Though really I'm just telling myself all this because you're probably just a manifestation of my subconcious which is unwilling to let you go.

Chris: You said probably! Beginning to doubt yourself eh?

Erica: Shut up! (*Pause.*) What did you tell me before you left to go to work... the day you... had the accident. (*Chris stares at her.*) Just before you got in the car?

Chris: You know what I said.

Erica: I can't remember.

Chris: Bullshit. You're trying to test me?

Erica: Just answer the question.

Chris: No way. I'm not 'proving' myself to you by answering a stupid question.

Erica: Answer the question!

Chris: No.

Erica: (*Hysterically.*) Now I can tell my psychologist that my hallucination is refusing to answer me.

Chris: (*Grumpily.*) Why bother tell him anything?

Erica: Because... He's going to help me.

Chris: You don't sound very convinced of that.

Erica: What other choice do I have?

Chris: (*Shrugs.*) Well if I were you I wouldn't tell him anything.

Erica: Why not?

Chris: Let's just say I doubt he'll be very helpful.

Erica: We'll just have to see won't we?

Chris looks around and smiles. A little girl is playing in the park.

Chris: Look at that kid.

Erica: Her hair is coming out of its clasp. Look at the dirt on her knees. Her face... it's... lit-up! (*Pause*) When does it all change Chris?

Chris: When we grow up.

Erica: She's smiling at us.

Chris: At you.

Erica: Oh right. Forgot no one else can see you. Which is further proof that you don't really exist.

Chris: Why should that mean I don't exist? No one else can see because they walk around with their eyes closed.

Erica: And what, I'm the only one with my eyes open? Think there'd be quite a few more traffic accidents if that were the case.

Chris: You're the only one who can accept that I might be real.

Erica: The moment I accept you're real is when the men in white coats come for me.

Lights dim.

Scene Three

Erica is in the office with the psychologist. She looks slightly dishevelled as though she hasn't been taking care of herself.

Erica: I went to the supermarket for groceries yesterday. Neccessity forced me. It's been weeks since I've gone and there was barely any food left in the house. (*Pause.*) I felt like I had a bubble round my head or something. I was looking at these people, mothers picking out avocadoes, children running down the aisles... And I knew my life was nothing like theirs. It was as if we lived in two completely separate worlds.

Psychologist: Separate, how?

Erica: They were all so... interested. In picking out groceries and in deciding on which brand of window cleaner. They were so focused on these tiny inconsequential things. And I stood there looking at them and I thought, I used to be one of you. I used to care whether I got Vanish washer or squeezy washer. I used to care. Now, I don't give a damn.

Psychologist: Why's that?

Erica: I'm not involved in everyday things anymore. I just sit at home and look at things. Sometimes I realise I've been sitting there looking at the same thing for over an hour, and if you asked me what it was I'd been looking at, I wouldn't have a clue. The only times I feel animated anymore is when I'm with Chris.

Psychologist: So the hallucinations haven't lessened?

Erica: He's with me most of the time.

Psychologist: Have you been in touch with any of your friends recently? Met up with them?

Erica: No.

Psychologist: I'd like you to make an effort to keep in contact with people Erica. You need to get out of your head. You need to remember, these are hallucinations. They are not real.

Erica: (*Pause.*) What if... what if it is real?

Psychologist: I know these delusions are very strong and very realistic Erica, but they *are* delusions. It is not possible that they are real.

Erica: How can you be so sure?

Psychologist: It is simply not possible Erica.

Erica: Who are you to say what is possible and what is not?

Psychologist: It's not me who is saying it but everyone, it is the collective wisdom of our society.

Erica: You mean the collective ignorance of our society?

Psychologist: Look Erica, this isn't an argument about philosophy. The bottom line is, you are living in our society, you must be able to function in it. You have to be able to get up in the morning, go to work, interact with people, sleep at night. There is no room for men from Mars, talking with spirits and seeing things that aren't there.

Erica: You have such a limited view. Don't you.. well, don't you believe in an afterlife?

Psychologist looks surprised and uncomfortable at the turn in the converstion.

Psychologist: Believing in an afterlife is all very well. But it is an *after*life. People usually believe the person is... somewhere else.

Erica: So it's okay to believe in whatever you want, but if you act on that belief that's when it stops being okay?

Psychologist: Well... yes. A lot of people believe they can sense the presence of a dead friend or family member nearby. But if you indulge this belief to the extent that it affects your ability to function, that's when it's not okay.

Erica: But I'm happy. Without him it's as if I can only see the world in black and white. When he's there I see in colour again.

Psycologist: Tell me, Erica, when was the last time you went to work?

Erica: I haven't been in a while. They understand.

Psychologist: Have you been eating regularly? Are your sleeping patterns normal?

Erica: (*Defensively.*) Yes.

Pychologist: I don't think you have Erica. Look at yourself. You're exhausted, underweight. You've been alone in the house for the past few weeks...

Erica: I haven't been alone.

Psychologist: You haven't been to work or been socalizing. You have to agree that you need some help. (*Erica doesn't reply.*) You have to reach out your hand Erica, before I can take it.

Erica: I don't need help.

Psychologist tries to reason with her.

Psychologist: If you continue to go along with this idea of Chris you are jeopardizing your future. You will never be able to keep a job or sustain a relationship. (*Erica gets up.*) Where are you going? (*Erica leaves.*) Erica! (*When she doesn't reply or return he gets up and makes his notes about the session.*) Friday, 10 a.m. Erica Roberts. Session's estimated progress not achieved. The patient is not co-operating enough. Next session will take place in two weeks time. (*Switches off recorder. Addresses the audience.*) I'm worried about Erica. Her condition is deteriorating. She can choose a fantasy world, which is more forgiving. Or she can choose the real world and face the truth. She will lose her fantasy world but gain her sanity. If she can no longer take care of herself, she will have to be committed to an institution for her own good. Well, we'll see what next week brings.

Lights dim as he begins washing his hands.

Scene Four

Bench outside office. Erica sits with Chris. She isn't looking at him. Quiet cello music plays.

Erica: Sometimes I think when I look out the window I see something completely different to everybody else.

Chris: You're brooding again.

Erica: Sorry. (*Turns away.*) I've got to stop talking to myself. It's not healthy.

Chris: I assume that also means I've got to stop answering.

Though how we'll ever have a conversation with you not talking and me not answering is beyond me.

Erica: Maybe it's better if we don't have any conversations.

Chris: Then what on earth would we do to fill the time?

Erica: You're not supposed to have time to fill! You're meant to be... wherever dead people are supposed to be.

Chris: That doesn't apply in my case.

Erica: And why not? What exactly is your case?

Chris: I was hoping *you* would tell *me* actually.

Erica stands up.

Erica: You don't exist! I'm just.. reliving memories.

Chris stands up and draws close.

Chris: Touch me Erica. I'm real.

Erica: No.

Chris takes her hand. She gasps. He puts it to his face.

Chris: I am as real as anything is. (*Looks at her intensely. The music gets louder.*) You have a chance Erica. You can escape. You can free yourself from this suffocating cage. All you have to do is trust me. Step into my world.

Erica: Will I condemn myself to madness or release myself from it?

Chris: Take my hand Erica.

Steps away from her into light and mist. He reaches out his hand. Erica takes his hand and steps into the light without looking back. Music becomes more intense.

Chris: Look around you.

Erica looks around the scene. It is bathed in a warm glow.

Erica: Everything is as it was and yet to me it's different. The bench no longer leans so heavily against the wall, it is upright and vigorous. The dull grey buildings are no longer dull, how could I ever have thought them dull! (*Reaches out and touches the tree nearby.*) Look at how the wind plays with the leaves of the Sycamore, they dance to their own tune. (*Shakes her head regretfully.*) I had forgotten how much beauty there is in the world.

Chris: It was always there. You'd just shut your eyes to it.

Erica: They're open now.

Erica and Chris walk away together. Music fades.

Scene Five

Psychologist is sitting in his office looking at files when Erica bursts in. Without speaking she drops a tape on his desk. He looks up from his notes in astonishment.

Erica: Listen to it!

Psychologist: Excuse me?

Erica: Listen to the tape!

Psychologist: Ah... okay.

Erica sits down opposite him and watches carefully as he puts the tape into a player and plays it. The tape begins playing.

Erica's voice: The following is proof of the existence of Chris and evidence of Erica's sanity.

Psychologist sighs and crosses his arms.

Chris's voice: You'll need a bit more than this to prove your sanity Erica ha, ha..

Erica's voice: Talk to him Chris.

Chris's voice: What?

Erica's voice: Talk to him!

Chris's voice: Eh.. okay. Hey there Doctor, how are you today? What did you have for breakfast this morning? I had Cheerios. That is what I have every morning. Except this one time when there were none left and............ And that silence is the sound of you not caring.

Erica's voice: (*Through gritted teeth.*) Talk to him about something slightly more relevant.

Chris's voice: Yes boss. You and I haven't had the pleasure of being acquainted yet, my good Doctor, but I know you more then you think. Let me give you a word of advice, we all need something to help us cope, but in the long term your way is not advisable. (*Erica can he heard coughing.*) Am I convincing you, Doctor, of my existence? Are you sufficently convinced or will I continue?

Erica's voice: That'll do. (*Erica turns the recording off. Regards the psychologist triumphantly.*) What do you have to say to that?

The psychologist is silent for a long moment.

Psychologist: Now really Erica, I thought we had gotten past these attempts at 'proving' Chris to be real. I can't think why you thought a tape of you conversing with yourself would have been evidence of anything. (*Erica is too stunned to say anything.*) Now can we get back to our work, and focus on improving your health. We need to urgently discuss how to get you through this crisis.

Erica: Are you for real?

Psychologist: I'm always for real Erica.

Erica: Why won't you even give me a chance to show you my side?

Psychologist: (*Ignoring her.*) Erica, you know that Chris cannot be real.

Erica: Why?

Psychologist: Because he is dead.

Erica: Just because something can't be proven doesn't mean it isn't real.

Psychologist: Why do you distrust the scientific view? Does your belief that Chris exists stem from that distrust?

Erica: (*Ignoring him.*) Can you honestly tell me that there is no tiny part of you that allows Chris to be real?

Psychologist: Do you want me to believe it so as to verify your own belief?

Erica: Do you answer every question with a question?

Psychologist: Of course I do, I'm a psychologist.

Erica groans and gives up trying to question him.

Erica: I don't distrust the scientific view of the world, I simply believe it has a limited grasp of that which cannot be calculated and measured.

Psychologist: Convenient, seeing as an hallucination certainly cannot be 'calculated and measured'. (*Takes a deep breath.*) He is not real. You must come to terms with this.

Erica is silent then launches her attack.

Erica: What about you? You spend your day listening to people whose lives have fallen part and then what? You just wash it all away and go home and pretend like everything's fine. You sit with your family and smile and laugh on the outside. You watch TV with your kids, you go to bed and you get up in the morning and you start all over? Is that reality??

Psychologist doesn't answer. Erica gets up, walks towards the door.

Erica: We all need something to help us cope, Doctor. And by the way Chris says the car keys you lost are in your bottom drawer.

Erica leaves. The psychologist remains seated. His brow is furrowed in thought. He reaches out and turns the radio on.

Radio: ...nine o'clock news. The body of three year old Maria Finnegan was found last night in the local canal... (*signal crackles*) ...urge anyone with information on her murder to come forward... (*signal crackles*) ...bank robbery... ...three people shot... (*signal crackles*) ...70 year old man attacked in home last night... ...critical condition... ...and now over to Thomas Kenny for the weather report. Well folks today's weather forecast is a cheerful one. I predict clear skies and plenty of sun...

Signal breaks down completely. The psychologist reaches over and turns the radio off. He stands up and walks to the sink, washes his hands and turns to leave. He pauses and looks back at his desk. Glancing around, he walks back to his desk and furtively opens the drawer. He breathes a sigh of relief. Then he pulls out some papers. From between the pages a set of car keys fall out. He stares at them in amazment. He picks them up slowly. He glances around once more and then hurries offstage. Focus switches to Erica and Chris on the bench outside the office.

Erica: Why aren't you... in... heaven or wherever?

Chris: Erica, you know I'm not the religious sort. This is my heaven. Besides I'm not done here yet.

Erica: What do you mean?

Chris: Don't you ever wonder *why* I'm here? (*Erica stares at him.*) It's not just for the good conversation!

Erica: Why?

Chris: I'm here because you need me. When you stop needing me, I'll stop being here.

Erica: I'll always need you.

Chris: No, you won't. I'm just... the stepping stone.

Erica: To what?

Chris: That's up to you.

Erica: Promise me you'll never leave me.

Chris: I'll never leave you. When you're ready, you'll leave me.

Lights dim.

Scene Six

Erica and Chris are with the psychologist in his office. Erica looks much healthier than before and radiant. The psychologist looks weary. Erica and psychologist are standing facing each other. They are clearly arguing. The psychologist's tone is appealing.

Psychologist: Chris is not real! He does not exist!

Chris: (*Makes an indignant noise.*) Is that so?

Erica: What makes you so convinced that your world is the real world? Are you so narrow minded that you cannot accept that there could be *more*?

Psychologist: (*Stiffly.*) My beliefs are not the issue.

Chris rolls his eyes and imitates the psychologists tone.

Erica: Ask him! Ask Chris!

Chris: He can't see me Erica. It is beyond his comprehension that I could exist.

Psychologist: You are deluding yourself!

Erica: What if I like deluding myself? What if I'm happier in my delusions?

Psychologist: You will not find happiness in a world that does not exist.

Erica: I will not find happiness in the world that does exist! It has shown me nothing but cruel indifference. I am sick of the world that does exist.

Psychologist: If you choose Chris, you choose to live in a false existence.

Erica: I choose happiness. And in the end isn't that what everybody wants? Whether it is real or imagined is not the point.

Chris: There's no point reasoning with his sort. He's as set in his ways as a mule.

Psychologist: Erica I appeal to you, listen. You must abandon this illusion. You are cutting yourself off from your family and friends, from the rest of the world!

Erica: The world that you live in is just as much an illusion!

Psychologist: Maybe – but at least I share my illusion with the rest of humanity.

Erica: How do you know how many people are caged in your collective illusion like mad animals wishing to get free? Why are so many people suffering from depression, anxiety, mental illnesses? (*Psychologist tries to protest but she continues.*) Why are people so afraid to stop and look, listen and notice life all around us, beautiful, bounteous and completely free? Why are people so reluctant to make eye contact? Is it because each person is afraid that he or she will be found out, pretending to be happy? How many times have you really looked at people on the bus or on the street, so many in some far off place, resentful of being disturbed, talking to themselves, afraid to be different! Wearing false smiles on their faces to mask their emotions! If that mask were to fall! If their true emotions were to come out! Oh, then we would see your reality!

Psychologist. (*Interrupting.*) Erica! I will have to call for assistance if you do not calm down!

Psycologist reaches for the phone. Erica talks over him, her voice rising with her temper.

Erica: You know in your heart that your argument is wrong, it is false, it depends on everybody pretending to be happy, not to notice, and all around you people are breaking under the strain. At least my illusion is liberating! I enjoy every breath of air, every moment in life! I am awake, I am free! And you want me to come back into the cage just because it is crowded with other people so I will not be lonely – but who said I was lonely – awakened to life, there is no sense of loss or loneliness.

Erica turns and leaves the stage. Chris follows. The psychologist sits, stunned, then his face hardens and he picks up the phone.

Woman's Voice: Emergency services, how can I help you?

Psychologist: A patient has just left the building. She has had a severe psychotic episode and is a danger to herself and potentially to others. Send the medics to apprehend her. (*Sits down. Rests head on hand. Sighs.*) It's for the best, for the best. It's the only way to handle these things. Only Wednesday and I'm exhausted. God I need a pick me up.

The psychologist pulls a small bag of white powder from his pocket. He takes a fifty euro note and rolls it. He pours the powder on his desk, arranges it and sniffs it through the note.

Voice on Phone: Doctor, you have half an hour before your next patient.

Psychologist: Yes, yes....

Lights go out.

Scene Seven

The psychologist's office. Some years have passed. Erica looks vibrant and healthy. She seems content. Sane. The passing of time is more noticeable in the psychologist who looks older, more haggard.

Psychologist: Well well, you're doing fabulously Erica. Your final tests are all clear and your medical team have nothing but good reports about you. By all accounts you are in recovery.

Erica: Thank you.

Psychologist: Have you signed the release form? (*Pushes a form towards her. She signs it.*) Well, that's everything. Your term at Saint Francis' Hospital is over. You are free to go.

Erica: Thank you. (*Gets up to go. Pauses.*) You're looking very tired Doctor. Not sleeping well?

She leaves him looking surprised. We follow Erica to the other side of the stage where she sits on the bench outside the office. The tree beside it is in full bloom. She laughs quietly.

Chris: That gave him quite a turn.

Erica: It certainly did.

Chris sits on the bench beside her. She takes his hand.

Chris: I told you I'd never leave you while you need me.

He kisses her. Lights begin to fade. She looks around contentedly.

Erica: It is beautiful here.

Cello music. Fade to black.

MKII

Robert Barrett

"Tenderfoot was easily the highlight of transition year. There was never a dull day; they ranged from doing improvisations in the little theatre upstairs, to building a full sized guillotine. It was a unique experience to see plays, some of which were my own, go from their most conceptual stage in the writers' minds, to first drafts and then go through production."

Character

Man

For solo performer.

I just had an argument with **her,**
Who do I think I am she says?
I'll tell ya who I am!

I'm a modern man,
A man for the millennium,
I'm the rust on your gears,
And the insect in your ear,
Digital and smoke free.
A diversified multicultural postmodern deconstructionist,
Politically anatomically and ecologically incorrect.
I've been uplinked and downloaded.
I've been inputted and outsourced.
I know the upside of downsizing.
I know the downside of upgrading.
I'm a high tech lowlife.
A cutting edge state-of-the-art bicoastal multitasker,
And I can give you a gigabyte in a nanosecond.

I'm new wave but I'm old school,
I ain't no Luddite,
But I'm gonna set the world alight.
I'm a hot wired heat seeking warm hearted cool customer,
Voice activated and biodegradable.
I interface from a database,
And my database is in cyberspace,
So I'm interactive,
I'm hyperactive,
And from time-to-time,
I'm radioactive.
Behind the eight ball,
Ahead of the curve,
Riding the wave,
And dodging a bullet,
I'm on point,
On task,
On message,
And off drugs.
I got no need for coke and speed,
I got no urge to binge and purge.
I'm in the moment,
On the edge,
Over the top,
But under the radar.
A high concept,
Low profile,
Medium range ballistic missionary.
A street-wise smart bomb.
A top gun bottom feeder.
I wear power ties,
I tell power lies,
I take power naps,
I run victory laps.
I'm a totally on-going bigfoot slam dunk rainmaker with a
proactive outreach.
A raging workaholic.
A working rageaholic.
Out of rehab,
And in denial.
I got a personal trainer,
A personal shopper,
A personal assistant,
And a personal agenda.
You can't shut me up,
You can't dumb me down.

'Cause I'm tireless,
And I'm wireless.
I'm an alpha male on beta blockers.
I'm a non-believer and an over-achiever.
Laid back but fashion forward.
Up front,
Down home,
Low rent,
High maintenance.
Super size,
Long lasting,
High definition,
Fast acting,
Oven ready,
And built to last.
I'm a hands on,
Foot loose,
Knee jerk,
Head case.
Prematurely post traumatic,
And I have a love child who sends me hate mail.
But I'm feeling,
I'm caring,
I'm healing,
I'm sharing.
A supportive bonding nurturing primary care giver.
My output is down,
But my income is up.
I take a short position on the long bond,
And my revenue stream has its own cash flow.
I read junk mail,
I eat junk food,
I buy junk bonds,
I watch trash sports.
I'm gender specific,
Capital intensive,
User friendly,
And lactose intolerant.
I like tough love.
I use the f word in my email,
And the software on my hard drive is hard core, no soft porn.
I bought a microwave at a mini mall.
I bought a minivan in a mega store.
I eat fast food in the slow lane.
I'm toll free,
Bite sized,

Ready to wear,
And I come in all sizes.
A fully equipped,
Factory authorized,
Hospital tested,
Clinically proven,
Scientifically formulated medical miracle.
I've been pre-washed,
Pre-cooked,
Pre-heated,
Pre-screened,
Pre-approved,
Pre-packaged,
Post-dated,
Freeze-dried,
Double-wrapped,
Vacuum-packed,
I'm a rude dude,
But I'm the real deal.
Lean and mean.
Cocked, locked and ready to rock.
Rough tough and hard to bluff.
I take it slow.
I go with the flow.
I ride with the tide.
I got glide in my stride.
I don't snooze,
So I don't lose.
I keep the pedal to the metal,
And the rubber on the road.
I party hearty,
And lunch time is crunch time.
I'm hanging in,
There ain't no doubt.
And I'm hanging tough,
Over an out.

TRAPPED BY FEAR

Aisling O'Leary

"When you are sixteen you don't think about writing a play. Or if you do, you don't think you'll see it produced in a theatre."

Characters

Kylie
Jack
Seán

Three people rush into a dark room, the last slamming the door behind her. She quickly glances for a lock of some kind, finds it and clicks it into place. She sighs and leans with her back against the door. The other two have collapsed to the ground, gasping. She smiles.

Kylie: How is everybody then? Alive?

Jack: I think so. Once my heart slows down and I stop seeing spots I'll be able to give you a definite answer.

Kylie: What about you, Seán?

Seán: (*Gasping.*) My legs... I've never run so... They're so sore...

Kylie: You're still alive though. Well, that seems to have been a success. We ran and they didn't catch us. Worked out just how I planned it.

Jack: Yeah, but where have we run to?

Kylie: A room, apparently. Dark by the looks of it.

Jack: I can see that, smartass. I mean where is the dark room in which we find ourselves at present?

Kylie walks over to the others and hunches down next to them.

Kylie: Does it matter? We should be okay here, for a while anyway. If we stay just a couple of hours, and then check outside, I'm sure we'll be fine to leave. We just have to hang on a while.

Jack: A couple of hours?

Kylie: Four or five. No more than that, then we can head out.

There is a silence as the boys think for a moment.

Seán: So we can sleep?

Kylie smiles.

Kylie: Yes. We can definitely sleep.

Seán: Sounds like a good plan to me.

Jack and Seán lie down but Kylie stays as she is for a moment. She stands up and looks towards the locked door. After a moment she walks over to it and sits with her back pushed against it. She reaches into her pocket, retrieves a chocolate bar and begins to unwrap it. She lets out a sigh and takes a bite. The lights dim and fade back up again to indicate a passage of time. Kylie stands up, walks over to the boys and prods Jack with her foot.

Kylie: Sleep time's over Jackie boy! Time to get up and move out!

He rolls over and stretches. Looks around the room. He remembers where he is, who he is with and his present situation. He looks up at Kylie.

Jack: What are you saying?

Kylie: It's time that we got out of here. Go see if we can find somewhere to crash that has real beds and food that isn't 90% sugar. It's time to move out!

He gets up and stares at her for a moment.

Jack: Move out to where? We don't know where we are. We don't even know if it's safe to leave yet.

Kylie: Well there's only one way to be sure, isn't there?

Kylie bends down and nudges Seán.

Kylie: Seán? You awake? It's time to go!

Jack: (*In his sleep.*) Yeah, let's move out.

Seán wakes up. He immediately starts to groan.

Seán: I feel like crap... I don't know what's wrong but my legs feel terrible.

Kylie: They're not still tired are they?

Seán: No. They're just so sore. It really hurts, Kylie.

Jack takes an interest. He sits down next to Seán. Kylie drops down to the ground as well. She brushes Seán's hair back and looks at his face.

Kylie: Can you walk?

Seán: I don't know. They feel really bad.

Kylie: Can you try?

He begins to stand but stumbles and falls back. Jack and Kylie catch him and ease him back down to the ground. They prop him against the wall.

Jack: What happened there?

Seán: (*Gasping.*) I don't know... I can't stand up, Kylie! Why can't I stand up?

He begins to get agitated. Kylie holds his hand and tries to calm him. Jack looks down at Seán's legs and then glances at Kylie.

Jack: Still wanna move out now?

Kylie: (*To Seán.*) Do you have any idea what happened? Did you hit anything when we were running or /

/ indicates an interruption.

Seán: I can't stand up! Please, help me!

Kylie: We need to get him out of here. We need to get him to a hospital.

Jack: We don't know where the nearest hospital is. Or if they'll even be able to help him. They're probably full up anyway or don't you remember the /

Kylie: Why are you always so negative? We might as well try. What's the worst that could happen?

Jack: We might not make it to a hospital.

No one speaks. The only sound that can be heard is Seán's deep, panicked breaths. Kylie puts her arms around him and holds him close.

Kylie: Seán? (*He grunts.*) Do you want to stay here or go?

Seán: I... don't know... I can't think...

Jack: I think we should stay here. I didn't see any point in leaving before and now that we'll have him weighing us down /

Kylie: Jack!

Jack: Well it's true! If we have even the slightest chance of surviving out there it'll be even less likely if we have to carry him with us! If you're so intent on getting him help, then you're gonna have to leave one of us here, because I'm not getting myself killed trying to drag him to a hospital!

Kylie: We have to leave eventually! And I think this is as good a time as any.

Jack: Personally, I think the best time to leave would be when we don't have an invalid to worry about. If you wanna leave so badly then you should wait until he gets better.

Kylie: But what if he doesn't get better?

Jack: Then we leave without him.

Kylie: How can you say that? He's your friend!

Jack: He is not my friend.

Seán: Kylie, please don't leave me here. I don't wanna be on my own. Please don't go.

Kylie glares at Jack and continues cradling Seán in her arms. Jack just shakes his head in a disgusted way and stands up suddenly. He walks to the end of the room and stares at the ground.

Kylie: Don't worry Seán, I won't leave you. We won't leave you.

Seán: Thank you... thank you...

Jack: So we're staying?

Kylie: Yeah, we're staying.

She lays Seán back down on the ground. She slides her jacket under his head as a pillow. She gets up and walks towards Jack. The two stare at each other for a few seconds.

Kylie: Morning. We're staying until morning, okay? After that I don't care what you say I'm taking Seán and getting out of here.

Jack: Your funeral.

Kylie: Shut up. And what the hell was wrong with you back there? How could you say that stuff with him just sitting there? A little insensitive, don't you think?

Jack: I'm just being realistic. We couldn't have made it with him slowing us down and you know it.

Kylie: You can be such an ass, you know that?

She sits down against the wall. He stays standing.

Jack: How come you're staying for him now but when I wanted to stay all you wanted was to get out as soon as possible?

Kylie looks up at him and shakes her head. She looks away.

Kylie: Such an ass…

Jack sits down. Turns his back to them. The lights fade and return to indicate another passage of time. Kylie now has her knees pulled to her chest, her head is resting on them and she is looking at the floor. Jack is lying face up on the ground, he is awake, and he is staring at the ceiling. Seán appears to be asleep at the far end of the room. Kylie lifts her head and looks at Jack. She runs her hands through her hair and takes a deep breath.

Kylie: You okay?

Jack: Bored. (*They sit in silence.*) You?

Kylie: Hungry.

Jack: Don't you have more food in your bag?

Kylie: Yeah, but just because I'm hungry doesn't mean I can eat…

She glances over at Seán who has his back to them. Jack turns and looks at her as she does so. He stares at her for a moment and then turns back to the ceiling.

Jack: I'm not going to apologise.

Kylie: Of course you're not. (*Silence.*) If you're bored you could make up a game.

Jack: To play by myself?

Kylie: Not necessarily.

Jack: So what do you think is wrong with him?

Kylie looks at Seán again.

Kylie: I really don't know. Maybe he hit him when we were running.

Jack: And he didn't notice?

Kylie: Well we were all running pretty fast. I don't know about you but the only thing on my mind was getting us somewhere out of sight. I don't know if I'd notice a small sting on my leg. It's possible they got him with something and it didn't set in until later.

Jack: Do you think it's fatal?

Kylie: I hope you didn't mean that to sound as happy as it did.

He sighs.

Jack: Why are you friends with him?

Kylie: I think he's sweet and funny.

Jack: He's sappy and annoying.

Kylie: You really don't like him, do you?

Jack: Nope. Never have. But you do, so I hang around with him anyway.

Kylie: You're actually making me feel guilty for being his friend. It's not as if I forced you to be nice to him or anything.

Jack: You don't think so?

Seán begins to stir. He rolls over and looks at the others.

Seán: Guys?

Kylie jumps up and goes to Seán. She sits next to him.

Kylie: You're awake.

Seán: Yeah, for a little while now.

Kylie: How are you feeling? Are your legs any better?

Seán: They're not as sore. Actually, they're kind of... numb. They don't hurt anymore, just numb. I don't know if that's better or worse. And my arm is tingly but I have been sleeping on it.

He lets out a half laugh.

Kylie: It doesn't sound better. I think we should get going to a hospital.

Seán: Actually, I've been thinking about that. I know my legs are in a really bad way but... I don't think we should leave.

Kylie stares blankly at him. Jack sits up and listens.

Seán: We're okay here. I mean, it seems pretty safe, doesn't it? We have enough food to last us a while.

Kylie: But, you're...

Seán: In no shape to leave any time soon. I didn't like what Jack said last night but it's true. It's dangerous to leave until we know it's safe. For now, I think we're kinda better off here.

Kylie: But aren't you worried about your legs? Last night you couldn't think straight you were in so much pain!

Seán: Well they don't feel sore now. And if it doesn't hurt then there's no need for a hospital.

Kylie: That is just stupid! We have no idea what's causing this. What if they hit you with something? You could get worse. We have to leave right now.

Jack: Why, because you say so?

Kylie: What?

Jack gets up off the ground and looks at Kylie.

Jack: We have to leave because you say so. Telling us what to do and making all our decisions for us. Tell me, who put you in charge?

She walks over and sizes up to Jack. Seán watches from his place on the ground.

Kylie: Well, somebody had to. You two were just freaking out and arguing with each other. If I didn't take charge the two of you'd probably be dead!

Jack: Thanks for that vote of confidence. You know, I could have taken care of myself.

Kylie: Somehow I really doubt that.

Jack: I want to stay. It's safe.

Kylie: For how long?

Jack: All those in favour of staying raise your hand.

Kylie laughs. Seán slowly raises his hand. Jack's hand goes up without hesitation. Kylie's face drops.

Kylie: Are you serious? You're voting?

Jack: Looks like we're staying here.

Kylie: I don't believe this...

Jack: Oh, you just don't like losing power of command. This is a democracy now.

Kylie: You really are such an ass.

Jack: Cry baby.

Seán: Come on guys...

Kylie: (*Ignoring Seán.*) I am not staying here! I'm leaving and if neither of you two want to come that's fine with me. But there's nothing you can do to stop me. And then you'll only have each other for company. And I guarantee you that you'll have a better chance of surviving out there with me than you'll have in here with one another.

Jack and Seán look at each other for a moment.

Jack: We can manage.

Kylie: Oh, you really think so? Two seconds after I'm out of here you'll be at each other's throats.

She picks up her bag and swings it onto her back. She grabs her jacket, it's on the ground, and heads towards the door.

Jack: Well, you're on your own. We're safe here /

Kylie: Stop saying that it's safe! Nowhere is safe! It doesn't matter how much food you have or whether or not you've been discovered yet. There is no place that's safe anymore. There is only temporary. And then you move and you keep moving.

Seán: Kylie.

Kylie: I told you I'm not staying!

Seán: I can't feel my arm.

There is a silence as Kylie and Jack take this in.

Kylie: What?

Seán: My left arm... I can't feel it.

Jack: Are you kidding?

Seán: Why would I joke about that? I can't feel my damn arm!

Kylie drops back down and looks at Seán. Jack stays standing. Kylie shakes her head.

Kylie: That's it. You can't stay here in that condition. You're coming with me and we're gonna get you help.

Jack: For God's sake, he said he didn't want to go!

Kylie: Well that was before he lost the feeling in yet another limb!

Seán: I still want to stay.

Kylie stares at him. She starts to laugh.

Kylie: You're crazy. You're both crazy! Why do you want to stay here when you can't move your legs or feel your bloody arm?

Seán: Because I can't move my legs or feel my bloody arm. Do you think I'll be able make it even two feet like this? (*She doesn't say anything.*) The way I see it I have three options. One, I leave now and definitely don't make it. Two, I stay, recover and head out

when it seems safe. Or three, I stay, don't recover and stay until I...
I don't know...

*Kylie looks at the ground. Then she stands up and faces the door,
her back to the others. She watches the door for a few seconds and
then turns back to the guys. She takes in a deep breath. Exhales.*

Kylie: So... I can't change your minds at all, can I?

Jack and Seán glance at each other.

Jack: I don't think so, no.

Kylie: Okay.

*She drops her jacket back to the ground and pulls off her bag,
letting it fall to the floor too. She walks back to the others and sits
down.*

Jack: What, now you're not going?

Kylie: Nope.

Seán: What changed your mind?

*Kylie looks up at Jack, then next to her at Seán. She makes the
decision to look at the ground instead.*

Kylie: I don't want to go by myself.

Jack: What?

Kylie: I don't want to go out there by myself. I'm scared of what
might be outside. I thought that if you two were with me then I'd be
able to get out and just start thinking. You know, focus on getting
the three of us somewhere where we could rest and eat. But if I go
out there on my own... all I'll be able to think about is how scared
I am. About where I'm headed... what I'm going to do... who's
following me... I know I won't last if I think like that. (*No one speaks
for a moment. Kylie looks up.*) But now that I know you guys won't
be coming, no matter what I say, I'm not leaving either. I'd prefer to
be doomed in here with my friends than doomed out there on my
own.

She avoids their eyes by pretending in inspect her fingernails.

Jack: How much of that was an attempt to get us to go with you?

Kylie: About five per cent.

*She is still looking at her nails. She lets out a little sniff and that is
enough for Jack to sit down next to her and wrap his arms around
her shoulders. She holds onto his hands and snuggles into him.
Seán coughs to get some attention.*

Seán: So we're all staying then?

Jack: Yeah, I think so.

They sit for a few moments. Then the lights fade and return indicating a passage of time. Jack is now at the far end of the room. He is looking through Kylie's bag. Kylie is sitting up near the door. Seán is lying down with his head on Kylie's lap. He is barely moving. Kylie is running her fingers through his hair as she watches the door. She turns to look at Jack.

Kylie: Is there anything left?

Jack stands up and shakes a packet of crisps.

Jack: And a juice box.

Jack walks over to the others and sits down. He nods to Seán.

Jack: How is he doing?

Kylie: Well he can barely move. Legs and arms are no use... I don't know if he's going to get any better.

Jack opens the packet of crisps and offers them to Kylie. She takes one, stares at it for a moment and then eats it.

Kylie: We're in trouble aren't we?

Jack: Just a little, yeah.

Kylie: What are we going to do?

Jack: We could make up a game?

Kylie: I kinda meant in the long run.

Jack: It could be a very long game.

She laughs a little and sighs.

Kylie: Okay, what did you have in mind?

Jack: I don't know! We'd make it up as we go along.

Kylie: Why do you want to make up a game?

Jack: Well, it was your idea. Do you remember? One of the first days we were here? You said if I was bored I could make up a game. Well I'm going to make one up.

Kylie: Wow. That was so long ago... I can't even remember when it was. I've lost track of time...

Jack: Come on! Don't get all dreary. When did our roles reverse, huh? Since when am I the chirpy one and you're the pessimist?

Kylie smiles at Jack and takes another crisp.

Kylie: I'm sorry for calling you an ass.

Jack: It's fine. I am an ass. But I have the ability to be a very nice one on occasion. So, a game. Let's see, how about if we have a tr /

BANG BANG! There is a pounding on the door. Jack and Kylie jump and Seán wakes up.

Seán: What's /

Kylie clamps a hand over his mouth. She and Jack look at each other, then at the door. The banging continues. A voice is heard.

Voice: Any persons within this room are ordered to vacate now.

Kylie eases Seán's head up and slides out from underneath him. Kylie walks quietly to her bag and opens a side pocket. She takes out a gun. The guys stare at her in horror as she walks, with the gun cocked in her hand, towards the door. She puts her ear to the wood and shuts her eyes.

Voice: I repeat. Any persons within this room are ordered to vacate immediately!

Silence. After a moment Kylie steps back and exhales audibly. She turns, looks at the others and shrugs.

Kylie: Gone.

Jack: What the hell is that thing?

Kylie: What, the gun?

Seán: Yes the bloody gun!

Kylie: I thought that we might need it at some point.

Jack: So you've had that in your bag since we got here? Why didn't you tell us?

Kylie: I don't know… it just didn't seem to matter.

Seán: Are you serious? Why wouldn't it matter?

Kylie: Well do you feel any different now that you know I have it?

Jack: I feel a little bit betrayed.

Kylie: How the hell did I betray you?

Jack: I thought you'd have told me something like this.

Kylie: Why does it matter?

Seán: I don't know which I'm more scared about. The fact that you were able to get your hands on a gun or the fact that you were about to use it on someone we didn't even know.

Kylie: Someone shows up at that door, starts banging away and shouting like that. Nothing good is coming from opening it. Doesn't matter what side they're on, they take a look at us and we're done for.

Jack: That's rubbish.

Seán: She has a point.

Jack: Shut up.

Kylie: Thank you Seán.

Seán: Shut up. I'm still mad.

Jack: Me too.

Kylie: You're angry that I didn't tell you about the gun? Okay. Well, now you know about it. Can we continue as we were?

Jack: No we can't! I want to know where you got that.

Kylie: Why do you care?

Jack: Where did you get it?

She sighs and shifts her weight from one foot to the other.

Kylie: I stole it.

Seán: What?

Kylie: I stole it. When we were in the service station grabbing all of the food. It was crazy outside and the shopkeeper had run out and left this gun lying there on the counter. As we were leaving I snatched it and put it in my bag. I didn't think much of it at the time. I just figured that anything and everything we could get our hands on would be helpful at some point, maybe.

Jack: I don't like it.

Seán: Me neither. It's dangerous. What if it goes off?

Kylie: There's no bullets in it.

Jack: Then why did you pick it up!?

Kylie: I didn't know at the time. But it's scary to look at. I could hit someone with it. It's not completely useless.

Jack: Well you can hold on to it. If they get in here I'm not gonna be the one found holding a gun, loaded or not.

Kylie: If they get in, unauthorised possession of a weapon won't be our biggest problem.

Seán: Depends on who it is. Which side. Which division. Do you think maybe they won?

Jack: Or maybe we did.

Kylie sits back down.

Kylie: Or maybe everybody lost.

Seán: Is that good or bad?

Kylie: Sucks for everyone would be my guess.

Kylie sits back down beside Seán. Jack gets up. He wanders over to the door and stares at it for a while. He scratches his chin, bites his nails, drums his fingers on his side and walks back to the others. He picks up the crisp packet that was left on the floor when the stranger knocked. He looks inside and takes one out, then passes it to Kylie.

Jack: So how about that game?

Kylie: What was that about? The walking up and back?

Jack: Oh nothing. I was just thinking.

Kylie and Seán glance at each other as Jack sits next to them.

Kylie: You sure?

Jack: Yeah, 'course. Now, the game.

Lights fade and return to indicate a passage of time. Seán is lying on the ground with Kylie's jacket under his head. Kylie is sitting next to him looking at nothing. Jack is pacing the room silently. He stops and drops to the ground next to Seán. Looks at him.

Jack: Hey! Seán! Wake up!

Seán: What's wrong?

Jack: Do you feel any better?

Seán: No feeling. Legs and arms are useless.

Jack bites his lip and runs his fingers through his hair.

Jack: No chance you could leave?

Kylie looks from nothing to Jack. She and Seán stare at him.

Seán: No, I doubt I could.

Kylie: Now you want to go?

Jack: Um, yeah I think so.

Kylie: But /

Jack: I know I was totally against it but I just have a good feeling about it now. I think it would be a good time to leave.

Kylie: What?

He shrugs.

Jack: I guess… hearing that voice yesterday. It occurred to me that there are other people out there.

Kylie: That's kinda stupid.

Jack: Well it makes sense to me. And I want to go.

Kylie: So the big scary voice telling you to 'vacate' makes you want to go outside?

Jack: I can't explain it… I just feel like this is a good time for me to leave.

Kylie: Time for 'you' to leave? Not 'us' to leave?

Jack: Well you can come if you want but it doesn't look like you would. I'm gonna go.

He gets up. Kylie & Seán watch as Jack puts on his jacket and heads for the door.

Kylie: Stop!

Jack: Why?

Kylie: Think about what you're doing!

Jack: A week ago you wanted to do the same thing! And you chickened out. Now I want to go so I'm going.

He stops and turns around. Kylie and Seán look relieved for a moment, they think he has changed his mind, but realise that he hasn't.

Jack: I love you Kylie. (*She says nothing. Just stares up at Jack.*) And Seán? I'm sorry. For all the crap I did, I'm sorry. Goodbye guys.

He turns to the door and stands for a few moments. Then he reaches out and unlocks it. Slowly he pulls it open. He takes a deep breath, turns back to smile at his friends and then steps out, closing the door behind him. Kylie pulls Seán onto her lap. The two never take their eyes of off the door. Eventually Seán speaks.

Seán: He's gone. He left. Just…

Kylie: I know. It's… amazing. He really left.

Seán: Do you think that he'll be okay?

Kylie: I hope so... maybe he should have taken the gun?

Seán: Let's hope he won't need it.

Lights fade and return as Kylie gets up and locks the door again. When the lights return a passage of time has elapsed. The bag that contained their food lies empty on the floor. Kylie is standing over it.

Kylie: Hey. (*Seán is propped up against the wall a few feet away. He grunts a reply.*) We're in trouble. (*Seán nods and grunts.*) Maybe Jack had the right idea? I mean, he wanted to stay more than anybody and then he left. It's like he knew before we did that we were gonna be screwed. (*She pauses to let Seán speak but no reply is forthcoming.*) Do you think we should go?

Seán: Can't...m...

Kylie: Don't try. We both know it won't work. Maybe everything's alright out there. Maybe it'd be safe for us to leave. Maybe Jack is out there right now and he's eating and drinking and having fun and saying 'oh yes I'll go and see them tomorrow and tell them about the wonderful world that lies outside the room'. And then we'll go. He'll come and get us and we'll all go home. (*Seán doesn't respond. Kylie begins to quicken in her speech.*) And we'll get you some help. The best doctors in the world. The whole wide world and they'll fix you. You'll be able to move and talk and do everything for yourself again and then you and me and Jack will just go back to hanging out together and it'll be like nothing ever happened. (*She looks at Seán. Nothing. No grunts or nods. Kylie walks up and down the room. She is shaking.*) I think we should go. I think that you and I should get up and go. We should grab our stuff, well my stuff because you don't have any stuff because you didn't think of packing anything, you silly thing, and we should just walk right out that door. Well, you can't walk out so I'll carry you out. Or drag you out. But don't you worry, I won't leave you here! You can be sure I'm not gonna just leave you here! That's something that Jack would do. He leaves people. He walks out on them when they're in a tiny, dark, dingy room with barely any food, and the only thing that's stopping them from going crazy is having somebody to talk to who isn't paralysed, and so caught up with that fact that they have no time to answer people properly, and just grunt all the time, and look sorry for themselves. That's what Jack does. I wouldn't do that to you. You know that. (*Seán does nothing.*) Fine. Fine! If you're not going to answer me when I talk to you then I just won't talk to you anymore. How about that, huh? Nobody wants to talk to Seán, the annoying little brat who can't move, and thinks he's such a big deal because of it. You're not that much of a big deal! You shouldn't be so conceited, Seán!

Kylie stops pacing and looks down at Seán. She bends down and looks at his face. She raises her hand to his face and strokes his cheek. After a moment she pulls her hand away and puts her hands over her mouth. She walks away from Seán's body very slowly. For a moment or two she stands, watching the body as if he will wake up any minute. When she knows this won't happen she bends down and gently lays him down on the ground. She slowly pulls off her jacket and places it over him. She stands over him for a while.

Kylie: I have to go. I'm so sorry.

Kylie picks up her bag and turns to face the door. After several failed attempts to move towards it she takes a deep breath and strides towards it. The moment she reaches the handle she shuts her eyes. With one turn and push the door is open and Kylie walks through.

Lights fade.

P.R.
Scott Byrne

"Tenderfoot has been my biggest achievement so far but I couldn't have done it without everyone else who took part. I was unbelievably lucky to get to spend three weeks with such talented people and to make some amazing friends. They deserve the credit, not me, and I owe them more than words can express. Tenderfoot has made me into an infinitely better person."

Characters

Seán, project manager
Alan, team member
Niamh, team member
Brian, intern
Deirdre, CEO social networking company
Spokesperson, social networking company
Journalists
Boy's mother, Mrs. Doherty
Boy's father, Mr. Doherty
T.D., McGrath

Scene One

It is a sunny morning in Dublin. Four people sit around a wooden table as the light streams into the room around them. The oldest member of the group, Seán, sits at the head of the table with Niamh to his right and Alan to his left. The youngest of the group, Brian, sits opposite him. Seán throws a pile of newspapers into the middle of the table.

Seán: Prepare yourselves for a week of hell people. The shit has hit the fan and we're the poor saps left to clean up the mess!

Alan: Yeah... but isn't that what they pay us for?

Seán: I know that but for fuck's sake... look at this. The Herald, Independent and Star. They all have it on the front page. We're at a disadvantage already.

Niamh picks up some of the newspapers and reads out the headlines.

Niamh: "Teenage boy kills himself after torment by cyber bullies." "Boy takes own life after bullying online." "Tragedy as teenager ends his own life."

Alan: Jesus... how did we get the short straw on this one? This is looking like a lose/lose situation.

Seán: That's for sure. But it's our job to change that... to limit the damage to the brand. What's your opinion on all of this, Brian... is it?

Brian looks up from his phone.

Brian: Yeah... eh, it's Brian. You... you want my opinion?

Seán: No, I want you to give me a back massage and a goose that shits golden eggs! Of course I want your opinion, that's what your here for is it not?

Alan: Relax Seán! Jesus Christ, what are you trying to do to the young fella? He's only an intern and you decide to tear his head off.

Seán: Sorry... (*looks at Brian*) but this is a big deal. Everyone needs to pull their weight, even interns. We can't afford to fuck around. So... back to the point – what is your opinion?

Brian: Well... twitter and facebook have been all over it. Everybody is sayin' how terrible it is and how those responsible need to be punished. I think someone set up a memorial page too.

Seán shakes his head and laughs.

Seán: Jesus son, I want your actual opinion. I couldn't give a fuck about what is being said on twitter and facebook. I want the opinion that's inside your head – that you've formed yourself.

Brian: Oh well, em... well, it's awful, obviously. The bullies who drove him to do it should be caught and punished.

Niamh: Well Sherlock, thanks for that observation. We'll keep you around for sure!

Niamh turns to Seán.

Seán: Now Niamh, play nice. Brian's here because he needs to see how we get results and there's no better time than now for him to learn.

Brian: So what is it that they want us to do with this? (*Gestures to the newspapers.*)

Alan: Clean up the mess basically. The website that the bullying took place on, our client, will be absolutely torn to shreds in the media for the next few days. Their sponsorships will drop off the face off the earth and visitor numbers will plummet.....

Niamh: Unless we do our jobs properly, advise them on how to wash their hands of this, divert blame elsewhere.... give the public a convenient scapegoat.

Brian: So... we're gonna make it seem like they had nothing to do with it... like it was someone else's fault that this happened?

Sean: It isn't the client's fault. They can't be held responsible for this. They couldn't have known what was gonna happen.

Brian: But this isn't the first time something like this has happened. Another kid killed himself after abuse on the site. They promised that they would put in place measures to deal with bullying. Either they lied or their measures didn't work.

Niamh: Look, we have to look at every available option that we have in order to get it into people's heads that our client had absolutely nothing to with this.

Brian looks stunned.

Alan: (*Looking at Brian.*) Real admirable job ain't it, they don't tell you about this in college do they? Better prepare yourself for a dose of reality.

Seán: Okay! That's enough from yous two. We need to start working on this now. Niamh... I want you to start working on the ads. Some shit about how the client treats bullying seriously blah blah blah. Get some help from the lads in the office. Alan... I want you to find out as much about this kid as you can, his friends, his family, his school, his relationships... anything and everything that can help us.

Niamh and Alan get up from the table and leave.

Seán: Brian, I want you to come with me.

Brian: Where?

P.R. Scott Byrne

Seán: We're gonna pay a visit to the client's main office. See how bad it is over there.

Brian: Em.... yeah, no problem.

Seán: Great.

They head out the door.

Scene Two

Brian and Seán arrive at their client's headquarters. There are several journalists gathered outside. They are talking to a company spokesperson outside the building.

Spokesperson: Listen... just listen, my employer had absolutely nothing to do with this.

Journalist: Do you deny that the teenager in question used your site up until he died?

Spokesperson: No... we don't dispute that at all but hundreds of thousands of people have used our site since it started. We can't be held accountable for each and every one of them.

Journalist: We realize that but reports have come through that numerous complaints were sent in relation to this kid being bullied and that no action was taken on your part.

Spokesperson: We treat all allegations of bullying very seriously.

Journalist: So... how will this affect the future of the company? This can't be good for business.

Spokespeerson: I'm sorry, I can't... I'm not in a position to comment on that.

Seán and Brian walk past, on their way into the building.

Seán: Looks like the opening scene of Saving Private Ryan, doesn't it? Uh... this is gonna be a long day.

Inside the building is chaos - people moving in all directions and shouting.

Seán: Their precious little world has imploded. These people are used to avoiding the outside world and now it's trying to kick the door in to talk to them. This little bubble they had goin' is gone... and they can't handle it. If their phone or computer doesn't have the answer they're fucked - like a squirrel trying to fly the space shuttle.

Brian: So where are we off to? Who wants to see us?

Seán: To meet the founder - she's upstairs. Advise her how to get through this whole mess with something resembling her company intact.

Brian: By telling her how to blame someone else for it... to lie through her teeth!!

Seán: Precisely... you catch on quick. Keep this up and I see a bright future ahead of you. Now come on...

Seán leads Brian through heavy double doors into a large office. There is a woman leaning against a desk flanked on both sides by people.

Seán: Ah Deirdre... how are you?

Deirdre: How do you think I'm doin' Seán? Jesus, I thought you were supposed to be smart. People are calling for my head on a stake, that's how I'm doin'. After the last time the public are bayin' for blood. (*Raises her hands.*) And for fuck's sake, who is this? (*Looks at Brian.*) You know we can't just let any Joe Soap walk in - not right now Seán.

Seán: Relax.. he's here to help, just like me, he's just a bit inexperienced.

Deirdre: Sure know when to show up buddy. So what have you got for me?

Brian: We were gonna ask you the same question?

Deirdre: Oh look he talks!

Brian: At least I didn't get a kid killed.

Deirdre takes a quick step towards Brian.

Deirdre: I'm sorry... didn't quite catch that.

Brian: I said...

Seán gets between them.

Seán: Should we get back to the problem at hand?

Deirdre: Yes we should. (*Steps back from Brian.*) So what do you want from me?

Seán: Anything you have that could possibly help us.

Deirdre: Like what?

Seán: You mightn't like this but we need to see what you have about this kid, all the messages he sent and received before he died.

Deirdre looks around the room.

Deirdre: Everyone except these two. Out. Now!

Deirdre moves behind her desk.

Deirdre: If people find out about this, we'll be...

Brian: Be what, more fucked than you already are... I don't think that's possible!

Seán: He has a point there Deirdre.

Deirdre: Fine, you can view the messages. I'll have everything available by tomorrow.

Seán: Brilliant, that's what I wanted to hear. I'll be in contact with you once we have a good look at them.

Seán and Brian head out through the double doors.

Seán: Jesus Brian, watch your mouth will you. We're meant to be helping but instead you try and start an argument! This client could be vital for the company in the future.

Brian: How do you reckon that?

Seán rubs his temples.

Seán: Sometimes you are so fucking ignorant it's breathtaking. Our client was due to float on the stock market in a month, the first major Irish social networking site. It's only valued at fifteen million euros but it's potential is massive. They could become an important global company and we'd be the P.R. firm that steered them through this crisis. Now, let's get back to the office.

Seán and Brian leave the building.

Scene Three

Scene takes place a few days later in the same office. The original four are all gathered around the table.

Seán: Alright... so dazzle me with what you've come up with. Niamh, how did it go with the adverts?

Niamh: Well... it was good. I've got a few different ideas for you to take a look at.

Niamh takes out some pages and posters for the ad campaign and Seán scans through a few.

Seán: Hmm, did you come up with these on your own?

Niamh: No, I got some of the other lads in the office to throw in any suggestions like you said.

Seán: Okay... so who came up with this masterpiece?

Seán holds up a poster. It's main line reads - "We are sorry."

Niamh: That would be Dan.

Seán: Who does he think we are? The fucking boyscouts!! Admitting that the client is actually involved. Does he think that somehow that will make things better?

Niamh: Seán, calm down. There are other posters, we don't have to use his.

Seán: You're right but if this is what Dan thinks is okay then he's working for the wrong people.

Niamh: It's a concept. Say the unexpected, what nobody thinks you'll say.

Seán has another look at the other posters.

Seán: These other posters are all good, they should do the job just fine. You'll have to start workin' on getting them out where the public can see them. Get the taglines on the radio as well. But good job Niamh, I'm impressed.

Niamh: Thanks Seán, I'll get to work on it.

Seán: Okay, Alan, how did it go researchin' this kid?

Alan takes out a notepad and flicks through it.

Alan: Hmm... let's see. He was 15 years old, only child, was in 4th year - seemed to do well in school. Looks like a pretty normal kid apart from the bullying.

Seán: Okay, but did you find out anything useful.

Alan: There is one thing... there seems to have been some trouble at home. His da lost his job two years ago.. there was a lot of pressure in the family. Seems he felt like his parents were too busy arguing to be there for him.

Seán: That's good, that's very good. This could be very useful to us.

Brian: What do you mean by that?

Niamh: He means that with this information we can divert attention to the fact that he was going through a hard time at home so when the abuse started he had nobody to turn to, nobody to offer support.

Brian: People won't buy that.

Niamh: People will. A person mightn't but people will. A person is smart - people are dumb and easily manipulated. We just need to plant the idea of an alternative story. It's worked as long as people have wanted to cover up the truth and it will work for us as well.

Seán: Okay, this is good... we're making good progress here. Alan... you did well but we need more. Niamh, good work with the ads. Now... Brian, how did you get on yesterday at the client's offices? *(Seán looks at Alan and Niamh.)* I asked Brian to go to the client's office yesterday, to have a look at the messages this kid received on the client's site before he died. So... what did you find there?

Brian: Plenty. I went through every message this kid received. From what I saw, it seems like the abuse started last year. There were a couple of kids sending him messages, he got about five or six everyday and all of them were abusive. *(Brian hands out sheets of paper to everyone around the table.)* I just printed out some copies of the messages that were sent to him.

Alan: Jesus, this kid really took some shit from these people.

Seán: So, what do you think of them Brian?

Brian: It's just... it's just unbelievable. How could people say these things to another human being? How could people let this happen, someone had to have noticed, someone should have done something about it.

Alan: Yeah, look at this stuff. How could you say this about someone and think that they would be okay?

Niamh: I'm just surprised that he put up with it for so long.

Seán: Good work Brian, we needed someone like you to show us the way.

Brian: Show you the way?

Seán: We needed to know how the average person would feel about this. You are the only person here who still thinks like someone out on the street.

Brian: Is that why you had me look through the messages? To see how I'd react?

Seán: Yeah. What was it you said? Someone should have done something. And thanks to Alan we're going to make his parents look like the monsters who should have seen what was happening to their own child.

Brian: But it wasn't...

Seán: Brian, relax. *(Stands up.)* It's best not to dwell on it. You've all done good work today. And remember, what the people don't know can't hurt the client but what the people think they know can help.

Scene Four

Alan and Brian arrive at a housing estate.

Alan: It's just around the corner.

Brian: How did you convince them to let us talk to them?

Alan: Told them that we were journalists. They've already dealt with plenty of them over the past few days so we should be grand.

Brian: Got it... so we are tricking a dead kids' parents into thinkin' we're journalists when we actually want to just fuck up their son's memory.

Alan: Look..... I don't like this anymore than you do but I've got bills to pay and a family to feed. Do you think that I enjoy this? I do this 'cause I have to not because I want to.

Brian: Sorry... I didn't know... I thought...

Alan: You thought what? That I'm like those two psychopaths Niamh and Seán!! Those two would do anything to get ahead. For fuck's sake, I'm almost sure Seán sold his own mother to get his job.

Brian and Alan arrive at the front door of the house. Alan rings the doorbell. The door is opened.

Alan: Hello Mr. Doherty, my name is Alan. We were wondering if we could talk to you about your son... if that's okay with you?

Mr. Doherty: (*Sighs.*) Okay... but only for a few minutes, okay?

Alan: Yeah, yeah that's fine, we won't take long.

Brian and Alan step into the house. They sit down on a sofa in the sitting room. Mr. Doherty comes in - followed by his wife.

Alan: Firstly... I'd like to say that I'm truly sorry for what's happened. I've two kids myself, nearly the same age as your son was.

Mrs. Doherty: Thank you... it's.. it's been very difficult... ever since... since... I'm sorry... (*She gets up and leaves the room.*)

Mr. Doherty: I'm sorry... it's not your fault. It has been very difficult, these past few weeks. Yous are just doin' your jobs, I... I think people need to hear my son's story... to know what he went through.

Alan: I completely agree. Your son won't have died for nothing... I'll promise you that. So... is there anything you can tell us about him, anything at all?

Mr. Doherty: He was just a normal kid... a good kid, never did anything to anybody. He just went about his business, kept his head down.

Alan: Yeah... it seems like he really was. How was he at home... any problems?

Mr. Doherty: (*Sighs.*) I just never thought that it would end up like this. People tell me. 'Oh, it's not your fault, you couldn't have seen this coming.' But I do feel like it's my fault... I should have been there to help him... to protect him but I didn't... and now... now he's dead.

Alan: I know it's difficult Mr. Doherty but is there anything that you can think of?

Mr. Doherty: I lost my job two years ago and it's put a lot of strain on all of us. There was this one time... he ran away one night, me and his mam.. we were fighting. He came storming down the stairs, said he was sick of it. Said I wasn't there for him when he needed me, I was always just mopin 'round the house, feelin' sorry for myself. And then he left, didn't see him until two days later. Hardly said a word to me after that... I just thought he was angry at me. (*Stands up.*) I'm sorry... but that's all I can give yous right now. I need to be with the missus... she acts like she's copin'... but she's not. Can yous show yourselves out... please. Thanks.

Brian and Alan leave the house, and head back to the office. Brian and Alan arrive at the main doors of their office building.

Alan: (*Stops just before the door and turns to Brian.*) Tell me I'm not like Niamh and Seán, tell me that I've something resembling a conscience. I'm not a bad person... am I? I don't wanna do this but I don't have a choice. I... I need to know Brian... I have to know... am I a bad person because I can't look my kids in the eyes some mornings. I can't look at myself in the mirror for Christ's sake. Brian... I need to know... you're the only one I actually believe.

Brian: I don't know Alan... I really don't know. I don't know what I think about anything to do with this.

Alan: (*Alan laughs.*) Typical... you open up to someone and all they can say is I don't know... well I suppose I should have expected as much. Well listen.... I'm gonna give you a piece of advice Brian, that's all. And it's get out of this business while you can. These people... they're poison, they'll make you think there's nothing wrong... but inside you'll know, and it'll eat away from the inside 'till there's nothing left. *(Alan stands up and wipes his eyes.)* Listen to me... talkin' shite out here to you while they're all inside. Better not keep them waitin'.

They head in through the front door.

Scene Five

The four are gathered around the table a few days later.

Seán: We're on the home stretch now... not much longer left if you ask me. Everything has gone to plan so far. Alan and Brian... you did well on the visit to the parents. Finding out that he ran away. Brilliant. I'll make sure to pass it onto my contacts in the papers. They'll eat this shit up.

Brian: Why don't we ever call him by his actual name? I mean we've all read the papers, we all know what his name is, we've all heard people talking about him... so why don't we call him by his name.

Alan: Because if we give him his real name... we admit to it. We admit that he was a living breathing person. If you give something a name you can relate to it.

Niamh: What Alan is trying to say... in an extremely long-winded way is that it is better for our sanity if we don't treat this kid like he actually existed. Otherwise you could drive yourself totally mad and we wouldn't want that.

Seán: Anyway... back to the point... there is just one last thing left to do.

Brian: What's that... go dance on this kid's grave - something like that?

Seán: Ah Brian, lighten up. And besides... I haven't danced on anyone's grave in ages. *(Smiles at Brian.)*

Seán's phone rings. He answers it and listens for a few seconds.

Seán: And how did you find this out? Right, okay, and you're completely certain about this? You are 100% sure? Right, well thanks for the heads up. *(He puts down the phone.)* Fuck, fuck, fuck! Why now, when we're almost done.

Alan: What's wrong?

Seán: Do you remember that TD we helped out a few years ago? The one with the drug problem?

Alan: Yeah... what about him?

Seán: He's due to make a speech tomorrow in the Dáil. On internet responsibility. Bollocks, out of all the people it just had to be him. If he makes his speech we're done, all this work for nothing. We have to do something about this.

Niamh: I'll take care of it. He still owes us for getting him out of trouble the last time. There's no way he's going to mess it all up, with everything that's riding on us succeeding here.

Seán: Okay... that's good, as long as we can deal with this guy quickly, then we're home free. So remember Niamh, there are a lot of people depending on you to succeed.

Niamh: I know Seán. I better be off, we haven't got much time left.

Niamh stands up from the table.

Seán: One more thing Niamh.

Niamh: What's that?

Seán: I want you to bring Brian with you.

Scene Six

Niamh and Brian are sitting in the TD's office.

Niamh: This has to be my punishment for that poster. Why would he suddenly think that I needed your help.

Brian: Maybe he didn't trust you.

Niamh: Ha! You wish. I've been doing this a lot longer than you so don't start thinking that your something special. And remember if you fuck this up in any way... it'll be your last action as an employee at the firm.

Brian: Thanks for the motivational speech. You could make a job out of it. Who is this guy? Seán said yous worked with him before.

Niamh: His name is Patrick McGrath. He was the kid's local TD so he's been under pressure to do something about it for a few days now.

Patrick McGrath walks into the office.

Mr. McGrath: Well, hello. How can I help you two? I can't stay long. I'm very busy at the moment.

Niamh: Mr. McGrath, please sit down. We know about the speech you're planning to make tomorrow. And we're here to advise you against it.

Mr. McGrath: Who told you about that? Why does it matter to you if I make the speech anyway?

Niamh: Mr. McGrath, stop talking and listen. It's not in our interest for you to make your speech tomorrow.

Mr. McGrath: So you're here to blackmail me then, is that how it is?

Niamh: We're not here to blackmail you Mr. McGrath just as long as you do as we tell you, okay.

Mr. McGrath: And what if I say no? What have yous got that could make me change my mind? I've got nothing to hide.

Niamh: I'm pretty sure that your wife wouldn't want to see these would she? Something tells me she wouldn't be to happy to see where your salary is going, would she? That's an expensive habit you have there.

Niamh hands McGrath several photos of him taking drugs.

Mr. McGrath: Where? How did you get these?

Niamh: I doubt that you remember it but we've met before. The last time you were in trouble.

Mr. McGrath: You... yeah, that's right, I remember now. You were with the P.R. firm, you were only starting out back then. You came here with Seán.

Niamh: Good to see that you remember. We decided to hold onto the photos from the last time in case we ever needed them.

Mr. McGrath: Why am I not surprised? Always knew this would come back to bite me. Who's this lad?

(Points at Brian.)

Niamh: He's the new guy in the office. I'm on babysitting duty.

Mr. McGrath: Ahh right, I see. Well, let me tell you something. She *(points at Niamh)* was just like you the last time I seen her. All bright eyed and busy tailed. Nervous little thing so she was.

Brian: You wouldn't think it. She scares the shite out of most of the people in the office, to be honest.

Mr. McGrath: Yeah, I can imagine. Hardly recognised her when I walked in first.

Niamh: Will both of yous shut up! We're here to change your mind about the speech not listen to yous two having a chat about me.

Mr. McGrath: Relax Niamh, there's no need to be like that. Look... if you really don't want me to make the speech, considering what